TM-E 30-451

HANDBOOK ON GERMAN MILITARY FORCES

1 SEPTEMBER 1943

Dissemination of restricted matter.—The information contained in restricted documents and the essential characteristics of restricted material may be given to any person known to be in the service of the United States and to persons of undoubted loyalty and discretion who are cooperating in Government work, but will not be communicated to the public or to the press except by authorized military public relations agencies. (See also par. 18*b*, AR 380–5, 28 Sep 1942.)

MILITARY INTELLIGENCE DIVISION

WAR DEPARTMENT

WAR DEPARTMENT,
Washington 25, D. C., 1 September 1943.

TM-E 30-451, Handbook on German Military Forces, is published for the information and guidance of all concerned.

[A. G. 300.7 (26 Jul 43).]

By order of the Secretary of War:

G. C. MARSHALL,
Chief of Staff.

Official:
J. A. ULIO,
*Major General,
The Adjutant General.*

Distribution: X

(For explanation of symbols, see FM 21-6.)

TABLE OF CONTENTS

	Paragraphs	Page
FOREWORD	1–4	1
SECTION I. Organization and Strength of Units	5–13	3
II. Administration, Command, and Staff	14–16	16
III. Recruitment and Mobilization	17–29	25
IV. Uniforms, Insignia, and Identifications	30–35	38
V. Infantry	36–45	51
VI. Cavalry and Reconnaissance Units	46–49	61
VII. Infantry Weapons	50–55	65
VIII. Field Artillery	56–62	83
IX. Panzer Troops	63–68	103
X. Engineers	69–81	128
XI. Signal Troops	82–88	159
XII. Chemical Warfare Troops	89–92	183
XIII. Supply and Administrative Services	93–98	101
XIV. SS, Police, and Other Militarized Organizations	99–103	221
XV. German Air Force	104–111	227
XVI. Tactics	112–122	319
XVII. Permanent Fortifications	123–125	333
XVIII. Coinage, Weights, and Measures	126–128	346
INDEX		349

LIST OF ILLUSTRATIONS

Figure		Page
1.	Medium half-track tractor and prime mover, widely used to transport troops and tow weapons	9
2.	Organization of the infantry division	10
3.	Composition of the infantry division	11
4.	Armament of the infantry division	11
5.	Composition of the motorized infantry division	12
6.	Armament of the motorized infantry division	12
7.	Organization of the Panzer division	14
8.	Composition of the Panzer division	15
9.	Armament of the Panzer division	15
10.	Composition of the mountain division	15
11.	Armament of the mountain division	16
12.	Coordination of the Armed Forces through the High Command	17
13.	Ranks in the German Armed Forces (revised June 1943)___faces	32

LIST OF ILLUSTRATIONS

Figure		Page
14.	Scale of peacetime base pay in the German Army	35
15.	Scale of wartime base pay in the German Army	36
16.	Markings on identification tags (*Erkennungsmarken*) of the old and new types	46
17.	Medium armored personnel carrier *(Sd. Kfz. 251)*	53
18.	Organization of the infantry regiment	54
19.	Composition of the infantry regiment	55
20.	Armament of the infantry regiment	55
21.	Organization of the infantry battalion	56
22.	Composition and armament of the infantry battalion	57
23.	Composition of the motorized infantry regiment in the Panzer division	58
24.	Armament of the motorized infantry regiment in the Panzer division	58
25.	Composition of the mountain infantry regiment	59
26.	Armament of the mountain infantry regiment	59
27.	Composition and armament of the old-type motorcycle battalion	60
28.	Composition and armament of the motorized antiaircraft machine-gun battalion	61
29.	Composition and armament of the reconnaissance battalion in the infantry division	62
30.	Composition and armament of the reconnaissance battalion in the motorized division	63
31.	Composition and armament of the reconnaissance battalion in the the Panzer division	63
32.	Composition and armament of the bicycle battalion in the mountain division	64
33.	Composition and armament of the GHQ bicycle battalion	64
34.	9-mm Luger pistol *(Pistole 08)*	66
35.	9-mm Walther pistol *(Pistole 38)*	66
36.	7.92-mm Mauser carbine *(Kar. 98K)*, with grenade discharger accessories	67
37.	7.92-mm rifle 41 *(Gewehr 41)*, right view, bolt opened	68
38.	Infantrymen ready to attack with stick hand grenades, model 24 *(Stielhandgranaten 24)*	69
39.	9-mm submachine gun *(Schmeisser M.P. 38)* with magazine attached and shoulder rest extended	70
40.	9-mm submachine gun *(Schmeisser M.P. 40)*, showing carrying belt and magazine	70
41.	7.92-mm light machine gun *(M.G. 34)* on bipod mount	71
42.	7.92-mm heavy machine gun *(M.G. 34)* on tripod mount	72

LIST OF ILLUSTRATIONS

Figure		Page
43.	7.92-mm light machine gun (*M.G. 42*)	73
44.	50-mm mortar (*l.Gr.W. 36*) with crew	74
45.	80-mm mortar (*s.Gr.W. 34*) being loaded	75
46.	7.92-mm antitank rifle (*Pz.B. 38*) with grenade discharger	76
47.	7.92-mm antitank rifle (*Pz.B. 39*) with stock and bipod extended	76
48.	37-mm antitank gun (*Pak 37*)	77
49.	37-mm antitank gun (*Pak 37*) with stick bomb	78
50.	50-mm antitank gun (*Pak 38*) captured at Tobruk	78
51.	50-mm antitank gun (*Pak 38*) in camouflaged position with crew	79
52.	50-mm antitank gun (*Pak 38*) towed by prime mover	79
53.	75-mm infantry howitzer (*l.I.G. 18*), horse-drawn	81
54.	75-mm infantry howitzer (*l.I.G. 18*), mounted on carriage with rubber wheels	81
55.	150-mm infantry howitzer (*s.I.G. 33*) in firing position	82
56.	Characteristics of artillery weapons	84
57.	Orienting a battery for accurate fire control	85
58.	105-mm gun-howitzer (*l.F.H. 18*)	87
59.	105-mm gun-howitzer and crew in action	88
60.	105-mm gun-howitzer with half-track prime mover	88
61.	150-mm gun-howitzer (*s.F.H. 18*), horse-drawn, with crew, in firing position	89
62.	150-mm gun-howitzer, tractor-drawn	89
63.	150-mm gun-howitzer, horse-drawn, tube section	90
64.	150-mm gun-howitzer, horse-drawn, carriage section	90
65.	105-mm gun (*F.K. 18*) firing	91
66.	105-mm gun, tractor-drawn	91
67.	150-mm gun in firing position	92
68.	150-mm gun with crew, drawn by medium half-track tractor (*Sd. Kfz. 8*)	92
69.	Composition and armament of the artillery regiment in the infantry division	93
70.	Composition and armament of the artillery regiment in the motorized division	93
71.	Composition and armament of the artillery regiment in the Panzer division	94
72.	75-mm mountain howitzer with shield	94
73.	75-mm mountain howitzer without shield	95
74.	Composition and armament of the mountain artillery regiment	96
75.	210-mm *Mörser Lafette 18*	98
76.	Carriage of 210-mm *Mörser Lafette 18*	98
77.	210-mm tube	99

LIST OF ILLUSTRATIONS

Figure		Page
78.	210-mm howitzer, old type	99
79.	Pz.Kw.III chassis mounted with 75-mm short-barreled assault gun	100
80.	Pz.Kw.III chassis mounted with 75-mm long-barreled assault gun	101
81.	Composition and armament of types of tank regiments	105
82.	Composition and armament of the latest type of tank regiment	105
83.	Composition and armament of the tank battalion in the tank regiment of the Panzer division	106
84.	Composition and armament of the tank battalion in the motorized division	106
85.	Composition and armament of the antitank battalion in the Panzer division	107
86.	Composition and armament of the antitank battalion in the infantry division	107
87.	Characteristics of tanks	faces 110
88.	Pz.Kw. I (Sd.Kfz. 101), light tank	112
89.	Chassis of Pz.Kw. I used as mobile platform for Czech 47-mm antitank gun	112
90.	Pz.Kw. II (Sd.Kfz. 121), light tank	113
91.	Pz.Kw. III (Sd.Kfz. 141), medium tank, with short-barreled 50-mm gun	114
92.	Pz.Kw. III (Sd.Kfz. 141), medium tank, with long-barreled 50-mm gun	115
93.	Pz.Kw. IV (Sd.Kfz. 161), medium tank, with short-barreled 75-mm gun	116
94.	Pz.Kw. IV (Sd.Kfz. 161), medium tank, with long-barreled 75-mm high-velocity gun (equipped with double-baffle muzzle brake)	116
95.	18-ton Somua (captured French tank used by the Germans)	117
96.	16.5-ton medium tank (Czech) (CZDV8H)	117
97.	Pz.Kw. VI, heavy tank, showing Christie-type bogie wheels	118
98.	Light armored car with 20-mm gun	119
99.	Light armored car, showing machine-gun armament	120
100.	Six-wheeled heavy armored car	121
101.	Eight-wheeled heavy armored car	121
102.	Characteristics of armored cars	122
103.	Characteristics of half-track prime movers and armored troop carriers	123
104.	20-mm dual-purpose gun	124
105.	88-mm multi-purpose gun (Flak 36)	124
106.	88-mm multi-purpose gun (Flak 41)	125
107.	28/20-mm Gerlich tapered-bore antitank gun	126
108.	76.2-mm Russian gun, captured and used by the Germans	127

LIST OF ILLUSTRATIONS

Figure		Page
109.	75-mm antitank gun (*Pak 40*)	127
110.	Characteristics of antitank weapons	127
111.	Composition and armament of the engineer battalion in the infantry division	130
112.	Equipment of the engineer battalion in the infantry division	130
113.	Composition and armament of the motorized engineer battalion in the motorized infantry battalion	132
114.	Equipment of the motorized engineer battalion in the motorized infantry division	132
115.	Composition and armament of the Panzer engineer battalion in the Panzer division	133
116.	Equipment of the Panzer engineer battalion in the Panzer division	133
117.	Composition and armament of the mountain engineer battalion in the mountain division	134
118.	Equipment of the mountain engineer battalion in the mountain division	134
119.	Tank-landing barge	137
120.	Method of blowing a portal	141
121.	Power saw with gasoline motor	143
122.	Assault boat loaded with infantry	145
123.	Ponton bridge under construction	147
124.	Herbert bridge	149
125.	Photographing Herbert bridge	150
126.	L.Z. bridge over the Meuse River at Maastricht	152
127.	L.Z. bridge completed	152
128.	Composition of the signal battalion in the infantry division	164
129.	Composition and armament of the type of signal battalion in the Panzer division	164
130.	Composition of the corps signal battalion	165
131.	Composition of one type of signal battalion in the Panzer corps	165
132.	Composition of the army signal regiment	166
133.	Frequency coverage (in megacycles) of German radio sets	168
134.	Principal German radios with comparable U. S. Army sets_faces	168
135.	Field radio	169
136.	Two-man pack transmitter (14 bands, 950 to 3,150 kilocycles), probably used in the forward echelon for reconnaissance and observation	170
137.	*20 W.S.d.*, 20-watt transmitter	171
138.	Rear view of *20 W.S.d.*, 20-watt transmitter	171
139.	*Ukw.E.e. 10 W.S.c.*, tank components of *Fu 5–SE 10 U*	172

LIST OF ILLUSTRATIONS

Figure		Page
140.	Man pack receiver, intercept and monitoring type *445BS* (4 bands, 100 to 6,670 kilocycles), used with pack transmitter *TORN Fuf* in the forward echelon	173
141.	Receiver, ground intercept and monitoring type (20 bands, 0 to 5 megacycles)	174
142.	Airborne transmitter, *FuG 16* (38.5 to 42.3 megacycles), used by single-seat fighters for communication	175
143.	Mobile transmitter, type *100WS*, used in the division command net	176
144.	Field telephones	178
145.	Reeling out field wire	181
146.	List of German war gases	189
147.	150-mm *Nebelwerfer 41* captured in North Africa	192
148.	Smoke unit learning to use 105-mm chemical mortars	193
149.	Flame-thrower (old type)	196
150.	Small-size one-man flame-thrower	198
151.	Medium flame-thrower	199
152.	Railroad motor-truck used for transporting supplies to the front	209
153.	Combat train (horse-drawn)	210
154.	Loading a transport plane with supplies for the front	211
155.	SS unit with 37-mm antitank gun	223
156.	Organization of the German Air Ministry	230–231
157.	20-mm AA/AT gun	247
158.	37-mm antiaircraft gun	248
159.	Parachutists receiving last-minute details and orders	254
160.	75-mm recoilless gun (*L.G. 40*) adapted for airborne units	255
161.	Characteristics of German airplanes .... faces	270
162.	*Messerschmitt 109F*, the standard German single-engine fighter	271
163.	*Focke-Wulf 190*, the newest type of German single-engine fighter	272
164.	*Messerschmitt 110* (twin-engine long-range fighter)	274
165.	*Messerschmitt 210* (twin-engine fighter, light bomber, and ground-attack plane)	275
166.	*Junkers 88C* (twin-engine night fighter and bomber)	277
167.	*Junkers 87* (famous *Stuka* dive bomber)	278
168.	*Junkers 52* (standard three-engine troop transport and cargo plane)	279
169.	*Henschel 129* (new ground-attack, low-level, and dive bomber, used primarily against tanks)	281
170.	*Heinkel 111* (twin-engine medium bomber)	283
171.	*Dornier 217* (twin-engine heavy bomber)	285
172.	*Focke-Wulf 200 Kurier* (four-engine heavy bomber, used for long-range bombing and attacks on Allied convoys)	287

LIST OF ILLUSTRATIONS

Figure		Page
173.	*Heinkel 177* (new twin-engine heavy bomber, used for long-range attacks)	288
174.	*Henschel 126* (standard Army cooperation plane, used for tactical reconnaissance and artillery spotting)	291
175.	*Focke-Wulf 189* (twin-engine short-range reconnaissance plane for Army cooperation)	292
176.	*Fieseler Storch 156* (single-engine short-range observation plane for Army cooperation)	293
177.	*D.F.S. 230* (standard glider, designed to carry 10 men with full battle equipment)	295
178.	*Gotha 242* (standard freight-carrying glider, with a useful load of 5,500 pounds)	297
179.	*Gotha 244* (troop-carrying glider, similar to the *Gotha 242*)	298
180.	15-mm aircraft cannon (*M.G. 151*)	303
181.	20-mm aircraft cannon (*M.G. 151*)	303
182.	Light machine-gun team, using the 7.92-mm machine gun (*M.G. 34*) with drum magazine, in typical attack tactics	326
183.	37-mm antitank gun with crew in position during street fighting in the Russian Ukraine sector	327
184.	Underground emplacement	335
185.	Emplacement with a tank turret	336
186.	Rectangular shelter	337
187.	Dragon's teeth antitank obstacles	339
188.	Promenade emplacement designed for enfilading fire	341
189.	Emplacement in the sand dunes in the Wassenaar district of the Netherlands	342
190.	Cliff pillbox	343
191.	Gun emplacement on a beach protected by barbed wire	344
192.	Antitank obstacles of the chevaux-de-frise trestle type	345

COLOR PLATES

Plate		
I	Army continental uniforms: officers and enlisted men	
II	Army continental uniforms: mobile troops	
III	Army tropical uniforms: officers and enlisted men	
IV	Army continental uniforms: mountain troops	
V	Air Force uniforms: officers and enlisted men	
VI	Air Force uniforms: miscellaneous	follows 50
VII and VIII	Army insignia of rank	
IX	Colors of Army arms	

FOREWORD

1. Purpose.—The purpose of this handbook, which is a revision of TM 30-450 (17 December 1941), is to give both officers and enlisted men of the U. S. Army a better understanding of their principal enemy in Europe. In order to fight the Germans successfully, it is vital for the U. S. soldier to know at least in broad outline the manner in which the units of the German Armed Forces are trained, equipped, and organized, as well as something about the chain of command and the method of close cooperation between the various branches.

2. Scope.—*a. Limitations.*—No attempt has been made to give complete details on any of the subjects discussed in the handbook. Further information on the individual arms or branches of the German Army is available in the numerous special publications which have been published or are in the course of preparation by the Military Intelligence Division. Moreover, this handbook does not concern itself with individual units, locations, campaigns, and commanders; these are dealt with in the Order of Battle of the German Army.

b. Inclusion of Air Force.—The German Air Force is given considerable attention, for although this handbook is intended primarily for the use of U. S. ground forces, no handbook on the German Army alone would give an adequate picture of the enemy that the U. S. soldier will encounter. The basic principle of the German military system is unity of command and close cooperation of all arms. It is imperative, therefore, that the Air Force be considered with the Army as an integral part of a single and closely-knit military organization.

3. Language difficulties.—Where there is an English equivalent for a German term or where the translation of German words gives to the reader a clear picture of their meaning, both the English and the German terms are often given. However, in the case of German ranks that have no exact equivalent in the U. S. Army, no translation is given, since it would actually be more misleading than helpful.

4. Revisions.—All errors or suggested changes and additions to this handbook should be reported to the Dissemination Unit, Military Intelligence Division, War Department, Washington 25, D. C.

Section I

ORGANIZATION AND STRENGTH OF UNITS

	Paragraph
General principles of organization	5
Arms	6
Organization of higher units	7
GHQ troops (*Heerestruppen*)	8
Infantry division (*Infanterie-Division*)	9
Motorized infantry division (*Infanterie-Division (Mot.)*)	10
Panzer division (*Panzer-Division*)	11
Mountain division (*Gebirgs-Division*)	12
Light division (*Jäger-Division*)	13

5. General principles of organization.—*a. Flexibility.*— In no 2 years since 1933 has the organization of the German infantry division remained the same. At any given date, wide differences have existed between supposedly similar types of organization, and it is clear that the organization of units in the German Army is never static. The Germans believe that the rapid progress of scientific research and development of weapons makes it imperative that organizational practice remain flexible if it is to be in a position to take prompt advantage of technical innovations as well as of lessons learned in combat.

b. Einheit principle.—(1) *General.*—The composition of German units is based on the *Einheit* principle of organization. The *Einheit*, or unit, principle of organization may be defined as follows: standard types of small units with standard organization, training, and equipment are adopted as the basis on which all larger organizations are built. Thus, for example, the basic infantry combat unit is the standard platoon, consisting of four light machine-gun teams (each supported by a rifle team) and a light mortar team. This basic combat unit is the foundation of all organizations the tactical employment of which is based on fire and maneuver. It is found in the regular infantry in all types of divisions, in the motorcycle company, and in the engineer company. Similarly, all signal units, whether belonging to the signal troops or attached integrally to larger infantry or artillery units, are composed of a combination of one or more basic radio and telephone groups, the equipment, organization, and training of which are identical. The same principle is applied in the organization of all field and combat trains. The *Tross*, or train, of each company, troop, or battery of the Army is identically organized, with only such minor differences as are necessitated by the means of transportation involved. Each *Tross* is composed of three *Einheit* groups—the *Gefechts-Tross*, or combat train, the *Verpflegungs-Tross*, or ration train, and the *Gepäck-Tross*, or baggage train. Similarly all battalion, regimental, or division ammunition and service trains are based on the standard light column (a complete operating unit of 15, 30, or 60 tons' capacity), whereas all supplies are initially made up for issue and transportation in multiples of 30-ton lots. This *Einheit* principle has important advantages. Through its application, supply and replacement of equipment are greatly simplified, while training and tactical employment of basic units of all branches of the service can be standardized and efficiently directed by the General Staff. In addition, the principle of flexibility is maintained, since larger organizations can be formed from combinations of these standard basic units.

(2) *Tactical self-sufficiency of combat units.*—Each combat unit in the German Army, from the basic infantry platoon to the complete division, is so organized, armed, and equipped as to be able to accomplish its mission independently. Thus each combat unit is provided organically with all the support weapons which it is expected to require to accomplish its normal mission without reference to other units. Conversely, no weapons are provided as organic armament which are not required for that mission. Thus the basic infantry platoon, which is the smallest tactical unit in the German Army, has light machine guns and a light mortar as

its organic support weapons. In accordance with the *Einheit* principle, the basic unit of all other branches is similarly armed and organized with a view to its self-sufficient employment. The same principle is applied in the organization and armament of the infantry battalion, regiment, and division, and of all other units.

(3) *Administrative self-sufficiency of combat units.*—With respect to personnel and transportation, each tactical unit responsible for administration is so organized as to be independent of the next higher unit. The administrative units of the German Army are the army, the division, and the battalion. All other tactical units are attached to one of these three for administration and supply. Each of these administrative units must draw its supplies from the next higher administrative unit, and each is organically equipped with sufficient transportation for this task. This principle of organization, together with the formation of the division trains into as many light columns as there are battalions in the division, is largely responsible for the extreme flexibility of German tactical units. With the administrative independence of the battalion, a widely varying number of battalions can be grouped under a single regimental headquarters, with their proportionate share of light columns attached to the division trains, without placing any additional strain on administration or supply. This principle is particularly applicable in the case of reinforcing artillery. It also permits the German standard division to be altered quickly to suit the tactical needs of the moment.

(4) *March-combat group.*—Each division or similar unit of the German Army is organized so that it can be broken up into two or more self-sufficient teams, or march-combat groups. The march-combat group of the infantry division is the infantry regiment reinforced by a battalion of light field howitzers, with possibly an antitank company and an engineer company attached. The ease with which these march-combat groups can be shifted to form larger command groups is due to the administrative organization of the battalion and the light column.

6. Arms.—Every unit in the German Army is classified under one or another of the following arms (*Waffengattungen*):

- a. Infantry.
- b. Cavalry.
- c. Panzer troops.
- d. Artillery.
- e. Chemical warfare troops.
- f. Engineers.
- g. Railway engineers.
- h. Signal troops.
- i. Transport troops.
- j. Army antiaircraft units.
- k. Medical units.
- l. Veterinary units.
- m. Military police units.
- n. Local defense units.
- o. Construction units.
- p. Administrative units.
- q. Propaganda troops.
- r. Motor vehicle park troops.

7. Organization of higher units.—*a. Divisions.*—The various arms are grouped together to form divisions. The division is the basic large unit of the German Army, and is the largest unit having a prescribed organization. The following types of divisions exist (although only the first five figure importantly in combat):

(1) Infantry division.
(2) Motorized division.
(3) Panzer (armored) division.
(4) Mountain division.
(5) Light division (an intermediate type).
(6) Cavalry division (only one of which now exists) (see par. 46).
(7) Security division (for mopping-up duties in the rear areas).
(8) Frontier guard division.
(9) Special duty division (for controlling miscellaneous units in Germany or occupied territory).
(10) Reserve division (for training and occupation purposes).
(11) Mobilization division (for receiving recruits for assignment to field or training units).

b. Corps.—Two or more divisions may be grouped for tactical purposes to form a corps. Each corps staff has a signal battalion and various service units permanently assigned to it, but the allotment of divisions is flexible, varying according to the situation. The following types of corps exist:

(1) Infantry corps (for controlling a group of divisions in which infantry divisions predominate).

(2) Panzer corps (for controlling a group of divisions in which Panzer divisions usually predominate).

(3) Mountain corps (for controlling a group of divisions in which mountain divisions predominate).

(4) Corps command (for controlling an area in occupied territory in which certain defensive units are located, but which may be brought up to normal combat strength and sent into action as an infantry corps).

(5) Reserve corps (for controlling a group of reserve divisions).

c. Armies.—Two or more corps may be grouped for tactical and administrative purposes to form an army. Each army staff has a signal regiment and certain administrative units permanently assigned to it, but the allotment of corps is flexible, varying according to the situation. The following types of armies exist:

(1) Ordinary armies.

(2) Panzer armies (for controlling a group of corps in which the Panzer element usually predominates).

d. Army groups.—For strategic purposes, two or more armies may be placed under an army group command, which usually controls an entire theater of operations or an important part of such a theater. Each army group has a signal regiment and a large staff to deal with the many operational and administrative matters in its territory, including the rear area.

8. GHQ troops *(Heerestruppen).*—*a. General.*—As has been shown, the headquarters of army groups, armies, and corps have no combat units in their permanent organization. Only signal units and certain service units are permanently assigned to such commands. For particular operations, in addition to the temporary allotment of armies to army groups, corps to armies, and divisions to corps, these higher units receive reinforcements from the GHQ pool. This pool consists of all artillery, Panzer troops, engineer units, signal units, chemical warfare battalions, and miscellaneous units which are not assigned to divisions or are not otherwise permanently allotted. In addition, units of the German Air Force, including antiaircraft units and army cooperation units as well as regular bomber and fighter formations, are allotted to the higher commands of the Army according to need.

b. Typical allotment to an army.—The following is a typical allotment of GHQ troops to an army as observed from a German document published during the French campaign of 1940:

(1) *Artillery.*
  One artillery regimental headquarters.
  Two heavy artillery battalions (240-mm guns).
  One heavy artillery battalion (150-mm guns).
  One observation balloon company.
  One meteorological platoon.

(2) *Engineers.*
  One engineer regimental headquarters.
  Two engineer battalions.
  One commander of construction units and staff.
  Four bridge-building battalions.
  Four bridge columns (trains).

(3) *Other GHQ troops.*
  One survey (mapping) company.
  One meteorological platoon.

(4) *Army headquarters troops.*
  One infantry company.
  One infantry antitank platoon.
  One armored car company.

c. Typical allotment to corps.—The following is a typical allotment of GHQ troops to a corps as observed from the German document mentioned in *b*, above:

(1) *Artillery.*
  Two artillery commanders and staffs.
  Two artillery regimental headquarters.

(1) *Artillery*—Continued.
   Two medium artillery battalions (105-mm guns).
   Four medium artillery battalions (150-mm gun-howitzers).
   Two heavy artillery battalions (210-mm howitzers).
   Two heavy artillery batteries (210-mm howitzers).
   One heavy artillery battalion (240-mm howitzers).
   One heavy artillery battalion (300-mm howitzers).
   Four heavy artillery batteries (300-mm howitzers).
   Two artillery observation battalions.
(2) *Engineers.*
   Three bridge columns.
(3) *Other GHQ troops.*
   One infantry battalion for special employment.
   One heavy antitank battalion.
   One antitank battalion.
   One chemical warfare regimental headquarters.
   One chemical warfare battalion.

Figure 1.—Medium half-track tractor and prime mover, widely used to transport troops and tow weapons.

8   HANDBOOK ON GERMAN MILITARY FORCES

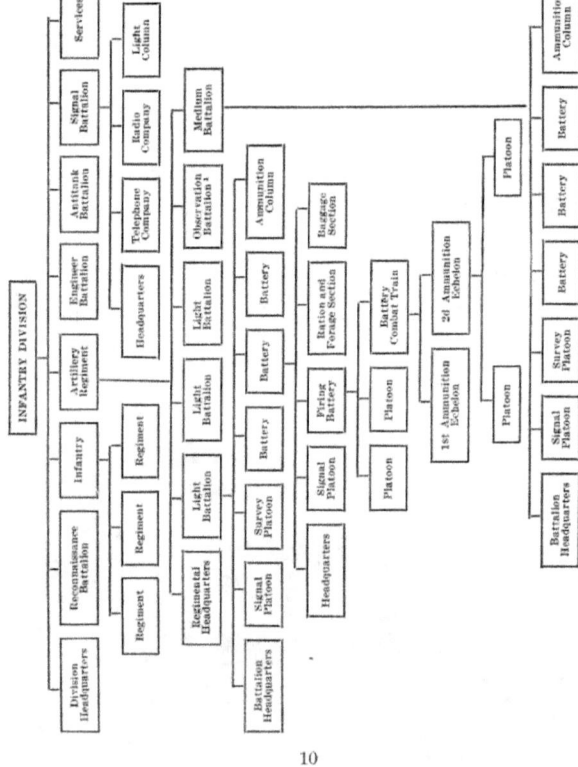

[1] The observation battalion is part of the GHQ pool.

Figure 2.—Organization of the infantry division.

ORGANIZATION AND STRENGTH OF UNITS

9. Infantry division *(Infanterie-Division)*.—The infantry division of the normal type consists of a headquarters, a reconnaissance battalion, three infantry regiments, an artillery regiment, an engineer battalion, an antitank battalion, a signal battalion, and services. (See fig. 2.) Its approximate strength in personnel and transport is shown in figure 3; in armament, in figure 4. (See sec. V, Infantry, p. 51, for further details.)

Units	O and EM	Mtrcl	Other Mtr vehicles	H-Dr vehicles	Horses
Division headquarters	152	17	31		20
Reconnaissance battalion	575	35	30	3	213
Three infantry regiments	9,477	135	219	642	1,923
Artillery regiment	2,700	38	35	226	2,211
Engineer battalion	800	43	87	19	52
Antitank battalion	599	64	113		
Signal battalion	474	32	103	7	52
Services	2,200	98	325	30	218
TOTAL	16,977	462	943	927	4,689

Figure 3.—Composition of the infantry division.

Weapons	Rcn Bn	3 Inf Regts	Arty Regt	AT Bn	Engr Bn	TOTAL
Machine pistols (excluding those in armored cars)		432				432
Machine guns, light	24	345	24	18	27	[1] 444
Machine guns, heavy	8	108				116
7.92-mm antitank rifles		81				81
20-mm antitank guns				12		12
37-mm antitank guns	3	36				39
50-mm antitank guns				24		24
50-mm mortars	3	81				84
81-mm mortars	3	54				57
75-mm infantry howitzers	2	18				20
150-mm infantry howitzers		6				6
105-mm gun-howitzers			36			36
150-mm gun-howitzers			8			8
105-mm guns			4			4

[1] Includes two in Div HQ and four in Div Sig Bn.

Figure 4.—Armament of the infantry division.

10. Motorized infantry division *(Infanterie-Division (Mot.))*.—The motorized infantry division differs from the infantry division of the normal type in that its units are motorized throughout and that it contains only two infantry regiments instead of three. The artillery regiment accordingly contains only two instead of three battalions of 105-mm guns, and two batteries of 150-mm howitzers. Each motorized infantry division also includes a motorcycle battalion, and there has been a tendency to add a Panzer component consisting of at least one battalion. The approximate strength of this division in personnel and transport is shown in figure 5; in armament, in figure 6. (See sec. V, Infantry, p. 51, for further details.)

Units	O and EM	Mtrcl	Other Mtr vehicles	L Armd-C	Hv Armd-C	Pz. Kw. II	Pz. Kw. III	Pz. Kw. IV
Division headquarters	152	39	31					
Panzer battalion	649	50	86			7	37	10
Motorcycle battalion	1,055	271	121					
Panzer reconnaissance battalion	637	116	104	18	6			
Two motorized infantry regiments	6,190	590	1,164					
Motorized artillery regiment	1,835	125	335					
Motorized engineer battalion	862	58	133					
Antitank battalion	509	64	113					
Motorized signal battalion	474	32	103					
Services	1,866	108	371					
TOTAL	14,319	1,453	2,561	18	6	7	37	10

Figure 5.—Composition of the motorized infantry division.

Weapons	Panzer Bn	Mtrcl Bn	Panzer Rcn Bn	2 Mtz Inf Regts	Mtz Arty Regt	Mtz Engr Bn	AT Bn	Mtz Sig Bn	TOTAL
Machine guns, light	99	58	51	236	18	27	18	4	511
Machine guns, heavy		14	2	72					88
Antitank rifles		9	3	54					66
20-mm tank guns	7		10				12		29
50-mm tank guns	37								37
75-mm tank guns	10								10
37-mm antitank guns				24					24
50-mm antitank guns		3	3				24		30
50-mm mortars		9	3	54					66
81-mm mortars		6		36					42
75-mm infantry howitzers	2	2		12					16
150-mm infantry howitzers				4					4
105-mm guns					4				4
150-mm gun-howitzers					8				8
105-mm gun-howitzers					24				24

Figure 6.—Armament of the motorized infantry division.

11. Panzer division *(Panzer-Division)*.—The several types of Panzer divisions that exist are alike in all respects except for the organization of the tank component. In the more recently organized Panzer divisions the reconnaissance battalion has been discarded and its functions have been taken over by the motorcycle battalion, which has been removed from the motorized infantry brigade. An armored car company has been added to the motorcycle battalion, and certain other adjustments have been made to the organization of the motorcycle battalion to make it suitable for divisional reconnaissance missions. (See fig. 7.) The approximate strength of the Panzer division in personnel and transport is shown in figure 8; in armament, in figure 9. (See sec. IX, Panzer Troops, p. 103, for further details.)

12. Mountain division *(Gebirgs-Division)*.—The mountain division consists of a headquarters, a bicycle battalion, two mountain infantry regiments, a mountain artillery regiment, a mountain engineer battalion, an antitank battalion, a mountain signal battalion, and services. Its approximate strength in personnel and transport is shown in figure 10; in armament, in figure 11. (See sec. V, Infantry, p. 51, for further details.)

13. Light division *(Jäger-Division)*.—The composition of the so-called "light divisions" of the German Army vary somewhat according to the special missions for which they were formed. They may be regarded as largely experimental intermediate units. In particular, the two which were used in North Africa, known as "Light Africa Divisions" *(leichte Afrika-Divisionen)*, were unique in their composition. Of the remainder, the majority contain two infantry regiments, an artillery regiment (sometimes motorized), a reconnaissance or bicycle battalion, and the usual engineer, antitank, and signal battalions. Their strength in personnel, transport, and armament is usually somewhat similar to that of the motorized infantry division (see par. 10).

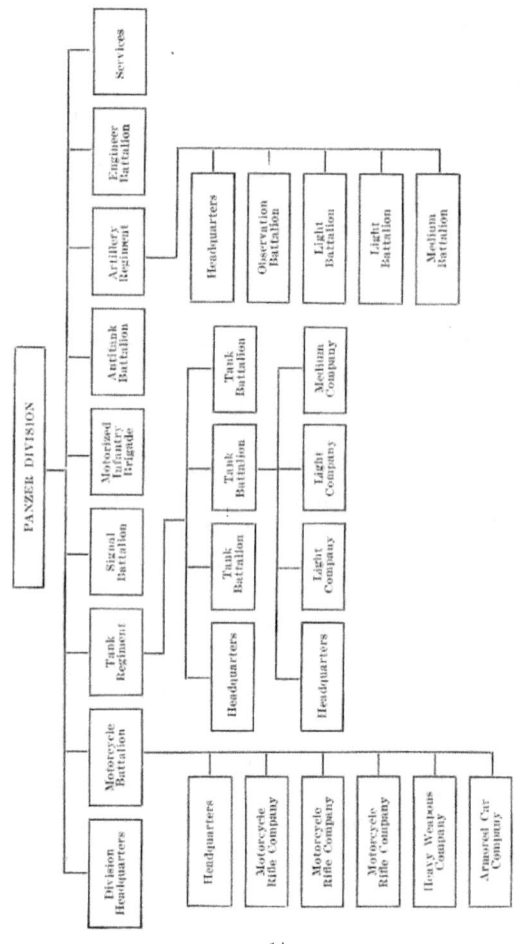

Figure 7.—Organization of the Panzer division.

14

ORGANIZATION AND STRENGTH OF UNITS

Units	O and EM	Mtrcl	Other Mtr vehicles	Lt Armd-C	Hv Armd-C	Pz. Kw. II	Pz. Kw. III	Pz. Kw. IV
Division headquarters	185	39	31					
Panzer regiment	2,416	170	353			28	114	30
Motorcycle battalion	1,153	236	150	18	6			
Motorized infantry brigade	4,409	314	713					
Panzer artillery regiment	2,102	132	455					
Panzer engineer battalion	979	101	220			2		
Antitank battalion	552	44	93					
Panzer signal battalion	420	27	85					
Services	2,157	120	446					
TOTAL	14,373	1,183	2,546	18	6	30	114	30

Figure 8.—Composition of the Panzer division.

Weapons	Panzer Regt	Mtrcl Bn	Mtz Inf Brig	Panzer Arty Regt	Panzer Engr Bn	AT Bn	Panzer Sig Bn	TOTAL
Machine pistols			156					156
Machine guns, light	376	87	358	24	48	16	22	931
Machine guns, heavy	24	12	48					84
Antitank rifles		9	36					45
20-mm AA/AT guns	28	18			2	12		60
37-mm antitank guns			18					18
50-mm tank guns	106							106
50-mm antitank guns		3	18			18		39
81-mm mortars		6	24					30
75-mm infantry howitzers	30	2	16					48
150-mm infantry howitzers			8					8
105-mm gun-howitzers				24				24
105-mm guns				4				4
150-mm gun-howitzers				8				8

Figure 9.—Armament of the Panzer division.

Units	O and EM	Mtrcl	Other Mtr vehicles	H-Dr vehicles	Horses or mules
Division headquarters	200	12	26		20
Bicycle battalion	551	57	37		
Two mountain infantry regiments	6,506	168	270	348	950
Mountain artillery regiment	2,500	12	23	178	1,785
Mountain engineer battalion	1,049	42	96	64	256
Antitank battalion	599	64	113		
Mountain signal battalion	476	28	102	7	56
Services	2,250	64	191	117	439
Total	14,131	447	858	714	3,506

Figure 10.—Composition of the mountain division.

Weapons	Bcl Bn	2 Mtn Inf Regts	Mtn Arty Regt	Mtn Engr Bn	AT Bn	Mtn Sig Bn	TOTAL
Machine guns, light	24	356	24	27	18	4	453
Machine guns, heavy	8	84					92
Antitank rifles		72					72
20-mm AA/AT guns					12		12
37-mm antitank guns	3	24					27
50-mm antitank guns					24		24
50-mm mortars	6	54					60
81-mm mortars	3	36					39
75-mm Mtn howitzers	2	12	36				50
105-mm gun-howitzers			12				12

Figure 11.—Armament of the mountain division.

Section II

ADMINISTRATION, COMMAND, AND STAFF

	Paragraph
Organization of High Command in war	14
Organization of subordinate commands	15
Regional organization (*Wehrkreise*)	16

14. Organization of High Command in war.[1]—*a. Unity.*—The outstanding characteristic of German military operations in the present war has been unity of command. The Army (*Heer*), Navy (*Kriegsmarine*), and Air Force (*Luftwaffe*) are not regarded as three separate services but as branches of a single service, the Armed Forces (*Die Wehrmacht*).

b. Supreme Command.—Hitler is the Supreme Commander of the Armed Forces, and both theoretically and practically exercises this command in person. Under him, the High Command of the Armed Forces (*Oberkommando der Wehrmacht*), headed by Field Marshal Wilhelm Keitel, is responsible for the whole organization, coordination, and employment of the Armed Forces in peace and war. Each of the three branches, in turn, has its own high command (Army High Command, Navy High Command, Air

---

[1] For the ranks in the German Armed Forces, see figures 13 (facing p. 32), 14 (p. 35), and 15 (p. 36); see also plates VII and VIII, following page 50.

Force High Command), which is responsible for carrying out in its own sphere with its own General Staff the directives of the High Command of the Armed Forces. (See fig. 12.)

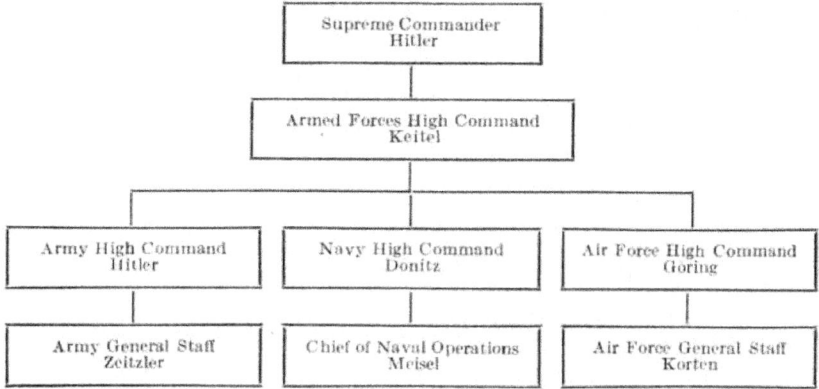

Figure 12.—Coordination of the Armed Forces through the High Command.

c. Armed Forces Operations Staff.—This staff, which is a part of the Supreme Command, is the body most concerned with advising and assisting Hitler in the planning and execution of military operations. It is stationed at Hitler's Field Headquarters and is equivalent to a joint General Staff of the three branches, having effective authority to carry out its decisions. Operations in any given theater are controlled by the local task-force commander, who is subject to the directives from Hitler's headquarters.

d. Formation of task forces.—When any given operation is contemplated, the following procedure is adopted:

(1) Hitler, after thorough consideration of the diplomatic and domestic political situation, assigns an objective to the Chief of the High Command.

(2) The Chief of the High Command studies the problem with the aid of the Armed Forces Operation Staff and issues a general directive.

(3) The Chief of the High Command calls a meeting of the

Commanders-in-Chief of the Army, Navy, and Air Force, at which the problem as a whole is discussed and a commander is nominated for the operation in question.

(4) After renewed consultation with the Chief of the High Command, Hitler appoints the commander for the operation, who may come from the Army, the Navy, or the Air Force.

(5) When the commander is appointed, he becomes a direct subordinate of the Chief of the High Command.

(6) The Chief of the High Command issues an explicit directive to the commander.

(7) The new commander selects his own staff, which may be composed of members of the three services.

(8) The staff prepares—
    (a) A general plan of operation.
    (b) A list of requirements.

(9) The commander of the operation submits his plans and his requirements to the Chief of the High Command for his approval. Generally the commander gets all that he requests, even including the specific units of his choice.

(10) The selected units become a task force.

(11) The commander of the operation prepares a training directive for the task force. All units in it are specially trained for a specified period. During this period, the commander's staff prepares detailed plans.

(12) Hitler and the Chief of the High Command set a date and time for the operation.

(13) The commander of the operation confers with all subordinate leaders and goes over the detailed plans of lower units prior to the beginning of the operation.

(14) The operation begins.

e. High Command of the Army.—The High Command of the Army (*Oberkommando des Heeres*) is headed by the Commander-in-Chief of the Army (*Oberbefehlshaber des Heeres*). He is the actual head of the Army without having the status of a cabinet member. He supervises the organization and training of the Army in time of peace and is field commander in time of war. This command includes both the exercise of field command and the administrative duties at home. This function for the present has been assumed by Hitler. The High Command of the Army (*Oberkommando des Heeres*) is organized into eight main sections, as follows:

(1) *Adjutant's Office* (*Adjutantur*).—The office acts as a central clearing office for incoming and outgoing mail. It is in no sense an equivalent of the U. S. Adjutant General's Department.

(2) *Personnel Office* (*Personalamt*).—This office has full appointive power, without recourse to higher authority, for all officers up to the grade of lieutenant colonel except for officers in the General Staff Corps. Appointments of colonels and generals are made by Hitler. General Staff Corps officers are appointed and promoted by the Chief of the General Staff. Otherwise, all matters regarding initial commissions, promotions, transfers, and retirements of officers are handled by the Personnel Office exclusively. Its power is very great, and it is shielded from interference. This office is the depository for all efficiency reports.

(3) *General Staff* (*Generalstab*).—Under the Chief of Staff of the Army there are five main departments, each under a Deputy Chief of the General Staff (*Oberquartiermeister I–V*). Each department consists of from one to five sections (*Abteilungen*). The organization is as follows:

    Oberquartiermeister I.—Operations.
        Abteilung 1.—Operations.
        Abteilung 5.—Transport.
        Abteilung 6.—Rear Echelons.
        Abteilung 9.—Topography.
        Abteilung 10.—Maneuvers and Operational Planning.
    Oberquartiermeister II.—Training.
        Abteilung 4.—Training.
        Abteilung 11.—Military Schools and Officers' Training.

Oberquartiermeister III.—Organization.
    Abteilung 2.—Organization.
    Abteilung 8.—Technical Services.
Oberquartiermeister IV.—Intelligence.
    Abteilung 3.—Eastern Section.
    Abteilung 12.—Western Section.
Oberquartiermeister V.—Historical.
    Abteilung 7.—Historical.

(4) *General Army Office (Allgemeines Heeresamt).*—This office performs numerous important functions including those of the Inspectorates of the various arms. Its organization is as follows:

    I.—Central Section, including Army Publications Administration.
    II.—Budget Section of the Army.
    III.—Mobilization and Organization Section.
    IV.—Ordnance Inspectorate.
    V.—Inspectorate of Infantry.
    VI.—Inspectorate of Cavalry and Horse-drawn Transport.
    VII.—Inspectorate of Artillery.
    VIII.—Inspectorate of Engineers.
    IX.—Inspectorate of Fortresses.
    X.—Weapons Section of the Panzer Troops, Cavalry, and Army Motorization.
    XI.—Inspectorate of Signal Troops.
    XII.—Inspectorate of Transport Troops.
    XIII.—Inspectorate of Chemical Warfare Troops.
    XIV.—Inspectorate of Railway Engineers.
    XV.—Medical Inspectorate.
    XVI.—Veterinary Inspectorate.

(5) *Ordnance Office (Waffenamt).*—This office is divided into the following eight sections:

    I.—Raw Materials Section.
    II.—Chief Engineer's Office.

  III.—Periodicals Section.
  IV.—Regulations Section.
  V.—Research Section.
  VI.—Development and Testing Group (with twelve subsections which deal with the weapons for the various arms).
  VII.—Industrial Mobilization Group.
  VIII.—Acceptance Section.
 (6) *Administration Office* (*Heeres-Verwaltungsamt*).—This office is divided into the following four sections:
  I.—Army Civilian Officials, Employees, and Finance.
  II.—Food and Supplies.
  III.—Barracks and Training Grounds.
  IV.—Administration of Army Buildings.
 (7) *Chief of the Mobile Troops* (*Chef der Schnellen Truppen*).—(*a*) This authority was created in 1938. It was given general training supervision over the following troops:
 Panzer.
 Cavalry.
 Motorized reconnaissance.
 Motorcycle.
 (*b*) The office of the Chief of the Mobile Troops is believed to have been largely superseded by the authority conferred on the Inspector General for the Panzer Arm (*General Inspekteur für die Panzerwaffe*), who was appointed early in 1943 and made responsible directly to Hitler.
 (8) *Inspectorate of Cadet Schools* (*Inspektion der Kriegschulen*).—This division of the Army High Command is of minor importance. Its functions are similar to what a "Bureau for West Point Affairs" would be if such a bureau were created in the U. S. War Department.
 15. Organization of subordinate commands.—*a. General.*—In the German Army there is no chief of staff in the division. The duties of the chief of staff and the chief of operations are performed by a General Staff Corps officer known as *Ia* (Op-

erations). All higher headquarters above the division have a chief of staff as in the U. S. Army.

  b. *Staff organization.*—The staffs of armies, corps, and divisions are all organized in the same way and consist of the following sections:

  (1) *Section I (Generalstab).*—(a) This section is staffed exclusively by General Staff Corps officers and is usually divided into four parts, as follows:

  Ia. Operations.
  Ib. Supply and Administration.
  Ic. Intelligence.
  Id. Training.

  (b) This General Staff section does not concern itself with any routine matters. In all German staffs the primacy of the operations officer is unquestioned. In corps and armies, when the chief of staff is absent, the operations officer acts in that capacity. In divisions the operations officer normally heads the staff, as there is no separate chief of staff.

  (2) *Section II (Adjutantur).*—This section is headed by a General Staff Corps officer and deals with all routine matters of administration.

  (3) *Section III (Feldjustizamt).*—This is the legal branch and is staffed by civilian officials (*Beamten*).

  (4) *Section IV (Intendantur).*—This includes representatives of all the various services, such as supply, medical, and veterinary.

  (5) *Section V (Wehrmachtsseelsorgedienst,* comprising *Heeresgeistliche*).—Chaplains' service.

  c. *Formation of staffs*—For organization of work, the sections of a staff are divided into three groups.

  (1) *Tactical group (Führungs-Abteilung).*—Comprises *Ia* and *Ic* of section I of *b* (1) (*a*), above.

  (2) *Supply group (Quartiermeister-Abteilung).*—Comprises *Ib* of section I of *b*(1) (*a*), above, and the whole of section IV of *b*(4), above.

ADMINISTRATION, COMMAND, AND STAFF 15

(3) *Personnel, etc., group (Adjutantur).*—Comprises sections II, III, and V of $b(2)$, (3) and (5), respectively, above. The postal section, pay section, divisional services, and divisional headquarters troops are attached to this section.

d. Attached officers.—The following officers are attached to the various staffs:

(1) *Army.*—(*a*) With the headquarters of each army is a senior officer of each of the following arms: cavalry, artillery, engineers, antitank, and signal troops.

(*b*) These officers act as technical advisers to the army commander and keep him in touch with all matters relating to their respective arms. They are known as *Höherer Kavallerieoffizier, Höherer Artilleriekommandeur,* etc.

(2) *Corps.*—(*a*) At each corps headquarters there is a senior officer of each of the following arms: engineers, signal troops, and antitank units.

(*b*) These officers come directly under the chief of staff of the corps. They command the units of their own arms within the corps and are responsible for their technical and tactical training. They are also available to give advice to the corps and division commanders. They are known as *Kommandeur der Pioniere, Kommandeur der Nachrichtentruppen,* etc.

(3) *Division.*—(*a*) An artillery officer, known as *Artillerie-Führer,* commands the artillery in a division and acts as artillery adviser to the division commander.

(*b*) The following officers are believed to be attached to the following groups of the division staff:

(1) *Tactical group.*
 Division artillery officer.
 Division engineer officer.
 Division signal officer.
 Antitank battalion commander.
 Officer in technical charge of the division motorized transport.

(2) *Supply group.*
Commander of the light columns and the division train.
Division provost marshal.
Division postal service commander.
Engineer officer ⎫
Signal officer ⎬ (for questions of supply matériel).

16. Regional organization (Wehrkreise).—*a. General.*—Germany is divided into a number of military districts (*Wehrkreise*). Before the present war each of these was commanded by a senior officer who also commanded the corps bearing the same number as the *Wehrkreis*.

b. List of military districts.—(1) The German army corps and *Wehrkreise* in 1939 were listed as follows:

Wehrkreis	Area included	Headquarters of *Wehrkreis* and of corps	Peacetime garrison divisions
I	East Prussia	Königsberg	1st, 11th, and 21st, and 1st Cavalry Brigade.
II	Pomerania and Mecklenburg.	Stettin	2d, 12th, and 32d.
III	Brandenburg	Berlin	3d and 23d, and 3d Panzer and 3d Light.
IV	Saxony and North Sudetenland.	Dresden	4th, 14th, and 24th.
V	Southwest Germany	Stuttgart	5th, 25th, and 35th.
VI	Westphalia and Lower Rhineland.	Münster	6th, 16th, and 26th, and 1st Light.
VII	Upper Bavaria	München	7th and 27th, and 1st Mountain.
VIII	Silesia and East Sudetenland.	Breslau	8th, 18th, and 28th, and 5th Panzer.
IX	Hesse and Thuringia	Kassel	9th, 15th, and 29th, and 2d Light and 1st Panzer.
X	Schleswig-Holstein and North Sea coastal area.	Hamburg	10th, 20th, and 22d.
XI	Hannover and Prussian Saxony.	Hannover	13th, 19th, and 31st.
XII	Middle Rhineland	Wiesbaden	33d, 34th, and 36th.
XIII	Franconia and West Sudetenland.	Nürnberg	10th, 17th, and 46th, and 4th Panzer.
XVII	Upper and Lower Austria.	Wien	44th and 45th, and 2d Panzer and 4th Light.
XVIII	Tyrol, Carinthia, and Styria.	Salzburg	2d and 3d Mountain.

(2) After the Polish campaign, *Wehrkreise XX* (Danzig) and *XXI* (Posen) were formed in the conquered territory.

(3) Alsace has been incorporated into *Wehrkreis V*; Lorraine and Luxemburg, into *Wehrkreis XII*; Eupen-Malmedy, into *Wehrkreis VI*; portions of northern Yugoslavia, into *Wehrkreis XVIII*; and the Bialystok district, into *Wehrkreis I*.

(4) The missing numbers in the above series were assigned to four special corps staffs for the tactical supervision of the peacetime Panzer, light, and motorized divisions (which have no corresponding *Wehrkreise*) (see par. 23c):

Corps	Corps headquarters	Divisions supervised
XIV	Magdeburg	2d, 13th, 20th, and 29th Motorized.
XV	Jena	1st, 2d, 3d, and 4th Light.
XVI	Berlin	1st, 2d, 3d, 4th, and 5th Panzer.
XIX	Wien	

Section III

RECRUITMENT AND MOBILIZATION

	Paragraph
General	17
Military service law	18
Period of service	19
Recruitment procedure	20
Active and reserve categories	21
Wartime modifications of draft procedure	22
Replacement training system	23
Professional cadre	24
Training	25
Housing, cantonments, and training areas	26
Pay and allowances	27
Mobilization in the past	28
Present principles of mobilization	29

17. General.—German recruitment and mobilization prior to and following the outbreak of the present war were organized and carried out in such a manner as to give Germany the best possible use of her manpower. Despite the years between 1918 and 1935, when Germany was forbidden by the peace treaties to have universal military training, the 4 years that followed were sufficient to provide enough trained soldiers to carry the Polish campaign to a victorious conclusion. The Nazi government also completed preparations to assure that there would be no repetition in 1939 of the German experience of 1914, when the hasty and ill-planned mobilization of hundreds of thousands of reserves in a short period of time threw German industry and agriculture into a state of confusion from which it never wholly recovered during World War I.

18. Military service law.—Universal compulsory military service existed in Germany for more than a century prior to World War I. It was expressly forbidden under the terms of the Versailles Treaty of 1919, but when Hitler came to power in 1933, he embarked on a vast rearmament program that included the training of a large army. The basic law governing the present system of military service was adopted on 21 May 1935. This law was far more sweeping in its provisions than that existing prior to 1919. Under the old law certain military categories were established and each was given a fixed schedule as to when its members would serve. Men omitted from these categories were not called for military service, and large groups were placed in deferred classes. The law introduced in 1935 made every German man available for military service. In the event of war the entire nation was placed at the disposal of the High Command, which decides the number and classes to be called to the colors. Thus the new law provided the legal basis for total mobilization of all Germans and placed the interests of the Armed Forces in wartime above all others in the state. Reserves may be called out at any time for training, even in peacetime.

19. Period of service.—The obligation to bear arms begins for all male Germans at the age of 18 and ends when they become

45. This applies, however, only to peacetime service, as in wartime the age limit may be extended by decree. When conscription was reintroduced, the period of active service was fixed at 1 year, but in 1936 this was extended to 2 years. Before the war, active military service usually began at the age of 20. The first registration (*Musterung*), however, took place when a young German became 18. This was accompanied by a preliminary medical examination, classification according to his physical fitness, and provisional assignment to a branch of the service.

20. Recruitment procedure.—This first registration is carried out in small local registration areas (*Musterungsbezirke*) with the cooperation of district police and other local civil authorities. The next stage in the recruit's career, the actual drafting (*Aushebung*), consists of a second and more thorough physical examination, a definite assignment to an arm of the service, and a decision regarding any request for deferment. Army officials handle recruiting for the Navy and Air Force as well as for the Army itself. If the recruit is fit (*tauglich*), he is sent home pending his call to the colors (*Einberufung*) and his induction (*Einstellung*). Between first registration and induction the recruit ordinarily performs his required labor service (*Arbeitsdienst*).

21. Active and reserve categories.—All German men more than 18 years of age (except those totally unfit for service) are classified in the following categories:

      Aktiv dienende—on active service.
      Reserve I—fully trained, under 35.
      Reserve II—partially trained, under 35.
      Ersatzreserve I—untrained, not called up, under 35.
      Ersatzreserve II—untrained, physically unfit, under 35.
      Landwehr I—trained, between 35 and 45.
      Landwehr II—untrained, between 35 and 45.
      Landsturm I—trained, over 45.
      Landsturm II—untrained, over 45.

22. Wartime modifications of draft procedure.—Draft of men for the German Armed Forces has been greatly accelerated since the outbreak of the war, though in its broad outlines it has remained the same. *Musterung* and *Aushebung* have now become one process, while the induction age has been lowered from 20 to 18, and older classes have been called up. Members of the *Ersatzreserve II* and *Landwehr II* are subject to call, and occupational and other deferments are strictly limited. Furthermore, a continual "combing-out" process is carried on to take men of military age from industry and agriculture and replace them with foreign laborers, women, or men unfit for military service. In a further effort to increase the number of men available for the Armed Forces, volunteers at the age of 17 are accepted for the Army as well as for special arms, while even younger men are being drafted for the auxiliary services.

23. Replacement training system.—*a. Recruiting service.*—In order to simplify the task of each German field army commander in wartime, the German Army is divided into the Field Army (*Feldheer*) and the Replacement Training Army (*Ersatzheer*). When the war broke out, the field armies moved out to take part in the various campaigns, leaving behind them the *Ersatzheer* to take care of all such details as drafting of personnel and their training for service in the field either as replacements or as new units. The deputy commander in each military district (*Wehrkreis*) took command when the regular commander moved out into the field. With the assistance of reserve officers from the district he carried out the recruiting and training plans formulated by the General Army Office (*Allgemeines Heeresamt*) in Berlin.

b. Local control.—Each military district is divided into recruiting areas (*Wehrersatzbezirke*), and these, in turn, are divided into recruiting sub-areas (*Wehrbezirke*). Although most of the military districts contain two or three recruiting areas, some districts in populous areas contain four, while others in

RECRUITMENT AND MOBILIZATION

thinly populated areas contain only one. The military headquarters of a *Wehrersatzbezirk* is known as a *Wehrersatzinspektion*, that of a *Wehrbezirk* as a *Wehrbezirkskommando*, and that of a *Wehrmeldebezirk* (reporting area) as a *Wehrmeldeamt*. There is no military officer on permanent duty in the local registration district (*Musterungsbezirk*), the smallest of the local replacement training service areas, and local police authorities represent the military.

c. *Recruiting areas.*—Greater Germany is divided as follows for purposes of recruiting:

Wehrkreis	Wehrersatzbezirk	Number of Wehrbezirke
I	Königsberg	7
I	Allenstein	4
II	Stettin	12
II	Schwerin	4
III	Berlin	10
III	Frankfurt-am-Oder	5
III	Potsdam	7
IV	Leipzig	11
IV	Dresden	12
IV	Chemnitz	9
V	Ulm	10
V	Stuttgart	13
VI	Münster	11
VI	Dortmund	8
VI	Düsseldorf	14
VI	Köln	9
VII	München	12
VIII	Breslau	13
VIII	Kattowitz	13
VIII	Liegnitz	7
IX	Kassel	9
IX	Frankfurt-am-Main	6
IX	Weimar	9

Wehrkreis	Wehrersatzbezirk	Number of Wehrbezirke
X	Schleswig-Holstein	6
X	Hamburg	6
X	Bremen	9
XI	Hannover	8
XI	Magdeburg	7
XII	Koblenz	10
XII	Mannheim	10
XIII	Regensburg	5
XIII	Nürnberg	11
XIII	Karlsbad	5
XVII	Linz	5
XVII	Wien	12
XVIII	Innsbruck	3
XVIII	Graz	10
XX	Danzig	7
XXI	Posen	5

It will be noted that in the above table the numbers XIV, XV, XVI, and XIX are missing from the list of Wehrkreise. This is explained by the fact that Wehrkreise are in reality corps areas, with one peacetime army corps located in each Wehrkreis and bearing its number. The four missing numbers were assigned to Panzer, light, and motorized corps, which had no corresponding Wehrkreise, as they drew their personnel from Germany at large (see par. 16b).

24. Professional cadre.—*a. Officer Corps.*—The German Officer Corps is normally a professional long-service body of officers devoting themselves exclusively to the practice of their profession. Their standard of living is not high, and in purchasing power their pay may be estimated at about two-thirds that of U. S. officers of equivalent rank. Prior to 1939, the strength of the German Officer Corps was estimated at a little under 30,000. For the present war, large numbers of retired officers have been recalled to duty, and in addition there is a very considerable body of young reserve officers who have been obtained from the ranks after service at the front and the completion of a 5-month training course.

b. Noncommissioned Officer Corps.—(1) *Time of service.*—The German Noncommissioned Officer Corps is composed largely of professional long-service volunteers. For the majority, the term German noncommissioned Officer Corps is composed largely of special administrative and technical ability, serve beyond the normal 12-year term, sometimes even up to 25 years. Prior to 1939, the Noncommissioned Officers Corps is believed to have approximated one-tenth of the total Army strength, or between 70,000 and 90,000 men. During the war, of course, it has been greatly expanded, and a special 4½-year term of service has been introduced.

(2) *Recruitment.*—The German Noncommissioned Officer Corps is built up by two methods, as follows:

(*a*) The bulk of noncommissioned officers are obtained within the units. Young recruits who desire to adopt the career of a noncommissioned officer apply to their company commander at any time during their tour of duty with the colors. The decision, however, as to whether the candidate will be accepted as a noncommissioned officer in his unit is not made until toward the close of the applicant's service, when the company commander has had a thorough opportunity to observe his character, intelligence, and ability to perform the duties of a noncommissioned officer. He must also have attained the rank of *Gefreiter* (acting corporal) during his normal service. The appointment to the grade of *Unteroffizier* is made by the regimental commander on the recommendation of the company commander.

(*b*) The second pathway to the career of a noncommissioned officer is through the noncommissioned officer schools. There are five of these schools in the German Army, each ranging in strength between 200 and 300. The course in these schools lasts 2 years. Volunteers are accepted between the ages of 18 and 20. The course, in general, is a practical one, although a few theoretical subjects are taught. Upon graduation, the successful students are appointed *Unteroffiziere* and assigned to regiments. These schools give the Army High Command the opportunity to equalize the quality of the noncommissioned officer in regiments. Many German regiments recruit from rural areas which do not furnish an adequate supply of noncommissioned officer material. To such regiments the High Command assigns young graduates of the noncommissioned officer schools.[2]

25. **Training.**—*a. Premilitary training.*—Before being called up for military service, all young men serve for some months in the Reich Labor Service. As a result, when German recruits join their organizations, they are hardened physically, and are accustomed to living in groups under military discipline. Important preliminary training in specialized branches is given in the naval and air sections of the Hitler Youth Organization (*Marine Hitler-Jugend* and *Flieger Hitler-Jugend*), in the glider schools, and in competitions held by the National Socialist Aviation Corps (*Nationalsozialistiches Fliegerkorps*, or *NSFK*).

b. Normal military training.—(1) *Winter.*—In peacetime the annual class of recruits joined the colors on or about 1 November. From 1 November until 1 March the emphasis in all training was placed on the development of the individual. Commencing in February, however, platoon and company tactical problems were given. During March the divisional inspections were held with respect to companies. In the last half of March and the first half of April, battalions and even regiments conducted tactical exercises of a nature which seldom called for the presence of other arms. During the winter season the staffs of higher units, beginning with the division, conducted a series of map problems, one-

---

[2] The German noncommissioned officer grades are not equivalent to those of the U. S. Army. The German *Gefreiter* is not a noncommissioned officer in the German definition of that term (see fig. 13).

and two-sided map maneuvers, tactical rides, and terrain exercises. Sometimes signal units participated in these exercises. Nevertheless, it is doubtful if one could speak of "combined training" in the peacetime program until 1 April.

(2) *Summer.*—Between 1 April and 1 August, annually, every German unit spent 3 weeks in one or another of the barrack camps located on the maneuver grounds. These camps are large and generally hold three regiments simultaneously. At all times it was the intention to place infantry and artillery together in these camps. During this field-training period the infantry and artillery were trained as a team. Here the tactics of the German march-combat group (the regiment of infantry and the battalion of field artillery) were developed.

(3) *Maneuvers.*—Large-scale maneuvers took place during September and October. These maneuvers were intended primarily to train the combined staffs, arms, and services. Usually they were of a divisional nature. At least in two *Wehrkreise*, however, and sometimes in three, corps maneuvers were held annually. Army maneuvers (involving from five to eight divisions) were held once every 2 years. Staffs and troops were present in full strength at all maneuvers. The supply services, however, were represented only partially, if at all, as the German Army felt that their presence did not repay in training value the expense entailed.

c. *Short-term training.*—Owing to the restrictions imposed by the Versailles Treaty, there was a period of 15 years during which Germany did not have universal service. The classes from 1919 through 1934 did not receive military training. Following 1935, Germany made strenuous efforts to train this great reservoir of military manpower by calling classes for 8-week periods of intensive training. Some groups appear to have undergone several of these periods.

d. *Wartime training.*—The same principles as outlined above still apply to wartime training, except that the schedule has been speeded up and is not so closely tied to the calendar. By the end of 1942, virtually all the combined training was shifted to occupied countries, especially to France, so that the troops in training might perform the additional duties of occupation forces and be available for defense against invasion.

  e. *Air Force training.*—Each soldier of the Air Force, upon being inducted into service, goes to an *Ersatz* (training) battalion, of which there is at least one in each *Wehrkreis*. Here he is given his basic training as a soldier and in addition certain preliminary mechanical training in Air Force specialties. During this period there are selected from the recruits those specially qualified for pilot training. From the *Ersatz* battalion the recruit is sent directly to his unit or in certain cases to large mechanics' training schools.

26. Housing, cantonments, and training areas.—*a. Barracks.*—Beginning in 1935, Germany engaged in a vast program of military construction to house her expanding Army. By the summer of 1940, the German Army was thoroughly equipped with modern barracks to accommodate at least 50 divisions. In living and messing arrangements, these barracks are approximately equal to the newest and best of the U. S. Army, and in certain educational and workshop facilities are reported to be in advance of present U. S. standards.

  b. Training areas.—The German Army now has at least 32 general training grounds (in Germany) which vary in size. Some contain areas of as much as 200 square miles; others are much smaller. Troop units are normally sent in succession to one or another of these troop training grounds for a 3-week field exercise and target training period. Each training ground possesses contonment barracks for from 2 to 3 regiments. All grounds have target ranges for small-arms firing, and about two-thirds possess artillery ranges. In addition, there are numerous special training grounds for the specialized arms, and there are several ordnance proving grounds.

27. Pay and allowances.—*a. Peacetime.*—The peacetime base pay rates for the various ranks in the German Army are shown in figure 14. In addition to these base pay rates, in peacetime officers received rental allowances, which varied according to the cost of living in different localities; officers and men re-

Pay group [1]	Service grade	Initial yearly pay [2]	After 2 years' service	After 4 years' service	After 6 years' service	After 8 years' service	After 10 years' service	After 12 years' service	After 14 years' service	After 16 years' service
1	Oberbefehlshaber der Wehrmachtteile Chef des Oberkommandos der Wehrmacht.	26,550								
2	Generaloberst General	}24,000								
3	Generalleutnant	19,000								
4	Generalmajor	16,000								
5	Oberst	12,600								
6	Oberstleutnant	9,700								
7	Major	7,700	8,400							
8	Hauptmann	4,800	6,000	6,900						
9	Oberleutnant	3,400	3,700	4,000	4,200					
10	Leutnant	2,400	2,700	3,000	3,440	3,700	4,000	4,200		
19	Stabsfeldwebel								2,550	2,742	2,944
20a 20b	}Oberfeldwebel	2,400						2,454	2,646	2,838
21a 21b	}Feldwebel	2,340						2,394	2,520	2,646
22a 22b	}Unterfeldwebel	2,040	2,160					2,322	2,424	2,514
23a 23b	}Unteroffizier	1,536	1,920					2,064	2,166	2,256
24	Obergefreiter	1,680	1,740	1,800						
25	Gefreiter	1,410								
26	Obergrenadier	1,260								
27	Grenadier	1,080								

[1] Groups 11 to 18 are not included in this table, as they apply only to special categories, such as bandmasters and medical and veterinary officers.
[2] The amount is given in *Reichsmark*; 1 *RM*=$0.40 (see par. 126).

Figure 14.—Scale of peacetime base pay in the German Army.

ceived liberal children's allowances for their minor children; and men who messed out of barracks received a food allowance. Officers were paid monthly in advance; men normally received their pay on the 1st and 21st of each month.

b. Wartime.—During the present war each member of the Armed Forces receives a greatly reduced "War Pay" (*Wehrsold*)

35

according to the schedule shown in figure 15. But there are liberal family allowances as well as a special bonus, usually one *Reichsmark* a day, for front duty. A further special bonus was given for service in Africa.

Pay group	Service grade	Yearly pay [1]
1	*Oberbefehlshaber der Wehrmachtteile*	3,600
	Chef des Oberkommandos der Wehrmacht	
2	*Generaloberst*	2,88
	General	
3	*Generalleutnant*	2,520
4	*Generalmajor*	2,160
5	*Oberst*	1,800
6	*Oberstleutnant*	1,440
7	*Major*	1,296
8	*Hauptmann*	1,152
9	*Oberleutnant*	972
10	*Leutnant*	864
11	*Stabsfeldwebel*	720
	Hauptfeldwebel	
	Oberfeldwebel	
	Unteroffizier	
12	*Feldwebel*	648
	Oberfähnrich	
13	*Unterfeldwebel*	540
	Fähnrich	
14	*Unteroffizier*	504
15	*Stabsgefreiter*	432
	Obergefreiter	
	Gefreiter	
	Obergrenadier	
	Grenadier	
16	*Obergrenadier* and *Grenadier* (less than 2 years' service)	360

[1] The amount is given in *Reichsmark*; 1 *RM* = $0.40 (see par. 126). For the discrepancy between peacetime and wartime base pay, see par. 27.

Figure 15.—Scale of wartime base pay in the German Army.

c. Professional.—Professional soldiers, however, receive in addition to their own pay a compensation allowance amounting approximately to the differences between it and the peacetime pay rates. This applies to other officers and long-term enlisted men, but not to ordinary wartime conscripts. Reserve officers may obtain a similar compensation allowance on application.

28. Mobilization in the past.—*a.* At the outbreak of war in 1914 the entire strength of the German nation was mobilized in a single week, a procedure which interrupted gravely the economic life of the nation. The effects of this 100-percent mobilization of trained man power were never afterward fully overcome. It was a very rigid procedure, and there was apparently no method of varying its extent or speed. In the course of 1 week, the active Army was brought to full strength and some 35 reserve divisions as well as a large number of fortress, *Landwehr*, *Ersatz*, and *Landsturm* units were created. In all, the active Army of 800,000 men was expanded to 3,900,000 in about 10 days' time.

b. As a result, not only was the Army cumbersome to handle, being composed of elements with wide divergences in training, efficiency, and equipment, but the whole life of Germany was disrupted to an almost disastrous extent. Agriculture was crippled, many branches of commerce and industry were temporarily paralyzed, and government administration was seriously hampered.

29. Present principles of mobilization.—*a.* These mistakes made in the last war were the subject of careful study and criticism by the German General Staff for many years thereafter, and a determined effort was made to prevent their recurrence. For the present war, German manpower has been mobilized gradually and selectively ever since the beginning of 1938, and the process is still continuing. Men are summoned to the colors individually by mail, not in annual classes by public proclamation. Only the number actually needed at any given phase of the war are called up, and great care is taken not to disrupt any one industry or individual factory, shop, office, or farm by an excessive or precipitous withdrawal of its manpower to the Armed Forces. This system, incidentally, has the advantage of secrecy. Furthermore, no units are formed entirely of new recruits, but all units contain more or less similar proportions of men with different degrees of training and belonging to the different age groups. This insures a high degree of uniformity of quality of all German combat units. Soldiers entering the German Army are assigned to either fighting or supply units according to their ages.

b. Early in 1943 the German Army announced that men in the fighting arms (infantry, Panzer, artillery, engineer, chemical warfare, and signal troop units) must be 37 or younger, whereas men in command headquarters and in higher units, supply troops, and men in engineer units employed in rear areas must be 38 or older. Fighting troops in tropical service must be 33 or younger, while supply troops serving in the tropics must be 34 or older. Only men 42 or older, or unable through physical disability to be on active duty, were allowed to remain in the zone of the interior, although an exception was made in the case of training personnel in training units.

Section IV

UNIFORMS, INSIGNIA, AND IDENTIFICATIONS[1]

	Paragraph
Army uniforms	30
Army insignia	31
Air Force uniforms and insignia	32
Uniforms and insignia of militarized and auxiliary organizations	33
Means of identification	34
Decorations and awards	35

30. Army uniforms (plates I to IV).—*a. General.*—The present type of uniform in the German Field Army has been evolved from that worn during World War I, the chief requirements being that it should be light, comfortable, weatherproof, and inconspicuous. The uniforms for officers and for enlisted men are basically the same in almost all particulars.

---

[1] Color plates of uniforms and insignia follow page 50.

Officers are distinguished from enlisted men only by insignia of rank and other comparatively minor markings and variations in their dress.

   b. Normal field uniform (plates I and II).—The following particulars apply to the uniforms of the great majority of German soldiers in the field:

   (1) *Field blouse.*—The field blouse (*Feldbluse*) is made of greenish-gray cloth, with a collar usually of a much darker shade of green. The collar may be folded back to make an open neck. No uniform shirt is worn under the blouse.

   (2) *Trousers.*—The trousers (*Hosen*) are of greenish-gray or gray cloth. Riding breeches for mounted officers and enlisted men are of the same color but with leather facings, and are worn with black riding boots.

   (3) *Overcoat.*—The overcoat (*Mantel*) is double-breasted and is made of greenish-gray cloth.

   (4) *Field cap.*—The field cap (*Feldmütze*), which is similar to the U. S. Army garrison cap, is made of greenish-gray cloth. It is worn by officers and enlisted men of all arms, except mountain troops and personnel of certain armored units (see *c*, below). The officer's field cap is of a better quality than the enlisted man's and has aluminum-colored piping along the top seam and top edge of the turnup. The field cap is so designed that it may be worn under the steel helmet. (A new field cap (*Einheitsmütze*) in the style of the mountain cap has recently been adopted.)

   (5) *Steel helmet.*—The steel helmet (*Stahlhelm*) is made of seamless sheet steel, and is painted both inside and outside with rust-resistant, dull field-gray paint. Officers and enlisted men wear the same helmet.

   (6) *Pack.*—The pack (*Tornister*) is a heavy square-shaped canvas bag with leather binding. A blanket, a camouflage cover, (which sometimes serves as a raincoat), and also at times the overcoat, are rolled and strapped around the pack. For mountain troops, the pack is replaced by a rucksack, a form of which, orig-

inally adopted by the *Afrika-Korps*, is coming to be used extensively throughout the Army.

(7) *Other equipment.*—Other equipment carried by the individual includes leather cartridge pouches, a shelter-half with ropes, a canteen and mess kit, a haversack, a gas mask, a gas cape (an impregnated cloth cover for protection against gas), entrenching tools, and side arms. Officers wear brown belts (sometimes with the strap of the Sam Browne type), and enlisted men black belts.

c. Field uniform of special units (plates II to IV).—(1) *General.*—Various units of the German Army with specialized functions wear adaptations of the normal field uniform or entirely different uniforms designed to facilitate the execution of their duties.

(2) *Panzer troops* (plate II).—Tank crews wear black uniforms with loose-fitting trousers and black field caps. Armored-car personnel wear a rush-green or grayish-green uniform of similar cut. On the black uniform the collar patch has the skull and crossbones insignia.

(3) *Mountain troops* (plate IV).—These troops wear a mountain cap (*Gebirgsmütze*) similar to the field cap worn by other troops, but with the addition of a visor of the same material; the ordinary type of field blouse; and greenish-gray or gray cloth trousers, fastened around the ankles by puttees, and high shoes. The olive-green double-breasted wind jacket is a distinctive accessory of the mountain uniform. For use in snow and in special types of terrain, mountain troops may also be equipped with snowshoes and various kinds of coveralls.

(4) *Chemical warfare troops.*—In addition to their normal uniforms, these troops are equipped with dark leather suits consisting of jackets and trousers, and a mask with goggles.

d. Special duty uniforms.—For unusual conditions of climate or terrain, special uniforms may be issued to any unit.

(1) *Winter uniforms.*—Lined two-piece suits with felt boots and face masks are issued for extreme cold. White coveralls with

hoods may be issued wherever snow makes camouflage necessary.

(2) *Tropical uniforms* (plate III).—Khaki and olive-colored uniforms with web equipment and linen-topped boots are frequently employed in hot and arid regions. (The tropical uniform has recently been adopted as the official summer uniform, and has been extensively used not only in Africa, but also in Italy, the Balkans, and the Crimea.)

31. Army insignia (plates I to IV, and VII to IX).[2]—*a. Unit insignia.*—No unit insignia are worn by German troops in the field in wartime.

b. National devices.—(1) *General.*—The regimental insignia of the type worn by the U. S. Army are replaced in the German Army by the national emblem, the national colors, and the national rosette.

(2) *National emblem* (plates I to IV, and IX.)—The national emblem (*Hoheitsabzeichen*), which consists of a gray, white, or silver-colored formalized eagle with widespread wings holding a swastika in its claws, is worn during service in the field as follows:

(*a*) On the peak of the field cap and mountain cap.

(*b*) On all blouses, above the right breast pocket.

A silver eagle with folded wings is worn on the left side of the steel and tropical helmets, on a black shield.

(3) *National colors* (plate I).—The national colors—red, white, and black—are worn in the form of a shield on the right side of the steel helmet.

(4) *National rosette* (plates I to IV, and IX).—The national rosette (*Reichskokarde*) is a small circular insigne in red, white, and black sewed on below the national emblem on the field and mountain caps. On visored service caps it is made of metal and flanked by oak leaves (see plate I).

c. Distinguishing color of arm (plate IX).—(1) *General.*— Each soldier wears the distinguishing color of his arm (*Waffenfarbe*). The most characteristic location of this color is on the

---

[2] For the ranks in the German Armed Forces, see also figures 13, 14, and 15.

piping around the edge of the shoulder strap, but it may also appear elsewhere.

(2) *Principal colors.*—The following are the principal distinguishing colors:

> Infantry—white (*weiss*).
> Mountain infantry—light green (*hellgrün*).
> Tank troops—pink (*rosa*).
> Motorcycle troops—grass green (*wiesengrün*) (probably now pink).
> Cavalry and cyclists—golden yellow (*goldgelb*).
> Motorized and Panzer reconnaissance—copper brown (*kupferbraun*) (now pink).
> Artillery—bright red (*hochrot*).
> Engineers—black (*schwarz*).
> Signal troops—lemon yellow (*zitronengelb*).
> Chemical warfare troops—bordeaux (*bordeauxrot*).
> Transport and supply troops—light blue (*hellblau*).
> Medical troops—dark blue (*kornblumenblau*).
> Veterinary troops—crimson (*karmesinrot*).
> Propaganda troops—light gray (*leichtgrau*).
> General Staff Corps—crimson (*karmesinrot*).

d. Insignia of rank (plates VII and VIII).—(1) *Shoulder straps.*—The insignia of rank are normally worn on the shoulder straps. It will be noted from the illustrations that the shoulder straps fall into five main groups according to the amount of cord or braid on the strap.

(2) *Collar patches.*—As an additional distinction, general officers wear a red collar patch with a stylized gold oak leaf. All lower ranks now wear a collar patch with a double band, with slight variation. Noncommissioned officers have an additional silver band around two sides of the collar patch.

(3) *Sleeves.*—With special types of uniforms which do not have shoulder straps or collar patches, such as snow suits, wind breakers,

protective suits for tank crews, canvas jackets, and work clothes, all ranks may wear a special sleeve insignia introduced in September 1942. These consist of woven oak leaves and bars, in gold for generals and light green for other ranks. These insignia are worn on the upper left sleeve.

32. Air Force uniforms and insignia (plates V and VI).—
a. General.—The basic uniforms of the German Air Force are blue-gray. Both the roll-collar type of blouse and the fly-front flight blouse (*Fliegerbluse*) are commonly worn. The field cap (*Fliegermütze*) is more rakish than the field cap of the Army.

b. National devices.—The national emblem (called *Hoheitszeichen* in the Air Force) is a "flying eagle" with a swastika in its claws. The national rosette is like that of the Army but with formalized spreading wings on each side of the oak leaves. These insignia, as well as the national colors, are worn in the same manner as in the Army. In addition, flying personnel wear a special badge on the left breast depicting an eagle with a swastika, the whole enclosed in a wreath.

c. Distinguishing colors.—The distinguishing color of arms in the Air Force is not only displayed in the piping of the shoulder patches as in the Army, but also forms the background on the collar patches. The following are the principal colors:

>Generals—white (*weiss*).
>Flying troops—golden yellow (*goldgelb*).
>Antiaircraft artillery—bright red (*hochrot*).
>Signal troops—golden brown (*goldbraun*).

d. Insignia of rank.—The shoulder straps worn by the Air Force bear the same insignia of rank as those in the Army. On the collar patches, however, are worn from one to four pairs of wings to distinguish ranks in the various groups, and those of officers contain either oak leaves or oak wreaths. Noncommissioned officers usually have in addition a band of silver braid around the lower edge of the collar.

e. Parachute troops (plate VI).—Parachute troops wear special loose-fitting blue-gray trousers and the flight blouse. For jumping, a knee-length coverall is worn over this uniform. Men who have made a minimum of six jumps wear a special badge depicting a silver diving eagle with a swastika in its claws, the whole enclosed in a gold-colored wreath.

33. Uniforms and insignia of militarized and auxiliary organizations.—*a. Waffen-SS.*—The *Waffen-SS* (see par. 100*b* (2)) wears a uniform identical to the Army field uniform. Its members can be distinguished from Army troops by the position of the national emblem, which is worn on the left sleeve instead of on the right breast, and the national colors on the steel helmet are replaced by the *SS* device. A further distinction is the special insignia of rank, which differ from those of the Regular Army and are worn on the collar patches. Also, oak leaves denote the higher ranks, while diamond-shaped devices, or pips, indicate the lower ranks of officers.

b. Storm Troopers (SA).—The regular uniform of the *SA* (see par. 103*e*) is the brown shirt and trousers, with a brown blouse and visored cap. Members wear a broad red arm band with a black swastika in a white circle. The band is worn on the upper left arm.

c. National Socialist Motor Corps (NSKK).—The *NSKK* (see par. 103*c*) wears a uniform consisting of a brown shirt and black breeches, and members may also wear brown blouses and brown coveralls. The national emblem is mounted on a wheel enclosing a swastika, and is worn on the cap or black crash helmet. Normally white Arabic numerals preceded by the letter "M" (indicating *Mot.*) on the right collar patch give the number of the unit. Insignia of rank are like those of the *SS* and *SA*, and are worn on the left collar patch, while additional insignia of rank are worn on the right shoulder. The *NSKK* wears the same arm band as the *SA*.

d. Reich Labor Service.—Members of the Reich Labor Service (*Reichsarbeitsdienst*), which is frequently designated by the abbreviation *RAD* (see par 103b), wear a uniform consisting of a brown shirt and a brown-gray blouse with a dark collar, a visored cap, and slacks or breeches. They also wear the Party arm band like the *SA* and *NSKK*. The insignia includes a white spade on a black background worn just above the arm band.

e. Technical Emergency Corps.—The field uniform of the Technical Emergency Corps (*Technische Nothilfe*), which is frequently designated by the abbreviation *Teno* (see par. 103d), is similar to that of the Army. There are two arm bands on the lower left sleeve, one bearing the words *Technische Nothilfe* in white, and the other the words *Deutsche Wehrmacht* in black. The national emblem is worn on the upper left sleeve, superimposed on a black triangle. The *Teno* emblem, a cogwheel, is worn on the collar patches.

f. National Socialist Aviation Corps.—Members of the *Nationalsozialistisches Fliegerkorps*, or *NSFK* (see par. 103f), wear a brown shirt and dark blue-gray blouse and breeches or slacks. They also wear either visored caps or berets. Their insignia are very similar to those of the *SA*.

34. Means of identification.—The two primary means of identification usually to be found on every German soldier are as follows:

a. Identification tag (fig. 16).—The identification tag (*Erkennungsmarke*) is issued on mobilization and is worn at all times by all personnel. The tag is of zinc and is oval-shaped, measuring about 2 by 3½ inches. It is divided into halves by a perforated line. Each half bears identical markings. When a man is killed, the lower half of the tag is broken off and sent to Germany and the upper half is buried with the body. Most identification tags which have been captured give a unit, a subordinate unit, a letter identifying the blood group, and a number. The identification tag seldom shows the unit in which the indi-

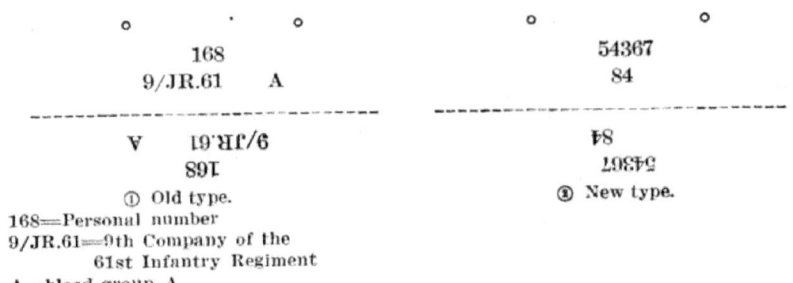

Figure 16.—Markings on identification tags (*Erkennungsmarken*) of the old and new types.

vidual concerned is currently serving (unless he had lost the original tag of his replacement unit and has received a new one from his present unit), but it may reveal the existence of a previously unidentified unit. A new type of identification tag recently captured does not bear the unit designation or blood group.

b. Paybook.—The paybook (*Soldbuch*) is issued on induction and is subsequently carried by the soldier at all times except when taking part in a raid. The paybook gives the following information concerning the soldier:

(1) The name and rank and the place and date of birth.

(2) A copy of the inscription on the identification tag.

(3) Personal data such as build, height, color of hair and eyes, civilian occupation, and religion.

(4) The unit in which he is serving, units of the Field Army (*Feldheer*) in which he served previously, and the replacement (*Ersatz*) unit into which he was originally inducted.

(5) The names and addresses of close relatives.

(6) A record of equipment issued.

(7) Dates of inoculations, details of eyesight, hospital record, and dental treatment.

(8) A record of pay group classification and of certain payments made to him.

(9) A record of furloughs, including dates and places visited.
(10) A list of decorations received.

35. Decorations and awards.—*a. Iron Cross.*—The Iron Cross award (*Eisernes Kreuz*) is for conspicuous bravery in face of the enemy or for outstanding services in leadership. The four classes of the Iron Cross rank in the following order:

Grand Cross of the Iron Cross (*Grosskreuz des Eisernen Kreuzes*).

Knight's Cross of the Iron Cross (*Ritterkreuz des Eisernen Kreuzes*).

Iron Cross, 1st Class (*Eisernes Kreuz, 1 Klasse*).

Iron Cross, 2d Class (*Eisernes Kreuz, 2 Klasse*).

Higher classes of the Iron Cross are awarded only to those already holding the lower class. The present Iron Cross, 1st and 2d Classes, differs from that of the last war in that the swastika and the year "1939" replace the initial "W" (*Wehrmacht*) and the crown. The Iron Cross, 1st Class, is usually worn on the blouse pocket of the left breast, and the Knight's Cross of the Iron Cross is suspended about the neck (see plate II). The bar to the Knight's Cross of the Iron Cross consists of three silver oak leaves on the medal ribbon. In addition, the oak leaves with swords, and the oak leaves with swords and diamonds, are awarded in very exceptional cases. The Grand Cross, which is approximately double the size of the Iron cross, 1st and 2d Classes, has been conferred only on *Reichsmarschall Göring*. Men who gained the Iron Cross in the World War I may be awarded a silver bar which bears the national eagle and swastika, and the date of the new award.

b. War Merit Cross.—The War Merit Cross (*Kriegsverdienstkreuz*) is awarded as a recognition of merit to persons not eligible for award of the Iron Cross. It has the following grades:

Knight's Cross of the War Merit Cross (*Ritterkreuz des Kriegsverdienstkreuzes*).

War Merit Cross, 1st Class (*Kriegsverdienstkreuz, 1 Klasse*).

War Merit Cross, 2d Class (*Kriegsverdienstkreuz, 2 Klasse*).

These awards may be made with or without swords. Swords are awarded for especially meritorious service in the zone of enemy action or for exceptional services in furthering the war effort. The cross is awarded without swords for meritorious services in which enemy action played no part. The War Merit Cross has a swastika in the center, embossed on a plain surface, and is edged with oak leaves. The 2d Class is in bronze. The 1st Class and the Knight's Cross are in silver. A bronze War Merit Medal with the legend *Für Kriegsverdienst* may also be awarded (usually to civilians).

c. German Cross.—The German Cross (*Deutsches Kreuz*), which was created in September 1941, consists of a dark-gray silver-edged eight-pointed star, about 2½ inches in diameter. In the center is a black, silver-edged swastika on a dull silver background surrounded by a gold or silver laurel wreath with the year "1941" at the bottom. The German Cross is worn on the right breast without ribbons. The German Cross in silver is awarded for repeated outstanding service in the military conduct of the war. It is awarded in gold for a repeated display of extraordinary valor or for repeated outstanding service in tactics.

d. Infantry Assault Badge.—The Infantry Assault Badge (*Infanterie-Sturmabzeichen*), in bronze, consists of a rifle with fixed bayonet encircled by a wreath of oak leaves, the whole surmounted by the German eagle and swastika. It is worn on the left breast pocket of the blouse immediately beneath the Iron Cross or any other decoration. It may be given to soldiers who have taken part in at least three attacks on the enemy position on 3 different days and have overcome the enemy in hand-to-hand combat.

e. Tank badge.—The Tank Badge (*Panzerkampfwagen-Abzeichen*), in bronze, is made up of a wreath of oak leaves surrounding a tank, the whole surmounted by the German eagle and swastika. It is worn on the left breast pocket of the blouse immediately beneath the Iron Cross or any other decoration. It may be given to soldiers of the Panzer troops who have engaged in at least three attacks on the enemy on 3 different days.

f. Assault Badge for Other Arms.—This award (*Sturmabzeichen anderer Waffengattungen*), in silver, depicts a stick grenade crossed with a bayonet and surmounted by the German eagle and swastika, the whole surrounded by a wreath of oak leaves. It is worn on the left breast. It is given to officers, noncommissioned officers, and privates of other arms which cooperate closely with the infantry or tanks, or to individual members of other arms who fulfill the conditions under which the infantry assault badge is awarded to infantrymen.

g. Wound Badge.—This award (*Verwundeten-Abzeichen*) is similar to the wound badge of the World War I, and consists of two crossed bayonets beneath a steel helmet bearing the swastika, the whole surrounded by a wreath of oak leaves. It is given in three classes, all of which are worn on the left breast pocket of the blouse, as follows:

>1st Class, in gold, for those wounded more than four times.
>2d Class, in silver, for those wounded three or four times.
>3d Class, in black, for those wounded once or twice.

h. Special decoration to soldiers for destruction of enemy tanks.—This decoration (*Panzer-Nahkampfabzeichen*), a narrow aluminum ribbon with black edging on which is affixed a miniature tank, is awarded to individuals for the destruction or incapacitation of an enemy tank by use of the antitank rifle, rifle, grenade, or explosives.

i. Campaign decorations.—(1) *General.*—In addition to the principal decorations and awards mentioned above, certain other emblems are worn by individuals who have taken part in offensive operations.

(2) *Narvik Shield.*—The Narvik Shield (*Narvikschild*) decoration is in the form of a shield showing the *Edelweiss* (of mountain regiments), an anchor surmounted by the German eagle hold-

ing in its claws a wreath which surrounds a swastika. This decoration is awarded in silver for the Army and Air Force and in gold for the Navy, and is worn on the upper left sleeve of the uniform. All members of the Armed Forces who participated in the Narvik action are eligible.

(3) *East Medal.*—The East Medal (*Ostmedaille*) was awarded to those members of the Armed Forces who served on the eastern front from November 1941 to April 1942. In lieu of the medal, soldiers may wear a dark red ribbon with white-black-white stripes.

(4) *Sleeve Band for Crete.*—An order of the *Oberkommando der Wehrmacht* on 16 October 1942 announced the award of the Sleeve Band for Crete (*Ärmelband Kreta*) to all members of the Armed Forces who participated honorably in the invasion of Crete. The decoration, consisting of a white arm band with gold borders and the inscription *Kreta*, is worn on the lower left sleeve of the uniform blouse.

(5) *Crimea Shield.*—The Crimea Shield (*Krim-Schild*) decoration is awarded to members of the Army, Navy, or Air Force who, in the period from 21 September 1941 to 4 July 1942, fulfilled one of the following conditions on the Crimean Peninsula: engaged in a major attack; were wounded; or remained on the peninsula for an uninterrupted period of 3 months. The shield is made up of a bas-relief of the Crimean Peninsula with the inscription *Krim 1941–1942*, surmounted by the German eagle holding in its claws a wreath surrounding a swastika.

(6) *Kholm Shield.*—The Kholm Shield (*Cholmschild*) was awarded to those members of the Armed Forces who participated honorably in the defense of Kholm, south of Lake Ilmen in the Soviet Union, from mid-January to mid-April 1942 under the leadership of *Generalmajor* Scherer. The decoration is worn on the upper left sleeve of the uniform blouse and shows the German eagle surmounting an Iron Cross below which is the inscription *Cholm–1942*.

HANDBOOK ON GERMAN MILITARY FORCES
PLATE II

ARMY CONTINENTAL UNIFORMS: MOBILE TROOPS

TANK TROOPS
Acting 1st Sergeant

ENLISTED MAN'S FIELD CAP

PANZER DEVICE
Worn on lapels

CAVALRY
Private, 1st Class

ARMORED CARS, ASSAULT GUNS
2d Lieutenant

PANZER LAPEL
Panzer Signal Unit

FIELD LAPEL
Assault Guns

From J.A.N. No. 1   TM-E 30-451

HANDBOOK ON GERMAN MILITARY FORCES
PLATE III

ARMY TROPICAL UNIFORMS: OFFICERS AND ENLISTED MEN

NATIONAL EMBLEM

CORPORAL'S CHEVRONS

BLOUSE AND BREECHES
1st Sergeant, Artillery

SHIRT AND SHORTS
Private, Signal Troops

OVERCOAT
Private, Transport Troops

COLLAR PATCH

SHOULDER STRAP
1st Sergeant, Artillery

From J.A.N. No. 1

TM-E 30-451

HANDBOOK ON GERMAN MILITARY FORCES
PLATE IV

ARMY CONTINENTAL UNIFORMS: MOUNTAIN TROOPS

SERVICE DRESS
2d Lieutenant, Signal Troops

SLEEVE DEVICE
Worn on right sleeve

REVERSIBLE JACKET
Captain

OFFICER'S
MOUNTAIN SERVICE CAP
Infantry

WIND JACKET
2d Lieutenant

MOUNTAIN CAP
(The new Army field cap resembles the mountain cap.)

From J.A.N. No. 1   TM-E 30-451

HANDBOOK ON GERMAN MILITARY FORCES
PLATE V

AIR FORCE UNIFORMS: OFFICERS AND ENLISTED MEN

HEADGEAR INSIGNIA

NATIONAL EMBLEM

NATIONAL COLORS
Worn on right side of helmet

EAGLE EMBLEM
Worn on left side of helmet

ENLISTED MAN
Private, Antiaircraft

NONCOMMISSIONED OFFICER
1st Sergeant, Flying Troops

OFFICER
Colonel, Construction Corps

OFFICER'S SERVICE CAP

ENLISTED MAN'S SERVICE CAP

OFFICER'S FIELD CAP

ENLISTED MAN'S FIELD CAP

HANDBOOK ON GERMAN MILITARY FORCES
PLATE VI

AIR FORCE UNIFORMS: MISCELLANEOUS

OFFICER'S SHOULDER STRAP (above)
COLLAR PATCH (below)
Colonel, Antiaircraft
(Generals: gold braid)

TROPICAL BLOUSE AND BREECHES
Sergeant, Signal Troops

NONCOMMISSIONED OFFICER'S
SHOULDER STRAP (above)
COLLAR PATCH (below)
1st Sergeant, Flying Troops

PARACHUTIST'S UNIFORM
Technical Sergeant

SUMMER FLYING SUIT
Master Sergeant

ENLISTED MAN'S
SHOULDER STRAP (above)
COLLAR PATCH (below)
Private, Signal Troops

From J.A.N. No. 1

TM-E 30-451

HANDBOOK ON GERMAN MILITARY FORCES
PLATE VII

ARMY INSIGNIA OF RANK

SHOULDER STRAPS

Shoulder straps indicate both rank and arm. The arm is indicated by colored piping around the edge of the strap.

GENERAL OFFICERS

FIELD MARSHAL
Generalfeldmarschall

GENERAL
Generaloberst

Noncommissioned officers are distinguished by collar braid, which borders the collar in whole or in part. This braid also indicates specialists (*Sonderführer*) of noncommissioned grades. Specialists of commissioned grades wear shoulder straps of their arm and grade, with red-white-black thread intertwined with the cords in the center of the strap.

GENERAL OFFICERS	FIELD OFFICERS	COMPANY OFFICERS
 LIEUTENANT GENERAL General der (*arm*)	 COLONEL Oberst Artillery	 CAPTAIN Hauptmann Tank Regiment
 MAJOR GENERAL Generalleutnant	 LIEUTENANT COLONEL Oberstleutnant General Staff Corps	 1ST LIEUTENANT Oberleutnant Military Police
 BRIGADIER GENERAL Generalmajor	 MAJOR Major Chemical Warfare Troops	 2D LIEUTENANT Leutnant Infantry

COLLAR PATCHES

GENERAL OFFICERS

OFFICERS, GENERAL STAFF

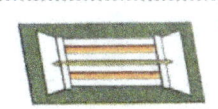
OTHER OFFICERS

HANDBOOK ON GERMAN MILITARY FORCES
PLATE VIII
ARMY INSIGNIA OF RANK

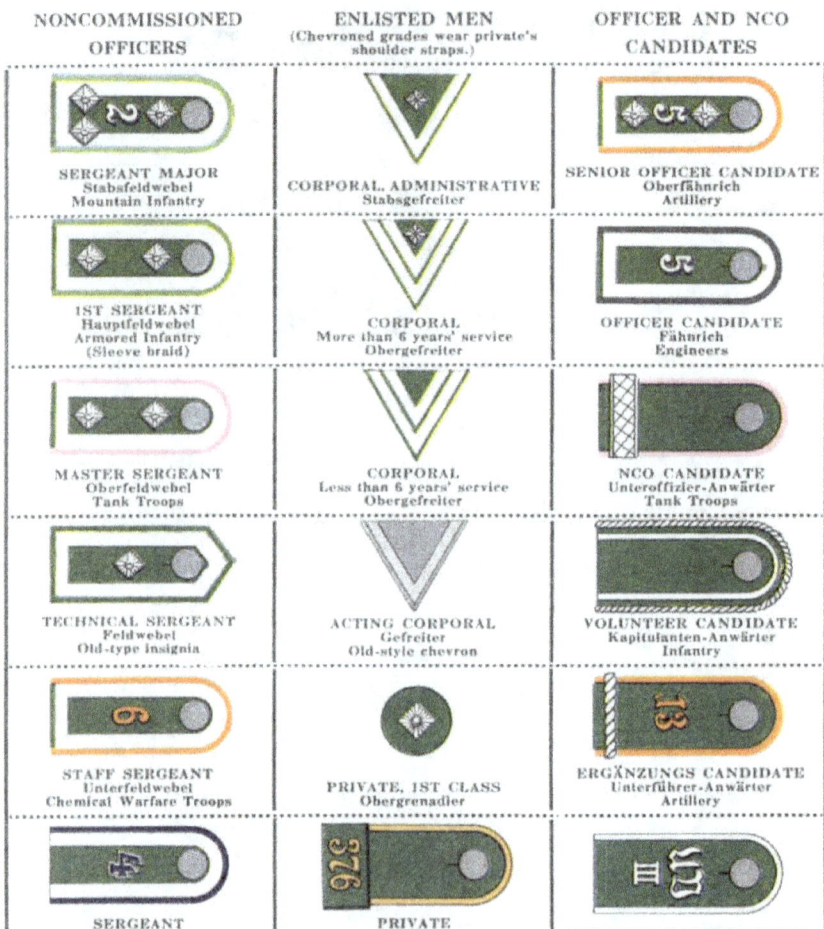

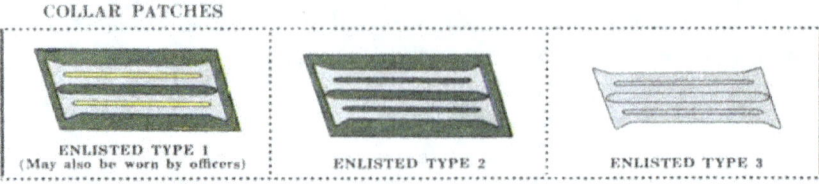

HANDBOOK ON GERMAN MILITARY FORCES
PLATE IX

COLORS OF ARMY ARMS

Colored pipings to indicate the arm appear on the shoulder strap, on the service cap, on the field cap, sometimes on the collar patch, and on that style of officer's field blouse which carries piping on the cuffs, on the collar, and on the edge of the blouse fly. The application of colors to motorcyclists and to other reconnaissance and mobile units remains uncertain, owing to organizational changes.

Color	Arm	Color	Arm	Color	Arm
Bright Red	GENERAL OFFICERS / Generale	Golden Yellow	CAVALRY, CYCLISTS / Kavallerie, Radfahrer	Violet	CHAPLAINS / Heeresgeistliche
Bright Red	ARTILLERY / Artillerie	Lemon Yellow	SIGNAL TROOPS / Nachrichtentruppen	Dark Blue	MEDICAL PERSONNEL / Sanitäts-Korps
Crimson	GENERAL STAFF CORPS / Generalstab	Light Green	MOUNTAIN INFANTRY / Gebirgsjäger	Light Blue	TRANSPORT, SUPPLY TROOPS / Fahrtruppen, Nachschubtruppen
Crimson	VETERINARY PERSONNEL / Veterinär-Korps	Grass Green	ARMORED INFANTRY / Panzergrenadiere	Black	ENGINEERS / Pioniere
Pink	TANK TROOPS / Panzertruppen	Grass Green	MOTORCYCLE TROOPS / Kradschützen (Probably Now Pink)	Light Brown	CONSTRUCTION TROOPS / Bautruppen
Orange-Red	MILITARY POLICE / Feldgendarmerie	Dark Green	CIVILIAN OFFICIALS / Beamten	Copper Brown	MOTORIZED, PANZER RECONNAISSANCE (Now Pink)
Orange-Red	ENGINEERING OFFICERS / Ingenieur-Offiziere (Disbanding)	White	INFANTRY / Infanterie	Gray Blue	SPECIALIST OFFICERS / Sonderführer
Orange-Red	OFFICERS, RECRUITING AGENCIES (Now White)	Bordeaux	CHEMICAL WARFARE TROOPS / Nebeltruppen	Light Gray	PROPAGANDA TROOPS / Propagandatruppen

From J.A.N. No. 1   TM-E 30-451

UNIFORMS, INSIGNIA, AND IDENTIFICATIONS 35

j. Miscellaneous.—(1) *General.*—Among other military medals likely to be found are the Memorial Medal, the Sudeten Medal, and the Memel Medal. All three medals are in bronze—the face shows two nude warriors bearing the German flag, with the national emblem as their stepping-stone.

(2) *Memorial Medal.*—The Memorial Medal (*Erinnerungs-Medaille*) marks the annexation (*Anschluss*) of Austria. The ribbon is dark red with black and white edging. The reverse side of the medal bears the inscription *Ein Volk, Ein Reich, Ein Führer* and the date *13 März 1938*.

(3) *Sudeten Medal.*—The Sudeten Medal commemorates the cession of the Sudetenland to Germany. The reverse side of the medal bears the inscription *Ein Volk, Ein Reich, Ein Führer* with the date *1 Oktober 1939*. The ribbon is black-red-black.

(4) *Memel Medal.*—The Memel Medal marks the return of the Memelland to Germany. The reverse side of the medal bears the inscription *Medaille zur Erinnerung an die Heimkehr des Memellandes* and the date *22 März 1939*. The ribbon is green-white-red.

Section V

INFANTRY

	Paragraph
Introduction	36
Infantry regiment (*Grenadier-Regiment*)	37
Infantry battalion in infantry regiment	38
Motorized infantry regiment (*Grenadier-Regiment (Mot.)*) in motorized division	39
Motorized infantry regiment (*Panzer-Grenadier-Regiment*) in Panzer division	40
Mountain infantry regiment (*Gebirgsjäger-Regiment*)	41
Motorcycle battalion (*Kradschützen-Bataillon*)	42
Motorized machine-gun battalion (*Maschinengewehr-Bataillon (Mot.)*)	43
Motorized antiaircraft machine-gun battalion (*Flugabwehr-Bataillon (Mot.)*)	44
Security regiment (*Sicherungs-Regiment*)	45

36. Introduction.—*a. General.*—Despite the important role which has been played by specialized branches of the German Army, the infantry has been and remains today the foundation for German offensive and defensive operations. Panzer divisions have penetrated enemy lines and operated as spearheads far behind them, but final decisions have been forced by aggressive, quick-marching, ground-holding infantry units provided with great firepower. The German Army has recognized the fundamental importance of the infantry by selecting particularly capable officer material for this branch, and by providing weapons to meet almost any situation that may confront an infantry unit from the squad up to the regiment. Each infantry unit is furnished with whatever it needs to meet the problems which will arise when it closes with the enemy. Heavy infantry weapons are provided in the infantry howitzer company with its three platoons of 75-mm (light) infantry howitzers and its one platoon of 150-mm (heavy) infantry howitzers. In this way, artillery does not have to be taken from main artillery objectives and the infantry has its own artillery close-fire support. Similarly, the infantry regiment has its own organic combat engineer, reconnaissance, antitank, and signal units, and its own supply column, making it almost as well-balanced and self-contained as a division.

b. Organization.—The Inspectorate of Infantry in the Army High Command is responsible, with few exceptions, for the organization, training, and equipment of the infantry throughout the Army. Exceptions are the motorized infantry regiments in Panzer divisions (*Panzer-Grenadier-Regimenter*) and motorcycle battalions, which together with Panzer and reconnaissance units are coordinated under the Inspector of Mobile Troops (*Inspekteur der schnellen Truppen*). The following principal types of subordinate infantry units exist:

(1) Infantry regiments (*Grenadier-Regimenter*), in light divisions called *Jäger-Regimenter*.

(2) Motorized infantry regiments (*Grenadier-Regimenter (Mot.)*), in Panzer divisions called *Panzer-Grenadier-Regimenter*.

(3) Mountain infantry regiments (*Gebirgsjäger-Regimenter*).

(4) Motorcycle battalions (*Kradschützen-Bataillone*).

(5) Motorized machine-gun battalions (*Maschinengewehr-Ba-*

Figure 17.—Medium armored personnel carrier (Sd.Kfz. 251).

taillone (Mot.)), a few in number, usually belonging to the GHQ pool.

(6) Motorized antiaircraft machine-gun battalions (*Flugabwehr-Bataillone (Mot.)*).

(7) Security regiments (*Sicherungs-Regimenter*).

37. Infantry regiment *(Grenadier-Regiment)*.—The German infantry regiment is a powerful, flexible unit controlling its own communications and supply. The infantry regiment is also provided with combat engineers, antitank defense, and close-support artillery in addition to its three battalions of infantry. (See fig. 18). The companies of the infantry battalions are

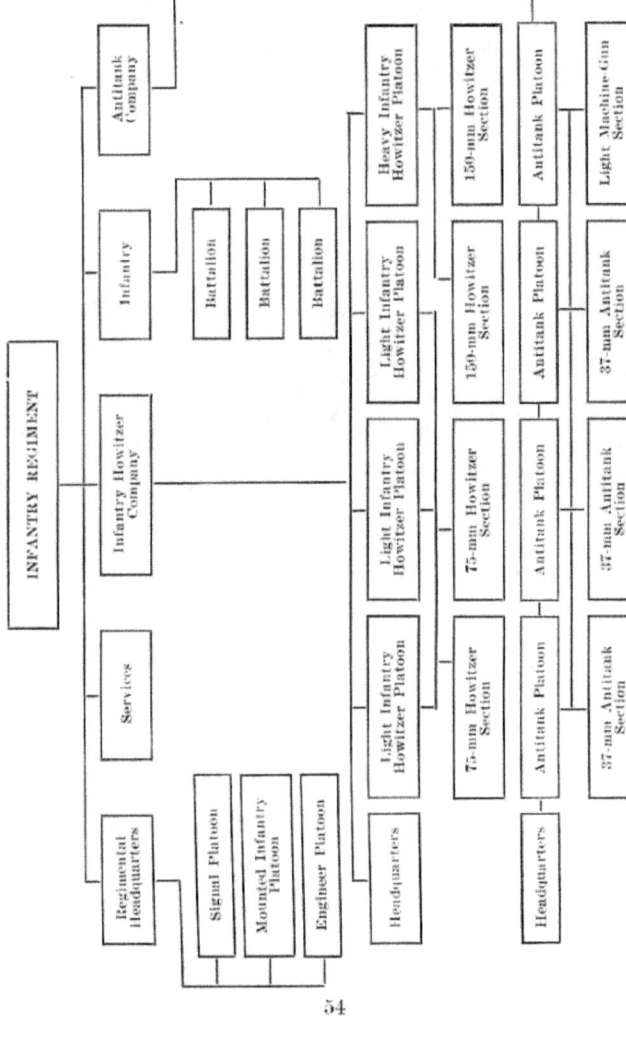

Figure 18.—Organization of the infantry regiment.

INFANTRY 37–38

numbered consecutively from 1 to 12 throughout the regiment, numbers 4, 8, and 12 being machine-gun companies. The approximate strength of the infantry regiment in personnel and transport is shown in figure 19; in armament, in figure 20.

Units	O and EM	Mtrcl	Other Mtr vehicles	H-Dr vehicles	Horses
Regimental headquarters	48	6	8	3	
Signal platoon	49			3	
Mounted infantry platoon	32			2	
Engineer platoon	57			7	
Infantry howitzer company	190	6		10	
Antitank company	170	23	30		
Three infantry battalions	2,514	45	33	150	
Services	99	7	2	39	
TOTAL	3,159	87	73	214	641

Figure 19.—Composition of the infantry regiment.

Weapons	How Co	AT Co	Engr Plat	3 Bns	TOTAL
Machine pistols				144	144
Machine guns, light		4	3	108	115
Machine guns, heavy				36	36
7.9-mm antitank rifles				27	27
37-mm antitank guns		12			12
50-mm mortars				27	27
81-mm mortars				18	18
75-mm infantry howitzers	6				6
150-mm infantry howitzers	2				2

Figure 20.—Armament of the infantry regiment.

38. Infantry battalion in infantry regiment.—*a. General.*—The infantry battalion consists of a headquarters, a signal section, three rifle companies, one machine-gun company, and trains. (See fig. 21.) Its approximate strength in personnel, transport, and armament is shown in figure 22.

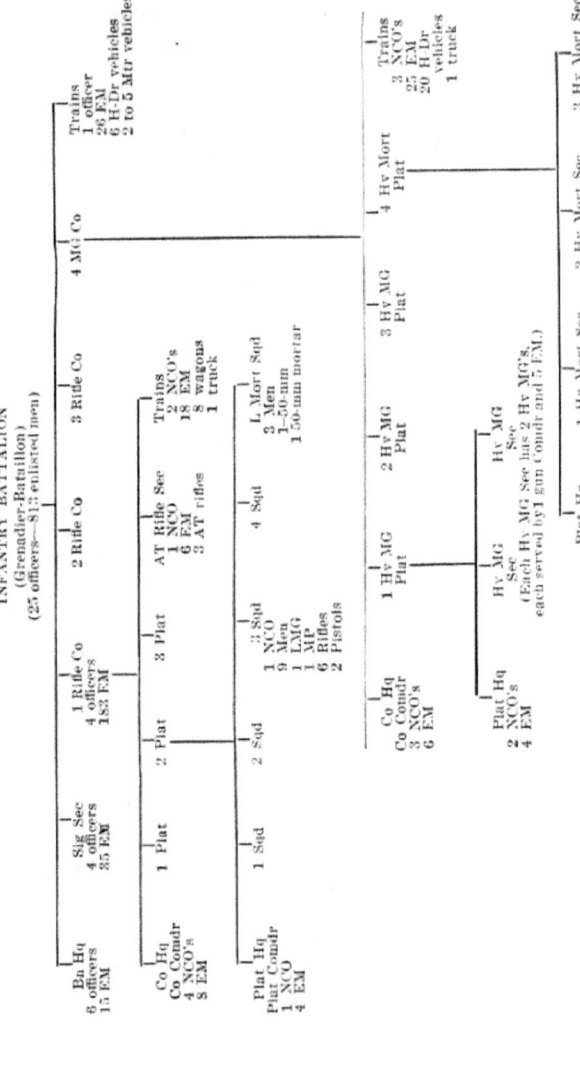

Figure 21.—Organization of the infantry battalion.

Units	O and EM	Mtrcl	Other Mtr vehicles	H-Dr vehicles	LMG	Hv MG	50-mm Mort	81-mm Mort	Machine pistols	AT rifles
Battalion headquarters	21	2								
Signal section	39		7	6						
Trains	27									
(1st) rifle company	187	3	1	8	12		3		16	3
(2d) rifle company	187	3	1	8	12		3		16	3
(3d) rifle company	187	3	1	8	12		3		16	3
(4th) machine-gun company	190	4	1	20		12		6		
TOTAL	838	15	11	50	36	12	9	6	48	9

Figure 22.— Composition and armament of the infantry battalion.

b. Composition of principal components.—(1) *Rifle company.*—The rifle company consists of a headquarters, an antitank rifle section armed with three antitank rifles, three rifle platoons, and a train. Each platoon is divided into one light mortar squad and four rifle squads; each rifle squad (squad leader and nine men) includes one light machine gun and one machine pistol. Platoon and company commanders also carry machine pistols.

(2) *Machine-gun company.*—The machine-gun company consists of a headquarters, three machine-gun platoons, one heavy mortar platoon, and a train. Each machine-gun platoon is divided into two machine-gun sections, each armed with two heavy machine guns. The mortar platoon consists of three mortar squads, each having one 81-mm mortar.

39. Motorized infantry regiment *(Grenadier-Regiment (Mot.))* in motorized division.—The motorized infantry regiment is identical in organization to the normal infantry regiment except that it has a motorcycle platoon instead of the mounted infantry platoon and that the regiment is completely motorized, with trucks replacing horse-drawn vehicles. The three independent platoons, engineer, signal, and motorcycle, are consolidated into a regimental headquarters company.

40. Motorized infantry regiment *(Panzer-Grenadier-Regiment)* in Panzer division.—The motorized infantry regiment, which forms part of the motorized infantry brigade *(Panzer-Grenadier-Brigade)* in the Panzer division, consists of a headquarters, a headquarters company (including a signal platoon, an antitank platoon, and a motorcycle platoon), two infantry battalions, an infantry howitzer company, and services. Its approximate strength in personnel and transport is shown in figure 23; in armament, in figure 24.

Units	O and EM	Mtrcl	Other Mtr vehicles
Headquarters	18	5	1
Headquarters company	152	26	23
Infantry howitzer company	101	10	20
Services	47	3	18
Two infantry battalions	1,968	128	291
TOTAL	2,286	172	353

Figure 23.—Composition of the motorized infantry regiment in the Panzer division.

Weapons	Hq Co	Inf How Co	2 Inf Bns	TOTAL
Machine pistols			78	78
Machine guns, light	3		116	119
Machine guns, heavy			24	24
Antitank rifles			18	18
20-mm antitank guns			3	3
37-mm antitank guns			9	9
50-mm antitank guns			9	9
81-mm mortars			12	12
75-mm infantry howitzers		4	4	8
150-mm infantry howitzers		4		4

Figure 24.—Armament of the motorized infantry regiment in the Panzer division.

41. Mountain infantry regiment *(Gebirgsjäger-Regiment)*.—*a. General.*—The mountain infantry regiment is specially organized for operations in rough country, having a considerably higher number of men in its three mountain infantry battalions than there are in the three infantry battalions in a normal infantry regiment. The regiment also has a large number of horses and mules for carrying loads over mountain trails which could not be crossed by vehicles. Most of the heavy weapons have been eliminated in order to facilitate mountain operations.

b. The mountain infantry regiment consists of a headquarters, a signal platoon, three mountain infantry battalions, an antitank company, and services. Its approximate strength in personnel and transport is shown in figure 25; in armament, in figure 26.

Units	O and EM	Mtrcl	Other Mtr vehicles	H-Dr vehicles	Horses or mules
Headquarters	31				
Signal platoon	43				
Three mountain battalions	3,006	84	135	174	
Antitank company	140				
Services	33				
TOTAL	3,253	84	135	174	475

Figure 25.—Composition of the mountain infantry regiment.

Weapons	3 Mtn Bns	AT Co	TOTAL
Machine pistols	117		117
Machine guns, light	172	6	178
Machine guns, heavy	42		42
Antitank rifles	36		36
37-mm antitank guns		12	12
50-mm mortars	27		27
81-mm mortars	18		18
75-mm mountain howitzers	6		6

Figure 26.—Armament of the mountain infantry regiment.

42. Motorcycle battalion *(Kradschützen-Bataillon).*—*a.* The motorcycle battalion was formerly an organic part of the motorized infantry brigade in the Panzer division. In newly formed Panzer divisions, however, the motorcycle battalion forms a separate unit, replacing the reconnaissance battalion. In order to give it added strength and firepower, each of these newer units contains an armored car company.

b. The old-type motorcycle battalion consists of a headquarters, three motorcycle companies, a motorcycle machine-gun company, a heavy weapons company, and services. Its approximate strength in personnel, transport, and armament is shown in figure 27.

Units	O and EM	Mtrcl	Other Mtr vehicles	LMG	Hv MG	AT rifles	50-mm Mort	81-mm Mort	50-mm AT guns	75-mm How
Battalion headquarters	78	12	21							
Three motorcycle companies	621	198	48	54	6	9	9			
Motorcycle machine-gun company	208	44	25		8			6		
Heavy weapons company	148	17	27	4					3	2
Services	50	3	20	3						
TOTAL	1,105	274	141	61	14	9	9	6	3	2

Figure 27.—Composition and armament of the old-type motorcycle battalion.

43. Motorized machine-gun battalion *(Maschinengewehr-Bataillon (Mot.))*.—Motorized machine-gun battalions are used to reinforce divisions generally in defensive sectors, and occasionally in offensive operations. Few of these units have been identified, and nothing is known about their organization beyond the fact that they belong to the GHQ pool.

44. Motorized antiaircraft machine-gun battalion *(Flugabwehr-Bataillon (Mot.))*.—Antiaircraft machine-gun battalions of this type may be attached to infantry divisions to strengthen their defenses, or they may be used as GHQ pool troops. This type of battalion consists of a headquarters, a signal section, three antiaircraft companies, and services. Its approximate strength in personnel, transport, and armament is shown in figure 28.

Units	O and EM	Other Mtr vehicles	Track-laying vehicles	LMG	20-mm AA/AT guns
Battalion headquarters	25	4			
Signal section	45	6			
Three antiaircraft companies	555	66	30	18	36
Services	30	15		2	
TOTAL	655	91	30	20	36

Figure 28.—Composition and armament of the motorized antiaircraft machine-gun battalion.

45. Security regiment *(Sicherungs-Regiment)*.—The Germans have formed special units known as security regiments, which operate in the rear areas of the armies, protecting lines of communication and mopping up guerrilla bands operating behind the German front. Such units are controlled either by a security division staff or by a special brigade staff. The German Army has made extensive use of such units behind German lines in the Soviet Union.

SECTION VI

CAVALRY AND RECONNAISSANCE UNITS

	Paragraph
General	46
Reconnaissance battalions (*Aufklärungsabteilungen*)	47
Bicycle battalions (*Radfahrabteilungen*)	48
Mounted cavalry units	49

46. General.—The German cavalry still retains its position as one of the arms of the German Army, although there have been no cavalry divisions in the Regular Army since the conversion of the 1st Cavalry Division to the 24th Panzer Division in 1942. (See par. 49.) The one cavalry division, a special *SS* unit, does not come under the control of the Inspector of Cavalry (*Inspekteur der Kavallerie*) in the Army High Command. The most important function of the cavalry arm at present is the training and control of the reconnaissance battalions which form an important part of most German divisions. In addition, in the GHQ pool there are independent bicycle battalions which also belong to the cavalry arm.

47. Reconnaissance battalions (*Aufklärungsabteilungen*).—*a. General organization.*—There are three usual types of reconnaissance battalions—those organized for normal infantry divisions, those for motorized divisions, and those for the old-type Panzer divisions. In the newly formed Panzer divisions the reconnaissance battalion is being replaced by a reinforced motorcycle battalion.

b. Individual units.—(1) *In normal infantry divisions.*—The reconnaissance battalion in the normal infantry division contains a battalion headquarters, a horse cavalry troop, a bicycle company, and a heavy weapons company. Its approximate strength in personnel, transport, and armament is shown in figure 29.

Units	O and EM	Bcl	Mtrcl	Other Mtr vehicles	Horses	L Armd-C	LMG	Hv MG	37-mm AT	50-mm Mort	81-mm Mort	75-mm How
Battalion headquarters	45		8	8								
Horse cavalry troop	205				213		9	2				
Bicycle company	181	126	22	7			9	2		3		
Heavy weapons company	144		5	15		3	6	4	3		3	2
TOTAL	575	126	35	30	213	3	24	8	3	3	3	2

Figure 29.—Composition and armament of the reconnaissance battalion in the infantry division.

(2) *In motorized divisions.*—The reconnaissance battalion in the motorized division contains a battalion headquarters, an armored car company, a motorcycle company, a heavy weapons company, and a light column. Its approximate strength in personnel, transport, and armament is shown in figure 30.

CAVALRY AND RECONNAISSANCE UNITS

Units	O and EM	Mtrcl	MT	L Armd-C	Hv Armd-C	LMG	Hv MG	50-mm Mort	20-mm guns	50-mm AT guns	75-mm How	AT rifles
Battalion headquarters	78	9	29			2						
Armored car company	150	14	12	18	6	24				10		
Motorcycle company	210	66	16			18	2	3				3
Heavy weapons company	150	18	31			4					3	2
Light column	49	9	16			3						
TOTAL	637	116	104	18	6	51	2	3	10	3	2	3

Figure 30.—Composition and armament of the reconnaissance battalion in the motorized division.

(3) *In old-type Panzer divisions.*—The Panzer reconnaissance battalion in the Panzer division has a battalion headquarters, two armored car companies, a motorcycle company, a heavy weapons company, and a light column. The approximate strength of this battalion in personnel, transport, and armament is shown in figure 31.

Units	O and EM	Mtrcl	MT	L Armd-C	Hv Armd-C	LMG	Hv MG	50-mm Mort	20-mm guns	50-mm AT guns	75-mm How
Battalion headquarters	78	9	29			2					
Two armored car companies	300	28	24	36	12	48				20	
Motorcycle company	210	66	16			18	2	3			
Heavy weapons company	150	18	31			4				3	2
Light column	49	9	16			3					
TOTAL	787	130	116	36	12	75	2	3	20	3	2

Figure 31.—Composition and armament of the reconnaissance battalion in the Panzer division.

48. Bicycle battalions (*Radfahrabteilungen*).—*a. General organization.*—Bicycle battalions are divided into two categories—those which are formed by the reorganization of reconnaissance battalions in mountain divisions and those which are GHQ pool troops and may be attached to infantry divisions.

b. Individual units.—(1) *In mountain divisions.*—The bicycle battalion in the mountain division consists of a battalion headquarters, two bicycle companies, and a heavy weapons company. The approximate strength of this battalion in personnel, transport, and armament is shown in figure 32.

Units	O and EM	Bcl	Mtrcl	Other Mtr vehicles	L Armd-C	LMG	Hv MG	37-mm AT guns	50-mm Mort	81-mm Mort	75-mm How
Battalion headquarters	45		8	8							
Two bicycle companies	362	252	44	14		18	4		6		
Heavy weapons company	144		5	15	3	6	4	3		3	2
TOTAL	551	252	57	37	3	24	8	3	6	3	2

Figure 32.—Composition and armament of the bicycle battalion in the mountain division.

(2) *In GHQ pool.*—The GHQ bicycle battalion consists of a battalion headquarters, a signal platoon, three bicycle companies, and a motorcycle company. The approximate strength of this battalion in personnel, transport, and armament is shown in figure 33.

Units	O and EM	Bcl	Mtrcl	Other Mtr. vehicles	LMG	Hv MG	50-mm Mort
Battalion headquarters	30	6	5	8			
Signal platoon	25	6	2	5			
Three bicycle companies	543	378	66	21	27	6	9
Motorcycle company	156		49	16	18	2	3
TOTAL	754	390	122	50	45	8	12

Figure 33.—Composition and armament of the GHQ bicycle battalion.

49. Mounted cavalry units.—The only mounted cavalry troops still remaining in the German Army are such cavalry regiments (*Reiter-Regimenter*) in the GHQ pool as have not been mechanized, and the horse cavalry troops, one of which is found in the reconnaissance battalion of each normal infantry division. The remaining cavalry regiments belong to training commands. It should be noted that the mounted platoon attached to the headquarters of each normal infantry regiment is not classified as cavalry but as infantry.

Section VII

INFANTRY WEAPONS

	Paragraph
General	50
Small arms and hand grenades	51
Automatic small arms and mortars	52
Antitank weapons	53
Infantry support artillery	54
Ammunition	55

50. General.—The weapons used by the German infantry, from side arms, hand grenades, rifles, machine guns, and mortars to the heavier infantry support guns, give the German soldier the greatest possible firepower not only against enemy infantry, but also against hostile armored forces. Although the German infantryman's weapons provide him with the means to defend himself, they are designed and allotted primarily for attack rather than for defense.

51. Small arms and hand grenades.—*a. Pistols.*—(1) *Luger.*—The Luger pistol (*Pistole 08*) is the most common German side arm (fig. 34). It is semiautomatic and recoil-operated, and has a caliber of 9 mm (.354 inch). It has an eight-round magazine which fits into the bottom of the butt. When empty, the gun weighs 1 pound 14 ounces. It fires a 9-mm rimless, straight-case cartridge and has an effective range of 25 yards.

(2) *Walther.*—The Germans have recently introduced the Walther pistol (*Pistole 38*), and eventually this weapon (fig. 35)

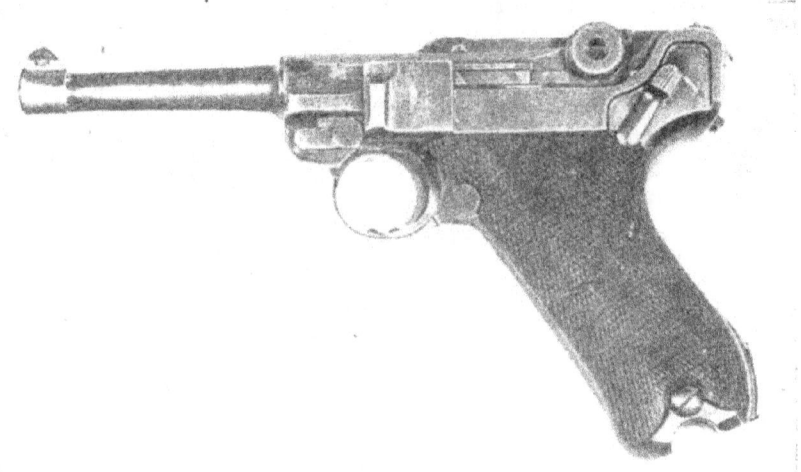

Figure 34.—9-mm Luger pistol (*Pistole 08*).

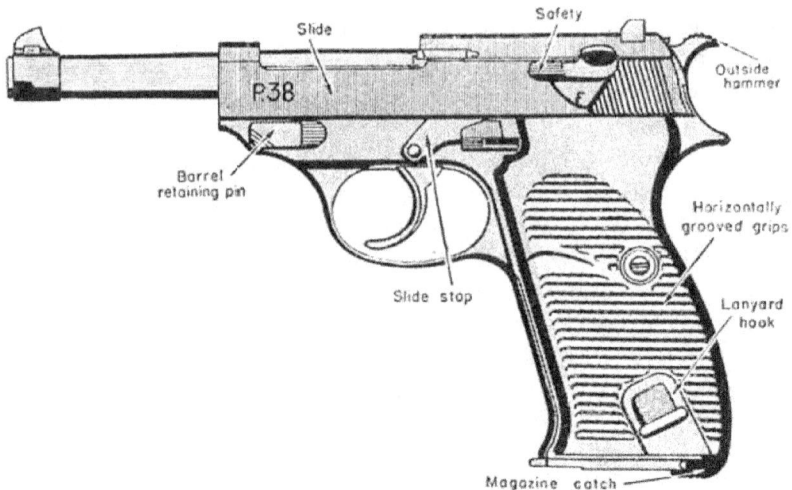

Figure 35.—9-mm Walther pistol (*Pistole 38*).

may replace the Luger. The Walther pistol is recoil-operated and has an eight-round magazine which fits into the lower rear of the butt. It has a caliber of 9 mm (.354 inch), weighs 2 pounds 1¾ ounces when empty, and has an effective range of 25 yards.

b. Rifles.—(1) *Mauser carbine, model 98K* (*Mauser-Karabiner 98K*).—The Mauser carbine, model 98K (*Kar. 98K*), is the standard shoulder weapon of the German Army (fig. 36). Bolt-operated and magazine-fed, it is 43½ inches long and weighs about 9 pounds. The rifle has open sights, the rear sight having a V-notch and being of a new Mauser tangent-curve type developed since World War I. The front sight is laterally adjustable within small limits in its dovetail slot to make it possible to zero the rifle

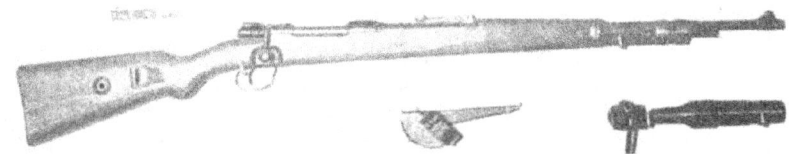

Figure 36.—7.92-mm Mauser carbine *(Kar. 98K)*, with grenade discharger accessories.

if this proves necessary. The front sight has no sideguards but is made strong enough to withstand rough service conditions. The leather sling of this short model is fastened at the front on the left side of the lower band, and at the rear through a transverse hole in the buttstock behind the pistol grip. It has neither a windage adjustment knob nor a peep-sight such as found on U. S. Army rifles, but it has an effective range of 800 yards. Its magazine holds five rounds of 7.92-mm ammunition. The rifle can be equipped with a grenade discharger, which is fitted to the bayonet lug. (The Germans employ high-explosive and armor-piercing rifle grenades.) There are several older models of this rifle, the *Gewehr 98*, the *Karabiner 98*, and the *Karabiner 98B*, all of which have longer barrels than the *Kar. 98K* but are otherwise almost identical to it.

(2) *Rifle, model 41 (Gewehr 41)*.—The Germans have introduced a new rifle (*Gewehr 41*) which is a gas-operated, magazine-fed, semiautomatic weapon (fig. 37). It weighs 10 pounds 14 ounces when empty. It holds 10 rounds in 2 five-round rifle clips and fires 7.92-mm ammunition. It has an over-all length of 45 inches and an effective range of about 800 yards.

c. Bayonet.—All German rifles are provided with a bayonet stud. The German bayonet, of the sword pattern, is 1 foot 3 inches long and weighs 1 pound 4 ounces.

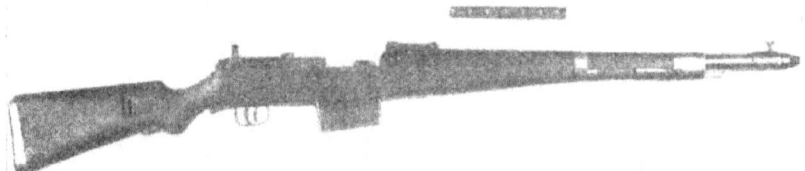

Figure 37.—7.92-mm rifle 41 (*Gewehr 41*), right view, bolt opened.

d. Hand grenades.—German soldiers are equipped with four types of hand grenades. These are model 24 (fig. 38) and model PH 39 stick hand grenades (*Stielhandgranaten*), the stick smoke hand grenade (*Nebelhandgranate 34*), and the egg-shaped hand grenade (*Eierhandgranate 39*). All except the smoke grenade are offensive-type grenades, with thin metal covering and a high explosive content in comparison with their weight. Thus they rely on their blast effect rather than on fragmentation to destroy enemy personnel and installations. The characteristics of the above three types of grenades are as follows:

	Over-all length	Weight	Time of delay fuze (seconds)	Effective blast radius (yards)
Model 24 (stick grenade)	1 foot 2 inches	1 pound 5 ounces	4 to 5	12 to 14
Model PH 39 (stick grenade)	1 foot 4 inches	1 pound 6 ounces	4 to 5	16
Model 39 (egg grenade)	3 inches (approximately)	12 ounces	4 to 5	

INFANTRY WEAPONS 51-52

Figure 38.—Infantrymen ready to attack with stick hand grenades, model 24 (*Stielhandgranaten 24*).

For use against pillboxes, the Germans sometimes remove the heads of six stick grenades, fasten them securely around a seventh, and use the whole as a demolition charge. The egg-shaped hand grenades are often used for booby traps.

52. **Automatic small arms and mortars.**—*a. Submachine guns.*—The German Army makes use of two types of submachine guns—the *Schmeisser M.P. 38* (fig. 39) and *M.P. 40* (fig. 40), both of which have been issued in large quantities and are reliable weapons. These guns are simple recoil-operated, magazine-fed weapons of metal and plastic construction. They both have a caliber of 9 mm and fire 7.92-mm ammunition. They are fed from 32-round removable box magazines. With loaded magazines they weigh 10 pounds 7 ounces, and have an effective range

Figure 39.—9-mm submachine gun *(Schmeisser M.P. 38)* with magazine attached and shoulder rest extended.

Figure 40.—9-mm submachine gun *(Schmeisser M.P. 40)*, showing carrying belt and magazine.

of about 200 yards. The guns fire the same rimless straight-case type of ammunition used in German side arms.

b. *Machine guns.*—(1) *M.G. 34.*—The standard machine gun in the German Army, the *M.G. 34*, can be fired as a light machine gun from a bipod mount (fig. 41). It can be used as a heavy machine gun when mounted on a tripod (fig. 42). It can also be used

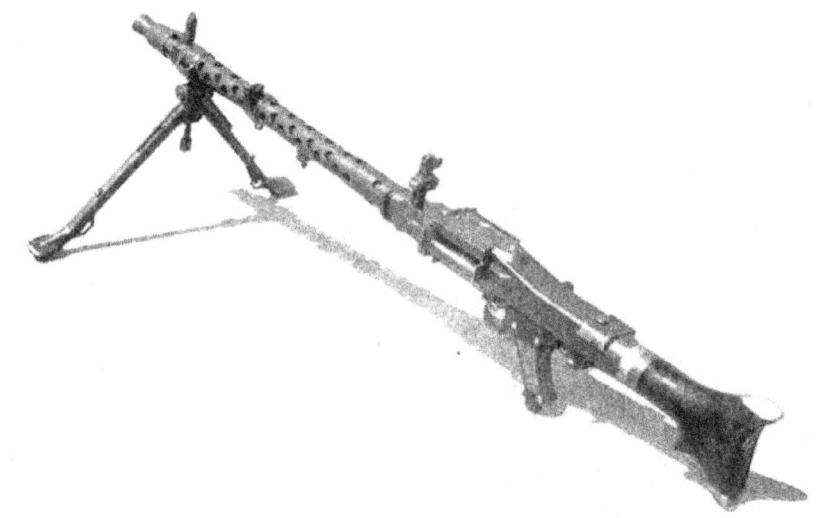

Figure 41.—7.92-mm light machine gun (*M.G. 34*) on bipod mount.

against hostile aircraft when mounted on a special antiaircraft mount, or even on the standard tripod mount when its crew have an adaptor and a special sight. All infantry squads as well as many other types of small German units are armed with the *M.G. 34*. The gun is an air-cooled, recoil-operated automatic weapon. After about 250 shots the heated barrel can be removed by a simple mechanism and a cool one put in its place. The gun is belt- or drum-fed. When on the bipod mount, it weighs 26.5 pounds, and on the tripod mount 68.5 pounds. The maximum range for both the heavy and the light mount is 5,000 yards, while the effective range for the heavy mount is 3,800 yards and for the light mount 2,000 yards. The gun can be fired either with semiautomatic or full-automatic fire and uses 7.92-mm ball, armor-piercing, or

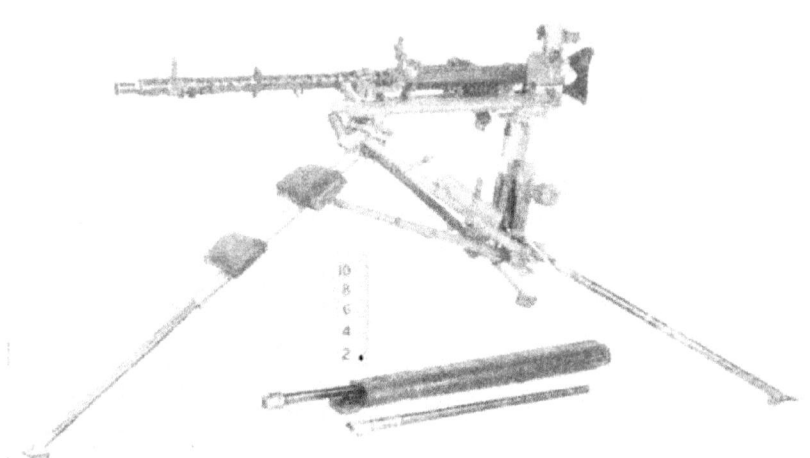

Figure 42.—7.92-mm heavy machine gun (*M.G. 34*) on tripod mount.

tracer ammunition. It has a cyclic rate of fire of from 800 to 900 rounds per minute.

(2) *M.G. 42*.—A newer dual-purpose machine gun, the *M.G. 42* (fig. 43), has appeared recently, and it will probably eventually replace the *M.G. 34*. Because of the wider use of stamping, welding, and riveting in its manufacture, the *M.G. 42* is easier to produce than the *M.G. 34* and is just as serviceable a weapon, although its finish is less smooth. Like the *M.G. 34*, it may be either belt- or drum-fed. It weighs 25.5 pounds with the bipod mount, and

67.5 pounds with the tripod mount. It has a cyclic rate of fire which varies from 1,050 to 1,100 rounds per minute.

c. *Mortars.*—(1) *5-cm.*[1]—The 5-cm (50-mm (1.97-inch)) mortar is the standard light mortar of the German Army (fig. 44). It is a light weapon, weighing only 31 pounds, and is easy to carry. It

Figure 43.—7.92-mm light machine gun (*M.G. 42*).

is a muzzle-loading, smooth-bore, high-angle-fire weapon and cannot be depressed below 45°. It is fired by a trigger arrangement. The weapon is operated by a three-man crew, two of them carrying the gun and the third carrying ammunition. It fires a high-explosive shell weighing approximately 2 pounds. Its

---

[1] Weapons with calibers below 20 millimeters are measured by the Germans in millimeters, whereas weapons with calibers of 20 millimeters and higher are measured in centimeters. (The conversion from centimeters to millimeters is simply a multiplication by 10.) As a rule throughout the text, calibers are represented in millimeters.

range varies from a minimum of 55 yards to a maximum of about 570 yards. Although a trained crew can fire about six rounds in 8 seconds, they cannot maintain this rate for any length of time.

(2) *8-cm.*—In addition to their light mortar, the Germans have

Figure 44.—50-mm mortar *(l.Gr.W. 36) with crew.*

a heavy 8-cm (80-mm) mortar (fig. 45), a muzzle-loading, smoothbore, high-angle-fire weapon similar to the U. S. Army 81-mm mortar. The shell is fired by contact with a firing pin situated on the inside of the breech at the lower end of the barrel. This weapon weighs 125 pounds, and can be carried either by three men or transported on a horse-drawn cart. Its effective range varies from a minimum of 437 yards to a maximum of 1,312 yards. The high-explosive shell weighs 7¾ pounds. The maximum rate of fire obtainable by a trained crew is 6 rounds in 9 seconds, but the usual rate is from 15 to 20 rounds per minute.

Figure 45.—80-mm mortar (s.Gr.W. 34) being loaded.

53. Antitank weapons.—*a. Antitank rifles.*—Two antitank rifles (*Panzerbüchse 38* and *39*) (figs. 46 and 47) are used by the Germany Army. These are single-shot weapons firing 7.92-mm (.312-inch) ammunition with a caliber .50 case. They have an effective range varying from 250 to 300 yards. In many cases these rifles are now being modified and converted into antitank grenade throwers.

Figure 46.—7.92-mm antitank rifle *(Pz.B. 38)* with grenade discharger.

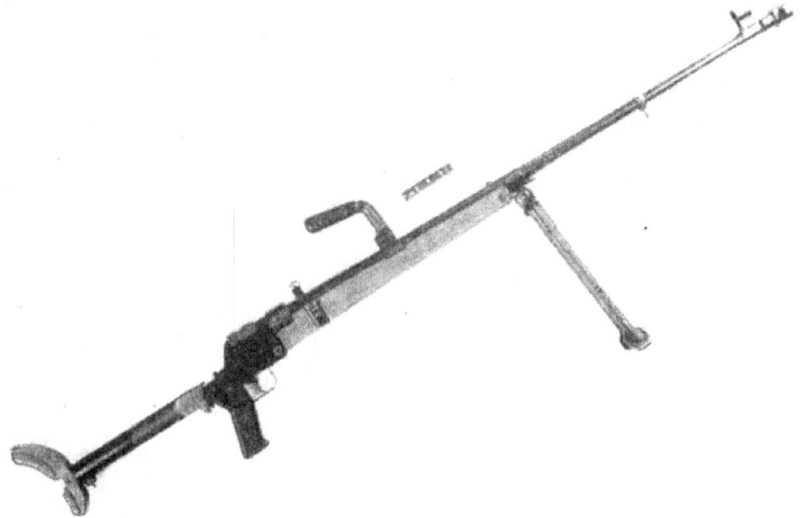

Figure 47.—7.92-mm antitank rifle *(Pz.B. 39)* with stock and bipod extended.

INFANTRY WEAPONS

b. *Antitank guns.*—(1) *3.7-cm Pak.*[2]—Although the *3.7-cm Pak* (37-mm (1.45-inch) antitank gun) has been partially replaced by the *5-cm Pak* as the principal German antitank weapon, the *3.7-cm Pak* is still widely used (fig. 48). The gun is part of the organic equipment of the German infantry regiment. It has recently been provided with a new type of armor-piercing ammunition which gives it a good penetration effect up to 400 yards. The gun weighs about 880 pounds, and is normally towed on its

Figure 48.—37-mm antitank gun *(Pak 37)*.

own wheels by a prime mover or carried in a truck. The muzzle velocity of the new type of armor-piercing ammunition is 3,450 feet per second. The effective range of the gun is 600 yards, its rate of fire is 8 to 10 rounds per minute, and it has a maximum elevation of 25° and a depression of 8°. It is operated by a crew of 6 men. A stick bomb 5.7 inches in diameter and 11 inches long with a rod that fits into the bore is used at short ranges (fig. 49).

---

[2] *Pak* is the German abbreviation for *Panzerabwehrkanone*, which means "antitank gun."

Figure 49.—37-mm antitank gun *(Pak 37)* with stick bomb.

Figure 50.—50-mm antitank gun *(Pak 38)* captured at Tobruk.

(2) *5-cm Pak.*—The *5-cm Pak* (50-mm (1.97-inch) antitank gun) (figs. 50, 51, and 52) was first introduced in the spring of

INFANTRY WEAPONS 53

Figure 51.—50-mm antitank gun (*Pak 38*) in camouflaged position with crew.

Figure 52.—50-mm antitank gun (*Pak 38*) towed by prime mover.

1941 to replace the *3.7-cm Pak*. It is mounted on a split-trail carriage, normally towed by a prime mover, and is expected eventually to become a part of the standard equipment of the German infantry regiment. The gun fires tracer and HE shells, as well as armor-piercing shells of a new type similar to those used in the 37-mm weapon. The muzzle velocity of the new type of AP ammunition is 3,940 feet per second, while the HE ammunition has a muzzle velocity of 1,800 feet per second. The effective range for the new type of ammunition is 500 yards, while the HE maximum range is 2,640 yards, with an effective range of 2,000 yards. The practical rate of fire for the gun is 10 to 15 rounds per minute. The gun weighs 2,145 pounds and has a maximum elevation of 27° and a depression of 18°. The gun is operated by a crew of 8 men.

54. Infantry support artillery.—*a. 7.5-cm infantry howitzer.*—The German 75-mm infantry howitzer, which is the basic light infantry support artillery weapon (figs. 53 and 54), is mounted on a carriage having either steel-type artillery wheels or pneumatic tires. The steel-wheeled carriage is used by airborne troops, and is sometimes referred to as the 75-mm mountain-infantry howitzer. The weapon is drawn either by 6 horses or by a motor vehicle. For pack transport it can be broken down into 6 loads of a maximum of 165 pounds each. The muzzle velocity of HE shell used in this weapon is 730 feet per second and its maximum range is 3,870 yards. Its maximum rate of fire is 15 to 20 rounds per minute. Its weight is 880 pounds. The gun can be elevated 73° and depressed 10°. It fires an HE shell weighing 12 pounds 2 ounces, and an armor-piercing shell. The gun is operated by a crew of 6 men.

b. 15-cm infantry howitzer.—The 150-mm infantry howitzer (fig. 55) is the standard German heavy infantry support weapon, firing a high-explosive shell weighing 84 pounds as well as a smoke shell, and can be used for either high or low trajectory fire. It is normally either horse- or motor-drawn. The gun has

INFANTRY WEAPONS

Figure 53.—75-mm infantry howitzer *(l.I.G. 18)*, horse-drawn. (This howitzer is also used by airborne units.)

Figure 54.—75-mm infantry howitzer *(l.I.G. 18)* mounted on carriage with rubber wheels.

a muzzle velocity of 790 feet per second and a maximum range of 6,000 yards and weighs 3,000 pounds. It is operated by a crew of nine men.

55. Ammunition.—*a. General.*—In the German Army, weapons with a caliber of 20-mm or less are measured in millimeters, while larger weapons are measured in centimeters (see p. 73, note 1). The nomenclature of German ammunition and guns is further complicated by the fact that in some cases

Figure 55.—150-mm infantry howitzer (s.I.G. 33) in firing position.

the Germans use only an approximate caliber to describe a weapon (for example, 7.9-mm for the 7.92-mm rifle and 8-cm for the heavy mortar, which is in reality an 8.1-cm weapon), whereas in other cases they use the exact caliber, as 3.7-cm for the *3.7-cm Pak*.

b. Types of ammunition.—The several types of ammunition of 7.92-mm caliber are all standard for German pistols, submachine guns, rifles, and machine guns. However, special types of this ammunition are used for special purposes. An example of this is the regular armor-piercing ammunition for German antitank rifles. This ammunition has a large case similar to that of the U. S. caliber .50 cartridge, but the projectile remains 7.92 mm. There are two types of light mortar shells, smoke and high-explosive, whereas the heavy mortars have an additional type, a smoke shell with a delayed action. Both the 37- and the 50-mm antitank guns are used primarily against armored vehicles, but they are also provided with high-explosive shells for use against personnel. (See par. 62 for types of ammunition currently used in German antitank weapons.) The 75-mm and 150-mm infantry howitzers (par. 54) fire high-explosive, armor-piercing, and smoke shells.

Section VIII

FIELD ARTILLERY

	Paragraph
Introduction	56
Divisional artillery	57
Artillery commanders and staffs	58
GHQ artillery units	59
Nomenclature	60
Methods of fire	61
Ammunition	62

56. Introduction.—*a. General.*—(1) The tabulation in figure 56 gives the characteristics of the principal German artillery weapons.

(2) The fundamental principle governing the German use of artillery is the concentration of overwhelming firepower at vital points to assure the advance of ground forces toward the main objective. To make such use of firepower possible, the control of artillery in each echelon is concentrated in the hands of a single field artillery commander. The fire of the guns is regulated from a fire direction center, which is organized on a battalion basis, receives data from observation points, can compute

Type	Length of bore (cals)	Muzzle velocity (fs)	Weight of shell (lbs)	Maximum range (yds)	Elevation	Depression	Traverse	Weight in action (tons)	Method of transport
88-mm AA/AT gun (3.46-in) (*Flak 8*), dual-purpose.	56	2,755	19.8 AP, 21 HE	16,200	85	3	360	8.07	MT.
105-mm gun (4.13-in) [*K.17 or K.17(t)*].	45	2,130	40.7	15,409	45	2	6	3.3	H-Dr or MT.
105-mm gun-howitzer (4.13-in) (being replaced by *I.F.H. 42*—no details available).	22.8	1,542	32.7 HE, 33 AP	12,000	40	5	56	2.1	H-Dr or MT.
150-mm gun (5.9-in) (*K.16*)	42	2,480	112.5 HE	25,000	42	3	8	10.7	H-Dr or motor tracked vehicles, 2 loads.
150-mm gun-howitzer (5.9 in) (s. *F.H. 18*).	22	1,705 HE	95.7 HE	14,570	50	3	60	5	H-Dr or MT.
155-mm G. P. F. gun (6.1-in) (French).	29.8	2,380	95	21,400	35	0	60	11.2	MT.
170-mm C. D. gun (6.7 in) (may be on railway mount).		1,970 to 2,300.	140	29,113 to 32,371.	70		360		Motorized, 2 loads (crew 12 men).
210-mm howitzer (8.27-in) (*M.18*) (Czech) (regarded by Germans as best all-purpose weapon yet produced).	25 to 30.	1,815	247	18,400	72		360	23	Motorized, 2 loads, 15½-ton tractor.
210-mm gun (8.27 in) (Czech)	40 ?	2,625		32,860	45	7	360		3 loads.
240-mm howitzer (9.4-in) (Czech).		1,670	365	24,000					Motorized, 3 loads; 25 mph on roads. 3 heavy cross-country vehicles.
280-mm gun (9.4-in) (Krupp, 1937).	46	2,780	396	35,000	45	4	360		
280-mm super-long-range gun (11-in)	125 to 130.	5,900	660	125 miles					
305-mm howitzer (towed gun fired from fixed emplacements) (12-in).	14	1,480	459	14,000				24	3 loads.
380-mm howitzer (15-in) (Czech)	17		1,640	18,500	65			81	
420-mm howitzer (16.5-in)(Czech)			2,220	16,900					
615-mm howitzer (24.24-in)			4,400 hollow-charge shell.	16,000 to 18,000.					4 loads, 4 mph.

Figure 56.—Characteristics of artillery weapons.

FIELD ARTILLERY 56

the fire for all the batteries in the battalion, and can thus direct the fire of all the guns in the battalion. The Germans stress fire control, and locate targets accurately by survey methods. Fire-direction charts and maps are habitually prepared in advance and used, and the range is never estimated. The Germans also place great emphasis on the use of lateral observers. In addition to the observation points provided by the artillery battalion (fig.

Figure 57.—Orienting a battery for accurate fire control.

57), there are further observation points provided by the observation battalion.

(3) Artillery officers are used as forward observers, and communicate with the direction center by wire or radio. Infantry officers are not used as forward observers for the artillery, and when artillery is being used to support an infantry unit, an artillery officer is attached to its staff as a liaison officer. He can

use the infantry communications net as well as the artillery net to communicate with the artillery. When divisional artillery units are reinforced by artillery from the GHQ pool, special artillery commanders and staffs from the GHQ pool are usually sent with these units (see par. 58). In such cases the GHQ pool commanders control the divisional artillery as well as the GHQ units, and coordinate the fire of all guns in order to meet possible changes in general plans. Division and even corps artillery units must be held in a state of readiness so that they can be regrouped rapidly, if this proves necessary, to support a main effort in a new zone of action. The scope of the Army artillery has been extended during the course of the present war. Originally all antiaircraft and naval coast artillery came under the control of the Air Force (*Luftwaffe*) and the Navy (*Kriegsmarine*), respectively.

(4) A considerable amount of Army coastal artillery (*Heeresküstenartillerie*) is now used to protect coastal areas between important naval installations, particularly at beaches where enemy landings might be attempted.

b. Organization.—German Army artillery organization comes under the control of the Inspector of Artillery (*Inspekteur der Artillerie*), who is responsible for its training and technical development. Much of the artillery is withheld in the GHQ pool, and is added for combat purposes to its relatively small organic divisional allotment. Units are also drawn from the pool to support army groups and armies in accordance with the estimated needs. The army groups or armies in turn usually place at least a part of these units at the disposal of corps or divisions. The artillery regiment in each infantry and motorized division has an observation battalion added from the GHQ pool, while in the case of the Panzer division the observation battalion is an organic part of the artillery regiment.

57. Divisional artillery.—*a. General.*—Divisional artillery regiments vary widely both as to size and equipment, depending upon the types of divisions to which they are attached.

FIELD ARTILLERY

b. Organization.—(1) *In infantry division.*—The artillery regiment in an infantry division consists of a regimental headquarters, including a signal section; three light battalions; and one medium battalion. Each light battalion consists of a headquarters, a signal platoon, a survey platoon, three batteries, in addition to a motorized ammunition column. The batteries in the light battalions have four 105-mm gun-howitzers each (figs. 58 to 60, 65, and 66). The medium battalion consists of a headquarters, a signal platoon, a survey platoon, two batteries each having four 150-mm gun-howitzers and a battery of four 105-mm guns and a motorized ammunition column. On the Russian front the 105-mm battery has in most cases been replaced by either a 150-mm gun battery (figs. 61 to 64, 67, and 68) or a 150-mm howitzer battery. The approximate strength, in personnel, transport, and armament, of the artillery regiment in the infantry division is shown in figure 69.

Figure 58.—105-mm gun-howitzer *(l.F.H. 18).* (The *l.F.H. 18* is fitted with a double-baffle muzzle brake.)

Figure 59.—105-mm gun-howitzer and crew in action.

Figure 60.—105-mm gun-howitzer with half-track prime mover.

FIELD ARTILLERY 57

Figure 61.—150-mm gun-howitzer *(s.F.H. 18)*, horse-drawn, with crew, in firing position.

Figure 62.—150-mm gun-howitzer, tractor-drawn.

Figure 63.—150-mm gun-howitzer, horse-drawn, tube section.

Figure 64.—150-mm gun-howitzer, horse-drawn, carriage section.

FIELD ARTILLERY

Figure 65.—105-mm gun *(F.K. 18)* firing.

Figure 66.—105-mm gun, tractor-drawn.

Figure 67.—150-mm gun in firing position.

Figure 68.—150-mm gun with crew, drawn by medium half-track tractor (*Sd.Kfz. 8*).

FIELD ARTILLERY

Units	O and EM	Mtrcl	Other Mtr vehicles	H-Dr vehicles	LMG	105-mm gun-howitzers	105-mm guns	150-mm How
Regimental headquarters		2	2	9				
Three light battalions		27	27	162	18	36		
Medium battalion		9	6	55	6		4	8
TOTAL	2,700	38	35	226	24	36	4	8

Figure 69.—Composition and armament of the artillery regiment in the infantry division.

(2) *In motorized division.*—The artillery regiment in a motorized division is identical to that in an infantry division except that there are only two light battalions instead of three, and that the entire unit is of course motorized. Each light battalion consists of a headquarters, a signal platoon, and three batteries, each having four 105-mm gun-howitzers, and a motorized ammunition column. The medium battalion has a headquarters, a signal platoon, a survey platoon, one battery of 105-mm guns and two batteries each having four 150-mm gun-howitzers, and a motorized ammunition column. The 105-mm battery has in many cases been replaced by either a 150-mm gun or a 150-mm gun-howitzer battery. The approximate strength, in personnel, transport, and armament, of the artillery regiment in the motorized division is shown in figure 70.

Units	O and EM	Mtrcl	Other Mtr vehicles	LMG	105-mm gun-howitzers	105-mm guns	150-mm How
Regimental headquarters	131	17	40				
Two light battalions	1,056	60	238	12	24		
Medium battalion	648	48	137	6		4	8
TOTAL	1,835	125	415	18	24	4	8

Figure 70.—Composition and armament of the artillery regiment in the motorized division.

(3) *In Panzer division.*—The artillery regiment in the Panzer division is identical to the artillery regiment in a motorized divi-

sion, except that Panzer artillery regiments include an observation battalion. The approximate strength, in personnel, transport, and armament, of the artillery regiment in the Panzer division is shown in figure 71.

Units	O and EM	M trcl	Other Mtr vehicles	LMG	105-mm gun-howitzers	105-mm guns	150-mm gun-howitzers
Regimental headquarters	131	17	40				
Observation battalion	267	7	40	2			
Two light battalions	1,056	60	238	12	24		
Medium battalion	648	48	137	6		4	8
TOTAL	2,102	132	455	20	24	4	8

Figure 71.—Composition and armament of the artillery regiment in the Panzer division.

(4) *In mountain division.*—The artillery regiment in a mountain division consists of a headquarters, a signal section, two or three light battalions, and a medium battalion. Each light battalion has a headquarters and three batteries of 75-mm mountain howitzers (figs. 72 and 73), while the medium battalion has three

Figure 72.—75-mm mountain howitzer with shield.

FIELD ARTILLERY 57

Figure 73.—75-mm mountain howitzer without shield.

batteries of 105-mm howitzers. The approximate strength, in personnel, transport, and armament, of the mountain artillery regiment is shown in figure 74.

Units	O and EM	Mtrcl	Other Mtr vehicles	H-Dr vehicles	Horses	LMG	75-mm Mtn How	105-mm gun-howitzers
Regimental headquarters								
Three light battalions						18	36	
Medium battalion						6		12
TOTAL	2,500	12	23	178	1,785	24	36	12

Figure 74.—Composition and armament of the mountain artillery regiment.

58. Artillery commanders and staffs.—*a. Commanders.*—The commander of the divisional artillery (*Artilleriefiihrer*, or *Arfü*) commands the divisional artillery when it is not reinforced from the GHQ pool, but when GHQ artillery units are attached to the division, the *Arfü* is usually placed under the command of an artillery commander (*Artillerie Kommandeur*, or *Arko*,) whose staff is supplemented in action by the larger staff of the divisional artillery regiment. An *Arko* may also be assigned to command an allotment of artillery to a corps, and in this case a GHQ artillery regimental staff and an artillery observation unit are normally included in the allotment. The artillery commanders are assigned as follows:

(1) *GHQ artillery general (Oberkommando des Heeres—General der Artillerie).*—This artillery general is the principal staff adviser on artillery employment at GHQ; he advises on the allotment of GHQ pool units to army groups and armies.

(2) *Artillery general (Stabsoffizier der Artillerie.)*—This artillery general is the adviser to the commander on artillery matters at army group and army headquarters and advises on the suballotment of GHQ artillery units to lower units. In a coastal area he is called *General der Küstenartillerie.*

(3) *Senior artillery officer (Höherer Artilleriekommandeur, or Höh Arko).*—The senior artillery officer is assigned with a

staff within army groups and armies for command over GHQ artillery units operating in an area larger than that of a single army corps.

(4) *Artillery commander (Arko).*—The artillery commander may command the artillery within a corps.

b. Staffs.—The staffs are as follows:

(1) *Artillery regimental staffs.*—These are special staffs formed on or after mobilization and staffs of peacetime division artillery medium regiments, which before the mobilization in 1939 were broken up and the battalions of which were used to form the medium battalions in the GHQ pool. The former are chiefly independent staffs. All GHQ artillery regimental staffs except coast defense staffs are fully motorized.

(2) *Battalion staffs.*—These are independent staffs controlling independent medium, heavy, and super-heavy batteries (motorized or railway) or coast defense batteries.

59. GHQ artillery units.—*a. Battalions and batteries.*—These units may be light, medium, heavy, or super-heavy, and may be horse-drawn, motorized, tractor-drawn, self-propelled, railway, or fixed. Motorized medium battalions formerly belonging to peacetime medium regiments consist of three batteries of four guns each. Heavy or super-heavy batteries may have only two guns or even one (see figs. 75 to 78).

b. Artillery observation battalions (Beobachtungsabteilungen).—These battalions provide and coordinate the reconnaissance and observation for artillery in combat, particularly for counterbattery fire, and plot the location of enemy artillery (and sometimes enemy heavy infantry weapons) by flash or sound-ranging. Usually these battalions are part of the GHQ pool, but a Panzer artillery observation battery is normally organically assigned to the divisional artillery regiment of a Panzer division. The organization of the observation battalion is as follows:

(1) *Headquarters battery.*—(*a*) *Signal platoon.*—This platoon connects headquarters and plotting centers.

Figure 75.—210-mm *Mörser Lafette 18*.

Figure 76.—Carriage of 210-mm *Mörser Lafette 18*.

FIELD ARTILLERY

Figure 77.—210-mm tube.

Figure 78.—210-mm howitzer, old type.

(b) *Meteorological platoon.*—This platoon measures meteorological factors affecting artillery fire.

(c) *Cartographic platoon.*—This platoon reproduces maps.

(2) *Survey battery.*—This battery performs normal survey duties.

(3) *Sound-ranging battery.*—This battery operates microphones in units of three or more.

(4) *Flash-ranging battery.*—This battery furnishes personnel to man observation points.

(5) *Observation balloon battery.*

c. *Assault gun battalions (Sturmgeschützabteilungen).*—These units have a headquarters battery and three batteries each equipped with seven 75-mm self-propelled guns (figs. 79 and 80). The GHQ pool also includes independent assault gun batteries similar to those in the battalions. These assault gun units are sometimes attached to divisional artillery regiments.

d. *Army antiaircraft battalion (Heeresflakabteilung).*—The antiaircraft battalion is fully motorized and usually has two or

Figure 79.—*Pz.Kw. III* chassis mounted with 75-mm short-barreled assault gun.

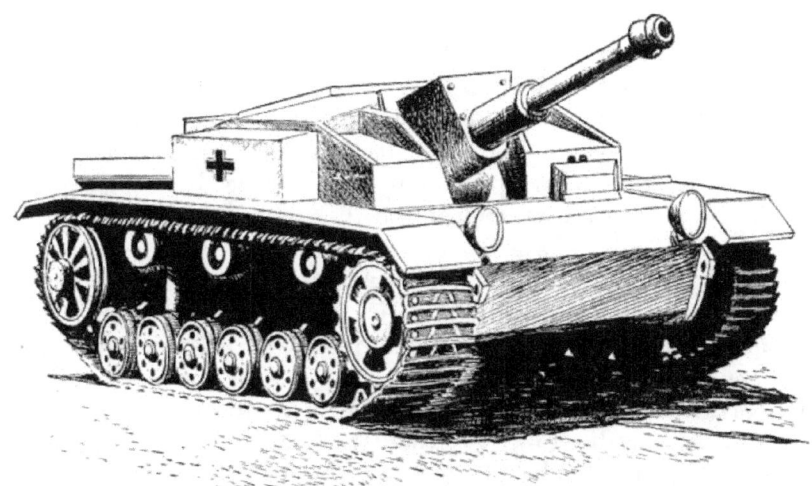

Figure 80.—*Pz.Kw. III* chassis mounted with 75-mm long-barreled assault gun.

three batteries consisting of four 88-mm guns each and one or two light batteries, each equipped with twelve 20-mm guns or nine 37-mm guns, and four light machine guns. The heavy weapons can also be used for defense against tanks, for assault against fortifications, and for other duties.

e. Survey and cartographic battalions (Vermessungs- und Karten-Abteilungen).—These units may be allocated from the GHQ pool to army groups or armies.

f. Miscellaneous units.—In addition, the following types of independent units are attached to GHQ pool:

(1) Velocity measurement platoon (*Velocitäts-Messzug*).
(2) Astronomical survey platoon (*Astronomischer Messzug*).
(3) Meteorological platoon (*Wetter-Peilzug*).
(4) Army map depot (*Armeekartenlager*).
(5) Army artillery equipment park (*Artilleriepark*).

60. Nomenclature.—*a. General.*—The Germans apply the terms "light" (*leichte*), "medium" (*mittlere*), "heavy" (*schwere*), and "super-heavy" (*schwerste*) to their artillery weapons (see fig. 56, p. 84).

61. Methods of fire.—German artillery makes extensive use of ricochet fire. In this type of fire the Germans set their shell fuzes so that the shells will strike the ground, and ricochet into the air and burst. They also employ time-fuze fire, which they try to regulate so that their shells will burst about 40 to 50 feet above the ground.

62. Ammunition.—*a. Types.*—Although high-explosive ammunition is the standard for all types of German artillery weapons, the Germans also make use of armor-piercing, incendiary, and smoke shells, and it is known that they have gas shells available for chemical warfare. The allotment of smoke shells to field artillery units is about 10 to 15 percent of the total ammunition, and smoke has proved extremely effective in concealing troop movements and lowering casualties. The Germans also make use of a hollow-charge-type shell against both armored vehicles and concrete field emplacements. German artillery does not employ shrapnel.

b. Supply.—(1) *In higher units.*—The normal chain of ammunition supply is from the railhead or the army ammunition park to the division ammunition distribution point by trucks of the divisional supply trains, thence usually in horse-drawn vehicles of the battalion ammunition columns to battalion or battery positions. If the distance from the railhead is too great for this method, ammunition sections from the army supply columns are interposed and work from the railhead to a point approximately halfway between it and the ammunition supply columns. Corps have no ammunition columns working with divisions, the corps columns all being required to maintain the artillery allotted to corps. The total number of rounds carried in the divisional trains and the battery ammunition sections is 468 shells for each light artillery piece and 250 for each medium piece.

(2) *In the battery.*—Each battery has 8 caissons, each car-

rying 48 rounds, organized into the 1st and 2d ammunition sections of 4 caissons each. Together they form a small and flexible battery ammunition train under the command of an officer. There is never more than 1 section present directly at the gun position. It may be disposed with 2 caissons on each flank, or the ammunition may be unloaded and 1 or both sections sent away for refilling according to the situation.

Section IX

PANZER TROOPS

	Paragraph
Introduction	63
Organic tank units	64
GHQ tank units	65
Tank maintenance	66
Armored combat vehicles	67
Antitank weapons	68

63. Introduction.—*a. General.*—German Panzer divisions with their great mobility and heavy firepower have formed the spearhead for most of the German attacks from the 1939 campaign in Poland to the campaigns of 1941 and 1942 on the eastern front. The experience of these battles has led to modifications in both the composition and the equipment of Panzer units, as well as in their tactical employment, but they still form the heart of the German Army's offensive power.

b. Development.—(1) The first German Panzer divisions consisted of a tank brigade, a motorized infantry regiment, and certain auxiliary units. The strength of the motorized infantry in these divisions was increased in 1939 and 1940 to two regiments. Thus, during the campaign in the west, at least some of the Panzer divisions included a tank brigade and a motorized infantry brigade, or a total of four tank battalions and four infantry battalions. During the first year of the campaign on the eastern front, Panzer divisions were used which had only one tank regiment composed of three battalions, and this is now the usual organization. However, some of the battalions have four companies (one medium and three light), and others have only three companies (one medium and two light).

(2) By early 1943, it is believed that the Germans had 27 Panzer divisions. At least 5 *SS* divisions and the *Grossdeutschland* Division have been provided with tank regiments; thus they also are equivalent to Panzer divisions. In addition, tank battalions have been attached to a number of the motorized divisions. Each division of all categories is also allotted an antitank battalion (*Panzerjägerabteilung*). The Panzer divisions designed for operation in Africa were organized in general similarly to the European Panzer divisions. However, in the African theater, more than in other areas, details of the organization varied in accordance with the type and amount of material available, the terrain, the nature of the hostile defense, and the mission.

c. Control.—The training and equipping of Panzer units, with the possible exception of the *SS* units, are controlled by the Inspector General for the Panzer Arm, *Generaloberst* Guderian. In addition to the tank units and antitank battalions which are organic parts of divisions, there are a number of independent Panzer units belonging to the GHQ pool. These include—

(1) Independent tank battalions.

(2) Heavy tank battalions.

(3) Independent flame-thrower tank battalions (*Flammenwerfer-Panzerabteilungen*).

(4) Heavy antitank battalions (*schwere Panzerjägerabteilungen*).

(5) Armored trains (*Eisenbahn-Panzerzüge*).

64. Organic tank units.—*a. Tank regiment in Panzer division.*—(1) *Types.*—It is believed that there are at least three types of tank regiments which may be encountered in Panzer divisions. Their basic strength in personnel, transport, and armament is shown in figure 81. One consists of two battalions of three companies each; another, of two battalions of four companies each; and the third, of three battalions of three companies each.

Units	O and EM	Mtrcl	Other Mtr vehicles	Pz. Kw. II	Pz. Kw. III	Pz. Kw. IV	MG	20-mm guns	50-mm guns	75-mm guns
Two battalions of three companies	1,700	120	255	21	77	28	263	21	71	28
Two battalions of four companies	2,011	134	284	21	111	28	331	21	105	28
Three battalions of three companies	2,416	170	353	28	114	30	400	28	106	30

Figure 81.—Composition and armament of types of tank regiments.

(2) *Latest type.*—The latest type of organic tank regiment, which is believed likely to become standard, consists of a headquarters (including a signal platoon, a light tank platoon, and a repair platoon), three battalions, a supply column, and a workshop company. Its approximate strength in personnel, transport, and armament is shown in figure 82.

Units	O and EM	Mtrcl	Other Mtr vehicles	Pz. Kw. II	Pz. Kw. III	Pz. Kw. IV	MG	20-mm guns	50-mm guns	75-mm guns
Regimental headquarters (including signal platoon, light tank platoon, and repair platoon)	128	10	15	7	3		13	7	1	
Three battalion headquarters	63	9	15							
Three battalion headquarters companies	666	78	135	21	9		87	21	3	
Three battalions	1,251	63	108		102	30	288		102	30
Supply column	56	4	18							
Workshop company	252	6	62							
Total	2,416	170	353	28	114	30	388	28	106	30

Figure 82.—Composition and armament of the latest type of tank regiment.

b. Tank battalion in tank regiment of Panzer division.—This battalion consists of a battalion headquarters (including a signal platoon, a light tank platoon, a motorcycle reconnaissance platoon, antiaircraft platoon, and a repair platoon), two light companies, and a medium company. Its approximate strength in personnel, transport, and armament is shown in figure 83.

Units	O and EM	Mtrcl	Other Mtr vehicles	Pz. Kw. II	Pz. Kw. III	Pz. Kw. IV	MG	20-mm guns	50-mm guns	75-mm guns
Battalion headquarters	21	3	5							
Battalion headquarters company (including signal platoon, light tank platoon, motorcycle reconnaissance platoon, antiaircraft platoon, and repair platoon)	222	26	45	7	3		40	7	1	
Two light companies	288	14	24		34		68		34	
Medium company	129	7	12			14	28			14
Total	660	50	86	7	37	14	136	7	35	14

Figure 83.—Composition and armament of the tank battalion in the tank regiment of the Panzer division.

c. Tank battalion in motorized division.—This battalion consists of a headquarters, two light companies, and a medium company. Its approximate strength in personnel, transport, and armament is shown in figure 84.

Units	O and EM	Mtrcl	Other Mtr vehicles	Pz. Kw. II	Pz. Kw. III	Pz. Kw. IV	MG	20-mm guns	50-mm guns	75-mm guns
Battalion headquarters				7	3		99	7	3	
Two light companies					34				34	
Medium company						10				10
Total	649	50	86	7	37	10	99	7	37	10

Figure 84.—Composition and armament of the tank battalion in the motorized division.

d. Antitank battalion in Panzer division.—This battalion consists of a headquarters, and three companies, two being armed with 50-mm antitank guns and one with 20-mm dual-purpose guns. Its strength in personnel, transport, and armament is shown in figure 85.

Units	O and EM	Mtrcl	Other Mtr vehicles	MG	20-mm AT guns	50-mm AT guns
Battalion headquarters	76	5	23			
Two companies (with nine 50-mm AT guns each)	138	11	26	6		18
One company (with 20-mm AA/AT guns on self-propelled mounts)	200	17	18	4	12	
Total	552	44	93	10	12	18

Figure 85.—Composition and armament of the antitank battalion in the Panzer division.

e. Antitank battalion in infantry division.—This battalion consists of a headquarters, three antitank companies, and an antiaircraft company. Its strength in personnel, transport, and armament is shown in figure 86.

Units	O and EM	Mtrcl	Other Mtr vehicles	MG	20-mm AT guns	50-mm AT guns
Battalion headquarters	57	6	15			
Three antitank companies	342	41	80	14		24
Antiaircraft company	200	17	18	4	12	
Total	599	64	113	18	12	24

Figure 86.—Composition and armament of the antitank battalion in the infantry division.

f. Antitank battalion in motorized or mountain division.—The composition and armament of the antitank battalion in the motorized or mountain division is similar to that of the same unit in the infantry division.

65. GHQ tank units.—*a. Normal-type and flame-thrower GHQ tank battalions.*—A number of independent tank battalions exist. These include both normal-type tanks and flame-thrower tanks (see par. 92 *b* (19) (*e*), p. 197). No details are known about their composition.

b. Heavy tank battalion.—The heavy tank battalion, equipped with *Pz.Kw. VI* tanks, was encountered for the first time in Tunisia early in 1943. This battalion consisted of a headquarters company and 2 combat companies. Each combat company was reportedly equipped with 9 *Pz.Kw. VI* tanks, and the headquarters company had 2 such tanks, making a total of 20 heavy tanks in the battalion. There are unconfirmed reports indicating that the battalion was at times provided with 23 *Pz.Kw. III* tanks armed with the short-barreled 75-mm tank guns. It is believed that these battalions are now a definite part of the German Army, belonging to the GHQ pool, and that their organization, like that of other tank units, is flexible.

c. Heavy antitank battalion.—It is believed that the heavy antitank battalions are organized in the same manner as the regular divisional antitank units, except that their antitank companies are equipped with 75-mm antitank guns instead of 50-mm.

66. Tank maintenance.—*a. General.*—Efficiency in the maintenance of motor vehicles, particularly in repair and recovery of armored vehicles, has been a noteworthy feature of German Panzer divisions to date. The motor maintenance units must cope with excessive wear and tear on heavy equipment, in addition to conditions imposed by combat. For the maintenance of vehicles, each Panzer division is normally provided with three workshop companies, and each tank regiment also has a workshop company. In addition, each tank battalion and regimental headquarters and each tank company have a maintenance section. Moreover, all tank personnel are trained mechanics and can carry out minor repairs. Workshop companies are believed to be completely independent in that they do not require the assistance of stationary installations for the performance of their tasks. Each workshop company produces its own power and light, and can charge batteries, carry out welding operations, vulcanize tires, and perform other similar tasks. Among other equipment it has a crane; a forge; milling, cutting, boring, and tool-grinding machines; and tool sets for locksmiths, tinsmiths, carpenters, and painters. The workshop company, in general, handles heavy repair jobs requiring up to 12 hours. Jobs requiring a longer period of time are sent back to rear repair bases.

b. Organization of maintenance.—(1) The workshop companies in Panzer divisions and tank regiments are believed to be similarly organized and equipped. The divisional companies reinforce the regimental companies as needed. Each workshop company is organized in general as follows:

> Company headquarters.
> Two or three workshop platoons.
> Recovery platoon.
> Armory.
> Signal communications workshop.
> Company transportation section.

(2) The maintenance section in a tank regimental or battalion headquarters consists of the following:

> One noncommissioned officer (tank mechanic), section leader.
> Three privates, tank mechanics.
> Two privates, tank mechanics and radio electricians (one also being a chauffeur).
> One private, chauffeur.
> Total personnel: one noncommissioned and six men.
> Total transportation: two trucks and one motorcycle.

(3) The maintenance section in a tank company consists of the following:

> One noncommissioned officer (tank mechanic), section leader.

Two noncommissioned officers, tank mechanics.
Eight privates, tank mechanics.
Two privates, tank mechanics and radio electricians.
Four chauffeurs.
Total personnel: three noncommissioned officers and fourteen men.
Total transportation: four trucks and two motorcycles.

c. Employment of maintenance organizations.—In general, the repair tasks which are undertaken by the maintenance units are allotted as follows:

Maintenance sections—jobs requiring up to 4 working hours.
Workshop units—jobs requiring up to 12 working hours.

On the march, maintenance sections move with their respective combat units. However, some may be attached to the combat trains if necessary. If a vehicle breaks down on the march, the maintenance section leader decides whether repairs can be completed by his section. In accordance with his decision, repair is started immediately or the vehicle is turned over to the workshop company. In combat, maintenance sections operate under the orders of the tank battalion commander. They are commanded by the battalion technical officer, and they usually follow along behind the assaulting tanks as closely as hostile fire and the terrain permit. If a disabled tank cannot be repaired on the spot, it is made towable and its position is reported to the recovery platoon of the workshop company. The recovery platoon usually operates aggressively under the direct orders of the workshop company commander. Normally, recovery vehicles accompany or are just in rear of the assaulting tanks. Drivers of these recovery vehicles cruise across the width of the regimental or divisional front searching for disabled tanks. Instances have been noted frequently where disabled German tanks have been repaired or towed to the rear while under fire. A tank commander acts on his own responsibility if he orders the driver of a recovery vehicle to tow his tank toward the rear. Even if it is later proved that the damage to the tank could have been repaired by a maintenance section, towing to the rear is still permissible if there is danger that the tank may be captured or destroyed by hostile fire. The recovered tanks are towed to an assembly point just behind the battlefield, where they are placed under the best available cover. The remaining towing vehicles then take the tanks back to the workshop on low trailers if the terrain permits.

67. Armored combat vehicles.—*a. General.*—Since the beginning of the Polish campaign in 1939, the Germans have increased the striking power of their tanks and armored cars. The earlier light tank types have been discarded, and the Germans now concentrate on various models of their *Pz.Kw. III* and *Pz.Kw. IV* tanks, and they have recently introduced the heavy *Pz.Kw. VI.* A *Pz.Kw. V* tank has also been reported, but no confirmed details on it are yet available. (For the principal characteristics of German tanks, see fig. 87.)

b. Light tanks.—The following German light tanks have been encountered in combat:

(1) *Pz.Kw. I (Sd.Kfz. 101).*—Tanks of this type were found in the Panzer divisions early in 1939 but have become obsolete and are no longer used as combat tanks (fig. 88). However, the chassis of this type of tank is used as a mobile platform for the Czech 47-mm antitank gun (fig. 89), and the 150-mm heavy infantry howitzer has also been encountered on this chassis as a self-propelled mount.

(2) *Pz.Kw. II (Sd.Kfz. 121).*—Owing to its thin armor and ineffective armament, this tank is becoming obsolescent as an armored combat vehicle, but it is still used in the Panzer division, principally as a reconnaissance, liaison, and command vehicle (fig. 90). Like the *Pz.Kw. I.*, the *Pz.Kw. II* chassis is used as a mobile platform for self-propelled weapons such as the 75-mm

Figure 88.—*Pz.Kw. I (Sd.Kfz. 101)*, light tank.

Figure 89.—Chassis of *Pz.Kw. I* used as mobile platform for Czech 47-mm antitank gun.

antitank gun (*7.5-cm Pak 40*), the Russian 76.2-mm antitank gun (*7.62-cm Pak 36 (r)*), and the 150-mm heavy infantry howitzer. It is also used as a flame-thrower tank (*Pz.Kw. IIF*).

c. Medium tanks.—The following German medium tanks have been encountered in combat:

(1) *Pz.Kw. III (Sd.Kfz. 141).*—The basic design of this tank apparently has proved satisfactory. At least 10 different models have been developed, and it remains the principal combat tank

Figure 90.—*Pz. Kw. II (Sd. Kfz. 121).* light tank.

in the Panzer division. In some models, additional armor has been improvised by bolting on extra plates. One model with increased basic armor has been devised. The different models present the same general appearance, but they can be distinguished from each other by changes in such external features as gun mantlets, driver's vision devices, track sprockets, and the size of the principal weapon. The four earlier models of this tank were armed with a 37-mm gun and two machine guns in the turret and

113

one machine gun in the front part of the hull. In the next three models, the 37-mm gun was replaced by the short-barreled 50-mm electrically-fired tank gun, and one machine gun (instead of two) was mounted in the turret (fig. 91). The machine gun in the forward part of the hull was retained. In later models, the basic armor was strengthened in some cases by bolting on additional plates at critical points and in others by increasing the thick-

Figure 91.—*Pz.Kw. III (Sd.Kfz. 141)*, medium tank, with short-barreled 50-mm gun.

ness of the basic armor to 50 mm on the front and rear. In the late models the original 50-mm tank gun has been replaced by a long-barreled 50-mm gun with a higher muzzle velocity (fig. 92), and in other late models a short-barreled 75-mm gun, similar to that used in the *Pz.Kw. IV* tank, constitutes the principal armament.

(2) *Pz.Kw. IV (Sd.Kfz. 161)*.—This tank has likewise been

developed step by step, although not quite to the same extent as the *Pz.Kw. III*. At least seven models of the *Pz.Kw. IV* exist. They are all similar in general appearance, but they can be distinguished from each other by changes in such external features as gun mantlets, minor changes in the turret, and the size of the principal weapon. The first six models of this tank all mounted the short-barreled 75-mm gun (*7.5-cm Kw.K.*) and one light machine gun in the turret (fig. 93). Another machine gun was mounted in the forward part of the hull at the right of the driver.

Figure 92.—*Pz.Kw III (Sd.Kfz. 141)*, medium tank, with long-barreled 50-mm gun.

During the development of the first four models, changes were made in the turret-gun mantlet, but it was not until the fifth model that the nose-plate armor was increased from 30 mm to 50 mm. The fifth model is also distinguished by changes in the turret roof, cupola, front drive sprocket, and driver's vision device. The seventh model was the first to be armed with the long-barreled 75-mm gun (*7.5-cm Kw.K. 40*), the muzzle of which projects well beyond the forward end of the hull and is fitted with a muzzle brake (fig. 94).

Figure 93.—*Pz.Kw. IV (Sd.Kfz. 161)*, medium tank, with short-barreled 75-mm gun.

Figure 94.—*Pz.Kw. IV (Sd.Kfz. 161)*, medium tank, with long-barreled 75-mm high-velocity gun (equipped with double-baffle muzzle brake).

Figure 95.—18-ton *Somua* (captured French tank used by the Germans).

Figure 96.—16.5-ton medium tank (Czech) *(CZDV8H)*.

(3) *Foreign tanks.*—Two foreign tanks, the French 18-ton *Somua* (fig. 95) and the Czech 16.5-ton medium (*CZDV8H*) (fig. 96), are also used by the Germans. Both of these models are lighter than the German medium tanks, and carry 47-mm guns as their principal weapon.

d. Heavy tanks.—The only German heavy tank which has been encountered in considerable numbers thus far in combat is the *Pz.Kw. VI* (fig. 97). This tank, with its 102-mm maximum armor thickness and long-barreled 88-mm gun, is a further indication of the general tendency throughout this war toward increased

Figure 97.—*Pz.Kw. VI*, heavy tank, showing Christie-type bogie wheels.

thickness in basic armor, and also armament with increased striking power capable of dealing with hostile tanks. Owing to the German emphasis on mobility and rapid action, it is believed unlikely that the maximum speed of these tanks will fall much below 25 miles per hour. It is to be expected that combat experience with the *Pz.Kw. VI* will be utilized in making modifications and improvements to be incorporated in later models of this or a similar heavy-type tank.

e. Armored cars.—The marked development noticeable in German tanks has not occurred in German armored cars. The

Figure 98.—Light armored car with 20-mm gun.

original designs of the three basic types of armored cars (four-wheeled, six-wheeled, and eight-wheeled) still exist (figs. 99, 100, and 101). However, as in the case of the tank, combat experience has shown the need for an armored-car weapon with increased striking power, and the eight-wheeled turretless armored car equipped with a 75-mm gun (instead of the 20-mm machine gun or the 37-mm gun in the normal model of this type) recently encountered in Africa is an indication of the trend in this

Figure 99.—Light armored car, showing machine-gun armament.

direction. The basic type of German armored cars are shown in figures 98 to 101. (For the principal characteristics of German armored cars and half-track prime movers and armored troop carriers, see figs. 102 and 103, respectively. See also figs. 1 (p. 9), 17 (p. 53), 66 (p. 91), 68 (p. 92), and 104 (p. 124).)

68. Antitank weapons.—*a. Development.*—The development in tank design and construction has been matched, if not surpassed, by corresponding developments in antitank weapons. The original 37-mm antitank gun (*Pak*) universally used by the

Figure 100.—Six-wheeled heavy armored car.

Figure 101.—Eight-wheeled heavy armored car.

Names	Weight	Crew	Armor	Armament	Wheels	Engine	Drive	Speed	Radius of action
SDKFZ 13 (4-wheel) Horch	4,480 lbs	2 or 3		1 LMG	4	Horch V 8, water cooled, 80-hp		40 to 50 mph.	
SDKFZ 221-2-3	Gross: 10,528. Net: 8,288.	3 (Comdr-gunner, loader-radio-man, operator).	Front, sides, top—8 mm. Visors—15 mm	1 2-cm Kw.K. 39 or Kw.K. 38. 1 7.92-mm M.G. 34 in turret, coaxial.		Horch V 8, water cooled, 66-hp or Opel Str 6, water cooled, 68-hp.		25 mph, 30 mph max.	124 to 155 miles
ASF 6 (medium) (6-wheel).	12,800	4 (1 driver, 2 gunners, 1 R/T operator).	14-mm	2b-mm Hv MG 1 LMG	6	6 cyl. in-line, 103 hp.	4-wheel drive (rear wheels)	50 mph	200 to 240 miles
SDKFZ 231 (8-wheel).	Gross: 16,800. Net: 18,928.	4 (Comdr-gunner, 2 drivers).	Up to 15-mm	1 2-cm auto cannon.	8	Diesel 90 hp. Büssing-Nag		53 mph.	106 to 187 miles.
SDKFZ 232 (8-wheel).	Gross: 18,704. Net: 17,024.	4 (Comdr-gunner, 2 drivers).	Up to 15-mm	1 M.G. 34 (coaxial in turret). 1 Machine carbine, unmounted. 1 2-cm auto cannon.	8	Büssing-Nag		53 mph.	106 to 187 miles
SDKFZ 263 (8-wheel)	Gross: 17,902. Net: 16,688.	5 (2 drivers)	Up to 15-mm	1 M.G. 34 (coaxial in turret). 1 Machine carbine, unmounted. 1 M G S¡ Machine carbine, unmounted.	8	Büssing-Nag		53 mph.	106 to 187 miles

Figure 102.—Characteristics of armored cars.

Name and type	Sd. Kfz. 10. 1-T light	Sd. Kfz. 11. 3-T light	Sd. Kfz. 6. 5-T medium	Sd. Kfz. 7. 8-T medium	Sd. Kfz. 8. 12-T heavy	Sd. Kfz. 9. 18-T heavy	Sd. Kfz. 250. 1-T light (armored)	Sd. Kfz. 251. 3-T medium (armored)
Personnel capacity (including driver)	10	8	15	12	14	9	10	12
Engine	100 hp Maybach	100 hp Maybach	130 hp Maybach	140 hp Maybach	185 hp Maybach	230 hp Maybach	100 hp Maybach	100 hp Maybach
Radius of action	Roads: 178 miles. Cross country: 93 miles.	Roads: 171 miles. Cross country: 84 miles.	Roads: 180 miles. Cross country: 72 miles.	Roads: 156 miles. Cross country: 62 miles.	Roads: 156 miles. Cross country: 62 miles.	Roads: 162 miles. Cross country: 62 miles.	Roads: 160 miles. Cross country: 80 miles.	Roads: 168 miles. Cross country: 84 miles.
Number of wheels	4 twin bogies.	6 twin bogies.	6 twin bogies.	6 twin bogies.	6 twin bogies.	6 twin bogies.	4 twin bogies.	6 twin bogies.
Road speed (maximum)	20 mph.	50 mph	50 mph	50 mph	50 mph	50 mph	50 mph	50 mph.
Weight (based on U. S. weights) (lbs)	Gross: 10,304. Net: 7,392.	Gross: 15,680. Net: 12,208.	Gross: 19,264. Net: 16,128.	Gross: 25,312. Net: 21,504	Gross: 32,480. Net: 26,432.	Gross: 38,752. Net: 33,824.	Gross: 13,304 Net: 10,000.	Gross: 18,816. Net: 15,000.
Armor							6-15-mm.	6-15-mm.
Armament							1-20-mm MG, 2-LMG 34.	1-20-mm MG, 1-LMG 34.

Figure 103.—Characteristics of half-track prime movers and armored troop carriers.

Figure 104.—20-mm dual-purpose gun.

Figure 105.—88-mm multi-purpose gun *(Flak 36)*.

FIRING POSITION

TRAVELING POSITION

Recuperator rod disconnected so that barrel may be retracted for traveling

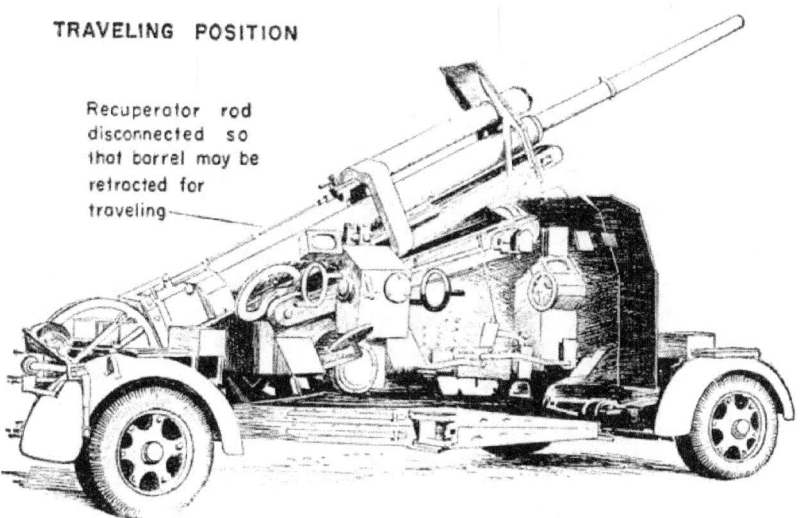

Figure 106.—88-mm multi-purpose gun *(Flak 41)*.

Germans in 1939 is rapidly becoming obsolete. By the end of 1939 the Germans had made considerable effective use of the dual-purpose 20-mm (fig. 104) and 88-mm antiaircraft-antitank weapons (figs. 105 and 106) against hostile armored vehicles. Early in 1941, the German Army used, in addition to the 37-mm *Pak*, a new 28/20-mm tapered-bore AT gun (initially used primarily by airborne and infantry units) (fig. 107), and a new 50-mm weapon known as the *Pak 38*. The Czech 47-mm AT gun on a self-propelled mount was also used as a stopgap (see fig. 89, p. 112). At the same time the 37-mm gun in German tanks was being replaced by the 50-mm tank gun (*5-cm Kw.K.*). Early in 1942, the Germans were using the Russian 76.2-mm (model 36) field gun as an antitank weapon (fig. 108). Airborne troops were also given in-

Figure 107.—28/20-mm Gerlich tapered-bore antitank gun.

creased protection against armored vehicles by the introduction of a new tapered-bore gun, the *4.2/2.8-cm Pak 41*. Later in 1942, two important new antitank weapons were introduced, the *7.5-cm Pak 40* (fig. 109) and the tapered-bore *7.5/5-cm Pak 41*. A French piece on a German carriage, known as the *7.5-cm Pak 97/38*, also made its appearance.

b. Characteristics.—(1) The characteristics of the most important German antitank guns are shown in figure 110.

Figure 108—76.2-mm Russian gun, captured and used by the Germans.

Figure 109.—75-mm antitank gun (*Pak 40*).

Type of gun	Inches (bore)	Muzzle velocity (fs)	Approximate weight	Type of AP projectile	Weight of projectile
28/20-mm *S. Pz. B. 41*	1.13	4,580		AP	4.6 ozs.
37-mm (*Pak*)	1.45	2,500	880 lbs	AP	1.5 lbs.
42/28-mm (*Pak 41*)	1.65	4,500		AP	0.796 lb.
47-mm (*Pak*) (self-propelled mount)	1.85	2,540	5 tons	AP	3.56 lbs.
50-mm (*Pak 38*)	1.97	2,700	2,145 lbs	AP	4.56 lbs.
75-mm (*Pak 40*)	2.95	2,830	1.5 tons	APCBC	15 lbs.
75-mm (*Pak 97/38*)	2.95	2,100		AP	14.1 lbs.
75/55-mm (*Pak 41*)	2.95	4,000	1.4 tons	T C core	5.7 lbs
76.2-mm (Russian)	3	2,200		APCBC	14.81 lbs.
88-mm (*Flak 36*)	3.46	2,600	7 tons	APCBC	21 lbs.

Figure 110.—Characteristics of antitank weapons.

(2) The ammunition for antitank weapons has developed as indicated below:

1939	1941	1942
AP shell	AP shell	APC shell
HE shell	APCBC shell (1.25 percent HE)	APCBC shell (0.31 percent HE)
	AP 40 shot	AP 40 shot
	HE shell	HE hollow-charge shell
		HE shell

c. Trend.—It appears likely that development in German antitank weapons in the immediate future will be concentrated on the 75-mm models. However, an improved 88-mm weapon on a suitable field mount and with a muzzle velocity higher than the 2,600 foot-seconds ascribed to the gun in the *Pz.Kw. VI* tank, is to be expected.

Section X

ENGINEERS

	Paragraph
Introduction	69
Battalions	70
GHQ units	71
Construction troops (*Bautruppen*)	72
Demolition equipment	73
Electrical and mechanical equipment	74
Floating equipment	75
Fixed bridges	76
Portable tank bridges	77
Mines	78
Antitank obstacles	79
Special equipment for use in assault	80
Vehicles	81

69. Introduction.—*a. General.*—In the German Army, engineer combat troops (*Pioniere*) are charged with bridging, ferrying, demolitions, the construction of obstacles, and the laying and removal of mine fields. German engineers pride themselves on being fighting troops and are frequently employed to defend the zones of obstacles which they have created. Selected engineers, known as storm-troop engineers (*Stosstruppspioniere*), are trained for infantry raiding parties, or as assault troops to take part in attacks on fortified positions. In addition to these units, there are specialized engineer troops known as fortress engineers (*Festungspioniere*) and railway engineers (*Eisenbahnpioniere*). Less technical duties are assigned to construction troops (*Bautruppen*). Aside from the regular engineer or construction units, there are pioneer platoons consisting of troops of the various arms which have had some training as engineers. One such platoon usually forms a part of the headquarters of infantry, motorized, Panzer, and mountain regiments; however, some of these regiments have as many as four pioneer platoons, while others have none. The platoons are specially trained for close combat, use of smoke and explosives, and assault operations against fixed defenses and enemy strongpoints.

b. Organization.—The General of Engineers and Fortresses on the Army General Staff acts as staff adviser on all questions of policy affecting engineer and construction troops, and serves also as Inspector of Fortresses. The responsibility for the training and equipment of engineer units is divided between the Inspectorate for Engineers, the Inspectorate for Fortress Engineers and Construction Troops (which is under the supervision of the Inspector of Fortresses), the Inspectorate for Railway Engineers, and the Inspectorate for Technical Troops.

70. Battalions.—*a. In infantry division.*—(1) *Composition.*—Each infantry division includes an engineer battalion, consisting of a headquarters, a signal section, two partially motorized companies, a heavy motorized company, a bridge column, and a light motorized engineer column. The strength of this battalion in personnel, transport, and armament is shown in figure 111; in equipment, in figure 112.

	O and EM	M trcl	Other Mtr vehicles	H-Dr vehicles	Horses	Hand grenades	LMG	Smoke generators	Small flame-throwers	Medium flame-throwers	Tellermines	S-mines
Battalion headquarters	41	7	3	3	10							
Two partly motorized companies	382	10	12	16	42	380	18	312			80	
Heavy motorized company	207	12	21			190	9	156			296	
Brigade column (with B equipment)	102	7	35									
Light engineer column	68	7	16			480		324	6	3	600	621
TOTAL	800	43	87	19	52	1,050	27	792	6	3	976	621

Figure 111.—Composition and armament of the engineer battalion in the infantry division.

	Small pneumatic boats	Large pneumatic boats	16-ton ramps	Compressors	Drilling equipment (sets)	Power saws	Welding equipment (sets)	Plain wire (concertina rolls)	Barbed wire (concertina rolls)	Mine detectors	Demolition stores (lbs)	Exploders	Instantaneous fuze (yds)	Hand searchlights	Sandbags
Two partly motorized companies	12	8		4	4	12	4	84		20	2,106	12	654		400
Heavy motorized company	4	3		3	3	9		76		10	2,091	9	654		600
Bridge column (with B equipment)	48	24	8					12							
Light engineer column				2	2	2	3	100	66		2,788	2	1,635	10	600
TOTAL	64	35	8	9	9	23	7	272	66	30	6,985	23	2,943	10	1,600

Figure 112.—Equipment of the engineer battalion in the infantry division.

(2) *Composition of principal components.*—(*a*) *Partially motorized company.*—The partially motorized company consists of a headquarters, company transport, and three platoons, each having three sections. It is armed with rifles, supplemented by nine light machine guns, and carries power tools, a few Tellermines, demolition stores, and several large and small pneumatic boats.

In this unit the equipment is carried in motor vehicles; apparently, the men customarily march on foot.

(b) *Heavy motorized company.*—The heavy motorized company is organized and equipped in somewhat the same way as the partially motorized company, except that this company is transported in trucks, has a repair section and a signal section, and carries more equipment and supplies.

(c) *Bridge column.*—The bridge column is a fully motorized unit normally consisting of three platoons, two of which are equipped with ponton bridge material and the third with supplementary equipment such as motor boats, outboard motors, pneumatic boats, and similar equipment. Where there is a tank bridge-laying platoon, this is the third platoon and the supplementary equipment platoon becomes the fourth platoon. Bridge columns transport and maintain the bridge equipment, but the erection of the bridges, constructed from this equipment, is the duty of the engineer companies described above. Bridge columns are normally equipped with B ponton and trestle equipment (see par. 75c).

(d) *Light engineer column.*—This column, a fully motorized unit, which carries the battalion reserve of tools, explosives, ammunition, wire, and supplementary equipment, combines the functions of the tools park and the reserve store park, both of which were formerly employed.

b. *In motorized division.*—Each motorized infantry division contains a motorized engineer battalion, which is organized in the same way as the equivalent unit in an infantry division, except that it has a repair detachment not found in the engineer battalion of the infantry division and also has heavy motorized companies instead of the partially motorized companies. The strength of this battalion in personnel, transport, and armament is shown in figure 113; in equipment, in figure 114.

HANDBOOK ON GERMAN MILITARY FORCES

	O and EM	Mtrcl	Other Mtr vehicles	Hand grenades	LMG	Smoke generators	Small flamethrowers	Large flamethrowers	Tellermines	S-mines
Battalion headquarters	71	9	19			*				
Three heavy motorized companies	621	36	63	570	27	468			888	
Bridge column (with B equipment)	102	7	35							
Light engineer columns	68	7	16	480		324	6	3	600	621
TOTAL	862	59	133	1,050	27	792	6	3	1,488	621

Figure 113.—Composition and armament of the motorized engineer battalion in the motorized infantry battalion.

	Small pneumatic boats	Large pneumatic boats	16-ton ramps	Compressors	Drilling equipment (sets)	Power saws	Welding equipment (sets)	Plain wire (concertina rolls)	Barbed wire (concertina rolls)	Mine detectors	Demolition stores (lbs)	Exploders	Instantaneous fuze (yds)	Hand searchlights	Sandbags
Three heavy motorized companies	12	9		9	9	27		228		30	6,273	27	1,962		1,800
Bridge column (with B equipment)	48	24	8					12							
Light engineer column				2	2	2	3	100	66	9	2,788	2	1,635	10	600
TOTAL	60	33	8	11	11	29	3	340	66	39	9,061	29	3,597	10	2,400

Figure 114.—Equipment of the motorized engineer battalion in the motorized infantry division.

c. In Panzer division.—Each Panzer division contains a Panzer engineer battalion. It consists of a headquarters, two light motorized companies, a Panzer engineer company, a bridge column, and a light engineer column. Its strength in personnel, transport, and armament is shown in figure 115; in equipment, in figure 116.

ENGINEERS

	O and EM	Mtrcl	Other Mtr vehicles	Panzer Sig car	Panzer Tr carriers	Pz. Kw. II	Hand grenades	Smoke grenades	LMG	20-mm guns (.79-inch)	Smoke generators	Small flame-throwers	Medium flame-throwers	Tellermines	S-mines
Battalion headquarters	71	9	19												
Two light motorized companies	420	36	72				380		36		312			616	
Panzer engineer company	219	15	33	1	6	2	450	90	12	2	144			188	
Two bridge columns	204	34	70												
Light engineer column	65	7	19				600	225			108	6	3	450	450
TOTAL	979	101	213	1	6	2	1,430	315	48	2	564	6	3	1,254	450

Figure 115.—Composition and armament of the Panzer engineer battalion in the Panzer division.

	Small pneumatic boats	Large pneumatic boats	16-ton ramps	Compressors	Drilling equipment (sets)	Power saws	Welding equipment (sets)	Plain wire (concertina rolls)	Barbed wire (concertina rolls)	Mine detectors	Demolition stores (lbs)	Exploders	Instantaneous fuze (yds)	Hand searchlights	Sandbags
Two light motorized companies	8	6		6	6	18		188		20	4,766	18	1,634		1,350
Panzer engineer company	2	2	12	1	1	3		54		10	7,065	6	654		625
Two bridge columns	48	32	128					24							
Light engineer column				1	3	2	2	90	60		4,538	2	1,635	5	1,200
TOTAL	58	40	140	8	10	23	2	356	60	30	16,369	26	3,923	5	3,175

Figure 116.—Equipment of the Panzer engineer battalion in the Panzer division.

d. In mountain division.—The engineer battalion in a mountain division consists of headquarters, signal section, two mountain engineer companies, a light mountain engineer column. A bridge column is attached to the battalion when necessary. The strength of this battalion in personnel, transport, and armament is shown in figure 117; in equipment, in figure 118.

	O and EM	Horses and pack animals	Mtrcl	Other Mtr vehicles	H-Dr vehicles	Hand grenades	LMG	Smoke generators	Small flame-throwers	Medium flame-throwers	Tellermines	S-mines
Battalion headquarters	113	44	7	4	8						80	
Two mountain engineer companies	554	212	4	2	56	380	18	312			308	
Light motorized company	210		18	35		190	9	156			300	
Light motorized engineer column	70		7	20		480		324	6	3	300	387
TOTAL	947	256	36	61	64	1,050	27	792	6	3	688	387
Bridge column (with B equipment)	102		7	35								
TOTAL with bridge column (with B equipment)	1,049	256	43	96	64	1,050	27	792	6	3	688	387

Figure 117.—Composition and armament of the mountain engineer battalion in the mountain division.

	Small pneumatic boats	Large pneumatic boats	16-ton ramps	Compressors	Drilling equipment (sets)	Power saws	Welding equipment (sets)	Plain wire (concertina rolls)	Barbed wire (concertina rolls)	Barbed wire (50-lb coils)	Mine detectors	Demolition stores (lbs)	Exploders	Instantaneous fuze (yds)	Hand searchlights	Sandbags
Two mountain engineer companies	12	4		6	6	12	2	84		32	20	2,118	12	654		400
Light motorized company	4	3		3	3	9		94			10	2,383	9	817		675
Light motorized engineer column				2	2	2	3	100	66			2,788	2	1,635	10	600
TOTAL	16	7		11	11	23	5	278	66	32	30	7,289	23	3,106	10	1,675
Bridge column (with B equipment)	48	24	8					12								
TOTAL with bridge column (with B equipment)	64	31	8	11	11	23	5	290	66	32	30	7,289	23	3,106	10	1,675

Figure 118.—Equipment of the mountain engineer battalion in the mountain division.

71. GHQ units.—*a. General.*—There are no regular engineer units assigned organically, aside from those battalions which form a part of every German combat division. All additional engineer units belong to the GHQ pool. These units are divided into combat engineers (*Pioniere*), fortress engineers (*Festungspioniere*), and railway engineers (*Eisenbahnpioniere*).

b. Combat engineers.—(1) *Engineer battalions.*—As far as is known, the GHQ battalions are organized on the same lines as the divisional engineer battalions and consist of a headquarters with a signal section, three heavy motorized companies, a bridge column, and a light engineer column containing tools and supplies. The strength of the battalion is approximately the same as that of the engineer battalion in a motorized division.

(2) *Bridging columns.*—These are mostly light bridge columns as in the infantry or motorized division, although there are columns with other equipment. Carrying units for heavier bridges are usually referred to as units of the equipment concerned, such as *Einheit leichtes zerlegbares Brückengerät* (light sectionalized bridge unit), *Einheit Herbertgerät* (Herbert bridge unit), etc. These units are sometimes under control of a special battalion staff known as *Stab Transportabteilung für schweres Brückengerät* (transport staff for heavy bridging).

(3) *Bridge-building battalions* (*Brückenbaubataillone*).—Bridging columns are carrying units only, and the bridges are erected either by the personnel of divisional engineer battalions or by special bridge-building battalions. These consist of a headquarters, 4 companies, an engineer tools platoon, and an engineer park company. The strength of the company is about 250 and the total battalion strength is about 1,250.

(4) *Assault-boat companies and detachments* (*Sturmbootkompanien und Sturmbootkommandos*).—The assault-boat company consists of a headquarters with a signal section and three platoons of three sections each. The strength is 194, and the unit is armed with 4 light machine guns and 3 antitank rifles. An unspecified

quantity of Tellermines and demolition stores is carried, as well as 36 assault boats. In recent practice, assault-boat detachments of varying sizes have been formed for service where required. One type has 3 platoons with a total of 81 assault-boats.

(5) *Assault engineering companies (Sturmpionierkompanien).*—These companies contain 2 platoons of engineers, trained in assault operations (principally against fortifications), and a third assault-boat platoon with 27 assault boats. The strength of a company is about 200.

(6) *Engineer landing companies (Pionier-Landungskompanien).*—These companies have a strength of about 200. Twelve landing boats are carried with 1 machine gun each, and an unknown number of assault boats equipped with outboard motors.

(7) *Technical battalions.*—These are industrial specialist units belonging to the engineers and are organized in battalions of three companies, not necessarily of the same kind. They are primarily concerned in the initial exploitation of occupied countries, the reconstruction of damaged installations, and similar tasks, which usually require them to work close to front lines. Industrial specialist units which have been reported include a staff (*Kommandeur technischer Truppen*), equivalent to a regimental staff; technical battalions composed of companies with varying specialties; technical battalions for mineral oil; electricity companies (*technische Kompanien E*); gas and water companies (*technische Kompanien GW*); and mining companies (*technische Kompanien BT*). The strength of these units is not known. The companies usually have three light machine guns each, and are probably trained as combat units.

(8) *Ferry construction battalions.*—Seagoing ferries are primarily the concern of the Navy, but lately they have been used by Army units (fig. 119). Certain construction battalions are specially trained in the assembly of such ferries and may also man them. When crews are to be furnished, a fifth company may be added to the battalion for this purpose. This company is a combat unit with nine light machine guns, and is evidently

designed for combined operations. Several battalions exist, but it is not known how many have a fifth company.

(9) *Engineer parks.*—(a) *Organization.*—One engineer park is allotted to each army. No recent information is available, but pre-war data indicate that the engineer park consists of a headquarters with a section for road-making equipment and a section for other equipment; two engineer park companies (subdivisions unknown), which are intended for maintenance and

Figure 119.—Tank-landing barge.

repair; and an engineer tools platoon, divided into two half platoons and a workshop section.

(b) *Strength.*—The strengths of the engineer park, the engineer park companies, and the engineer tools platoon are, respectively, 4 officers and 70 enlisted men, 3 officers and 190 enlisted men, and 1 officer and 102 enlisted men, or a total for the whole engineer park of 11 officers and 552 enlisted men. Equipment includes a half set each of B and C bridging equipment with 25 vehicles (the proportion of C equipment would probably now be lower), one L. Z. bridge, 8 sets of road-making equipment, 8 sets of equipment for repair of concrete roads, and 2 sets of equipment for repair of macadam roads. Details of the road equipment are not available, but it is believed that the total of such equipment is sufficient to employ about 3 road construction battalions.

c. Railway engineers.—(1) *General.*—Railway engineers belong to the engineer arm and are to be regarded as fighting troops in the same sense as other engineer units. Certain classes of the original personnel were drawn from the German state railways, but present replacements are almost entirely from railway engineer depot units of the Army. They are mainly employed on railway construction and maintenance in the forward areas, though some units are certainly concerned in railway operation as well. A large part of their duties consists of the construction of heavy bridges, and they may be found erecting such bridges as the *L. Z.* bridges (see figs. 126 and 127, p. 152) for roads as well as railways. These units should be distinguished from units of the railway troops (*Eisenbahntruppen*), which are concerned with the maintenance and operation of railways in rear areas and are not engineer units.

(2) *Individual units.*—(*a*) *Regiments.*—Railway engineer regiments have two battalions of four companies each, which may be partly or wholly motorized. There is no indication of their strength.

(*b*) *Bridge-building battalions.*—The railway engineers include both railway bridge-building battalions and railway construction battalions. The bridge-building battalions are believed to contain four companies, a railway engineer tools platoon, and a railway park company. The construction battalions probably have four companies also, but no details are available.

(*c*) *Specialist companies.*—In addition to the above units, there are independent railway construction companies; railway pier-building companies (*Eisenbahn-Pfeilerbaukompanien*); railway telephone companies; railway signal companies (*Eisenbahnstellwerkkompanien*); railway water-point companies (*Eisenbahnwasserstationskompanien*); light railway companies (*Feld-*

bahnkompanien); railway operating companies (*Eisenbahnbetriebskompanien*); cableway detachments and sections (*Seilbahnkommandostruppen*); and underwater welding sections (*Eisenbahnunterwasserschneidetruppen*). The functions of these companies are indicated by their titles, but it is not evident in all cases whether they are concerned with construction, maintenance, or operation. No details are available regarding their organization.

(*d*) *Railway engineer parks and workshop companies.*—These are part of the rear echelon of the railway engineers, and there is no information as to their organization. They are controlled by a special railway engineer staff (*Eisenbahnpionierstab z. b. V.*) in Berlin.

d. Fortress engineers.—Fortress engineers are primarily concerned with the layout, construction, upkeep of fortresses, and the preparation of obstacles and demolitions in fortress areas. They are specialists and, except in theaters where their technical skill is required, are not likely to be encountered in the field. The general outline of the fortress engineer organization is as follows: each military district (*Wehrkreis*) has a fortress engineer headquarters (*Festungs-Pionier-Kommandeur*); under this are staffs equivalent to regimental staffs (*Festungs-Pionierstäbe*), each of which normally controls two sector groups (*Festungs-Pionierabschnittsgruppen*). There are also fortress construction battalions, fortress engineer parks, fortress engineer supply staffs, and other units or staffs. Certain specialist units of fortress engineers connected with water supply were employed in Africa. These units included light and heavy water supply companies (*Wasserversorgungskompanien*), water distillation companies (*Wasserdestillationkompanien*), and water purification columns (*Filterkolonnen*). Military geological stations (*Wehrgeologenstellen*) belonging to the fortress engineers also have been encountered.

72. **Construction troops** *(Bautruppen).—a. General.*—Although construction troop units do not come under the Inspec-

torate of Engineers, but under the separate Inspectorate of Construction Troops, they perform many tasks which are performed by engineers in the U. S. Army, leaving the combat engineers (*Pioniere*) free for operations in the forward areas.

b. Organization.—The following types of construction units are known: construction battalions (*Baubataillone*); road-construction battalions (*Strassenbaubataillone*); light road-construction battalions (*leichte Strassenbaubataillone*); and light bicycle road-construction battalions (*leichte Radfahr-Strassenbaubataillone*). The construction battalion contains a headquarters, 4 companies, and a supply train. The supply train may or may not be motorized; the companies are not. The road-construction battalion consists of a headquarters, 4 road-construction companies, and a partly motorized equipment section. The companies contain a headquarters, with a signal section and 3 platoons, a motorized equipment column, and horse-drawn transport. The light road-construction battalion has a headquarters and 4 light road-construction companies, but has no equipment section. The companies are considerably smaller than those in the road-construction battalion and have no signal section. The light bicycle road-construction battalion is similar to the light road-construction battalion but contains 4 light bicycle-equipped road-construction companies. These units have been employed for the removal of obstacles in the path of Panzer divisions, and for road-building, wiring, mining of shelters in rock, and similar tasks. They are known to have assisted the front-line engineer units in bridge construction. The strength of the construction company is about 400; that of the battalion, about 1,900. The strength of the company in the highway construction battalion is about 360; the battalion strength is about 1,500. The strength of the company in the light road-construction company and light bicycle road-construction battalion is about 180, with the total battalion strength about 750.

73. Demolition equipment.—*a. Explosives.*—The standard German explosive is TNT, which is normally supplied in blocks weighing 100 grams (3½ ounces), 200 grams (7 ounces), 1 kg (2⅕ pounds), and 3 kg (6⅗ pounds) (fig. 120). The two smaller sizes are wrapped in wax paper and the larger sizes are in zinc containers. All sizes are provided with one or more threaded

Figure 120.—Method of blowing a portal.

holes for taking a detonator; no intermediate primer is necessary.

b. Fuzes and igniters.—The German safety fuze is similar in appearance to that of the U. S. Army, and burns at a rate of approximately 2 feet per minute; the instantaneous fuze has a green covering and is handled in the normal manner. The standard German igniter used for initiation of the safety fuze is the *Zündschnuranzünder 29* (*ZDSCHN ANZ 29*), which functions by withdrawal of a coiled wire through a match composition pellet. A later type, *ZDSCHN ANZ 39*, exists, but no details concerning it are known.

c. Exploders.—Several types of exploders for electrical firing of demolitions are in use. The latest pattern (*Glühzundapparat 40*) is a low-tension exploder which will fire through an external resistance of 255 ohms.

74. Electrical and mechanical equipment.—*a. Compressors and power tools.*—There are two sizes of compressors carried by German engineers, the small (*kleiner Drucklufterzeuger 34*) and large (*grosser Drucklufterzeuger 34*). No details are available on the former; the latter is mounted on a trailer, has an overall weight of approximately 1,900 pounds, and a capacity of 106 cubic feet of air per minute, delivered at a pressure of 88 pounds per square inch. Pneumatic tools driven by these compressors include drills, hammers, pile drivers, and probably small pumps. Power saws issued to engineer companies are normally gasoline-driven (fig. 121), but there are reports that electrically driven saws also have been used.

b. Field generating sets.—A large number of field generating sets, both alternating and direct current, ranging from 0.8 to 35 kilowatts, are in use in the German Army. No details are available.

c. Field searchlight projectors.—Small searchlights, 12 inches in diameter, are carried in engineer units as shown in figures 112, 114, 116, and 118 (pp. 130, 132, 133, and 134, respectively). The larger searchlights used for antiaircraft defense are manned by personnel in antiaircraft units of the air force and not by engineer personnel.

d. Mine detectors.—The Germans use two methods for detecting buried mines: probing and electro-magnetic. The probing technique is similar to U. S. methods; a special tubular steel rod is usually employed for this purpose. The electro-magnetic method of mine detection depends on the change in inductance of an oscillating circuit when placed near a conducting body. In practice, the circuit is embodied in a search coil mounted on the end of a rod of convenient length and moved over the surface of

Figure 121.—Power saw with gasoline motor.

the ground to be investigated. Mines are detected by the change of inductance, which is evidenced by variations in the note sounded in a pair of headphones worn by the operator. Several types of electro-magnetic detectors with different circuits are in use in the German Army, and are commonly named after the town in which they were originally produced: that is, Berlin, Köln, Frankfurt, or Aachen.

75. Floating equipment.—*a. Assault boats (Sturmboote).*—These are light wooden, keelless boats, which will carry seven men in addition to the crew of two (fig. 122). They are used in the initial stages of an assault-crossing and are powered by a 12-horsepower, 4-cylinder outboard motor, which drives a propeller through a 13-foot shaft contained in a tubular housing. Four men are required to carry the motor and eight to carry the boat. Boats can be nested in groups of three on special trailers for transport. The maximum speed of the boat when loaded is probably between 15 and 20 miles per hour.

b. Pneumatic boats.—(1) These boats are used in the second stage of an assault crossing. They are made of rubberized fabric in the form of an elongated ring, bulkheaded off into several air chambers so that the boat cannot easily be sunk. They can be used for ferrying, or for rafting and bridging, when they are fitted with various types of light wooden superstructures. The boats are made in two sizes, the larger of which can be inflated by hand bellows in about 15 minutes.

(*a*) *Small size.*—The smaller boat, which is 10 feet long and 4 feet wide, will carry one passenger in addition to the crew of two. It has an available buoyancy of about 600 pounds, weighs 110 pounds, and rolls up into a cylinder 5 feet long and 2 feet in diameter. It is not commonly used for rafting, but can be fitted with either a duckboard type of wooden structure to form a light infantry assault bridge, or with a double-track superstructure to form a bridge capable of supporting motorcycles.

(*b*) *Large size.*—The larger boat, which is 18 feet long and 6 feet wide, will carry one rifle or machine-gun section, in addition to the crew of seven. It has an available buoyancy of about 2½ tons, weighs 330 pounds, and rolls up into a cylinder 7 feet long and 3 feet in diameter. Boats can be joined together to form 2- and 4-ton rafts, and the rafts can be coupled together to form bridges, the exact rating of which is not known.

c. B ponton and trestle equipment (Brückengerät B).—This equipment was introduced into the German Army about 1934, and

ENGINEERS

Figure 122.—Assault boat loaded with infantry.

is the standard bridge carried by engineer battalions in motorized infantry divisions and in most infantry divisions, where it is replacing the obsolescent C equipment (see *d*, below). It is of normal design, consisting of balks, chesses, and guardrails, supported on undecked steel pontons, which can be used singly or joined together stern-to-stern to form ponton piers (fig. 123). The ponton measures 24 feet 7 inches by 5 feet 9 inches, and weighs 1,654 pounds. In addition to a crew of 4, it has a carrying capacity of 15 men with field equipment, or 10,000 pounds, with 9 inches freeboard. The balks are steel I-beams, 7 inches by 3 inches by 21 feet, weighing 315 pounds; the chesses are 10 inches by 2 inches by 12 feet by 7 inches, weighing 55 pounds. Trestles are of steel and weigh about 1,100 pounds. With this equipment, bridges and rafts of 4-, 9-, and 18-ton ratings can be built. In practice, the 18-ton bridge can be considerably over-loaded, probably up to 26 or 27 tons. The 4-ton bridge is constructed by using 1 ponton per bay, centered under the ends of the balks and requires special ponton transoms and saddles to support the balks. The 9-ton bridge may be built in the same manner as the 4-ton bridge by replacing each single ponton with 2 pontons joined longitudinally. These 2 bridges cannot be divided completely into rafts; they are therefore conveniently formed by bridging out rather than by the use of rafts. An alternative method of building the 9-ton bridge is to form rafts with 2 pontons per raft. Since, with this method, the junction of the balks falls between pontons, special ponton transoms and saddles are not required. The 18-ton bridge also is built by the latter method, with each ponton replaced by 2 pontons joined longitudinally. The superstructure of these bridges is progressively strengthened by the addition of balks, and in the case of the 18-ton bridge, by doubling the chesses and guardrails. For assisting bridging operations, motorboats are provided. These are powered with a 100-horsepower, six-cylinder, water-cooled gasoline engine, and each has a capacity of 6 men. They are capable of moving a treble 18-ton raft at 6 miles per hour.

Figure 123.—Ponton bridge under construction.

d. C ponton and trestle equipment (Brückengerät C).—This appears to be an earlier type than the B equipment which is now replacing it (see *c*, above). Pontons are similar in design to the B type, but are of wooden construction and are smaller, measuring 12 feet long and 5 feet wide, and weighing about 300 pounds. The pontons are open and splayed and can be nested for transport. The superstructure consists of balks and chesses joined together to form complete units of roadway, measuring approximately 23 feet by 2 feet. Four types of bridge can be built: an assault bridge of single strips of superstructure supported on single pontons; a 1-ton bridge consisting of a five-strip-wide superstructure supported on double ponton piers; a 4-ton bridge similar to the 1-ton, but with twice the number of piers; and a 5.3-ton bridge in which each floating bay is supported on three piers. The latter bridge is especially designed to take the 5.3-ton six-wheeled armored car.

e. D ponton and trestle equipment (Brückengerät D).—This equipment is used by motorized pioneer platoons and will take loads up to 9 tons. It is of the ponton, trestle, and girder type. No details are available, but the girder appears to be about 30 feet in length, and to be composed of a center box section with two triangular end sections.

f. K ponton and trestle equipment (Brückengerät K).—This is the standard bridge carried by engineers in the Panzer division. The pontons are of a three-section type and the superstructure is similar to the U. S. small box-girder bridge. Bridges of two, three, and four girders can be built, the full girder length of 64 feet being normally used. The track load-carrying capacity and corresponding spans are probably equal to, or greater than, the following:

4-girder, 48-foot span	25 tons.
4-girder, 64-foot span	21 tons.
2-girder, 32-foot span	21 tons.
2-girder, 64-foot span	10 tons.

ENGINEERS

g. S ponton and trestle equipment (Brückengerät S).—This ponton bridge is used only for heavy traffic across wide rivers, and its construction must be regarded as a major engineering operation. The pontons are sectional, and the roadway, which is 16 feet 6 inches in width, will accommodate two lines of traffic. Wheeled vehicles up to 24 tons and tracked vehicles up to 30 tons can be

Figure 124.—Herbert bridge.

accommodated for single-line traffic; the maximum load is reduced to 16 tons if two-way traffic is allowed.

h. Herbert bridge.—This heavy ponton bridge, with a built-up girder superstructure, originally formed part of the equipment of the Czechoslovakian Army. (See figs. 124 and 125.) It will take 20-ton tracked vehicles over a maximum unsupported span of 82 feet, and with closer spacing of pontons it could prob-

Figure 125.—Photographing Herbert bridge.

ably support a 35-ton tank. It can be used only on the largest rivers, and the construction and launching require too much time for consideration in assault operations. The Herbert equipment, therefore, may be classified as a semipermanent bridge, and its use is probably confined to rear areas. The pontons are of steel or light alloy, gunwale-loaded, and are used to a minimum freeboard of 12 inches: the bow is provided with a raised bulwark to assist in the rough water experienced on large rivers. The ponton sections are decked and provided with hatches, and it is possible for the maintenance crew to rest and sleep inside. The weight of a ponton is approximately 10 tons, and displacement with the freeboard mentioned is nearly 60 tons. The main girders carrying the roadway are composed of sections in the form of pyramids, 6 feet 6 inches high, with bases 8 feet 3 inches long by 4 feet 6 inches wide. Transoms are hung in special stirrups from the apex of each pyramid, and the transoms in turn carry the balk. A standard bay is 82½ feet long, that is, of 10 pyramid sections, pin-connected. The equipment also includes trestle piers of shore bays at river crossings or shallow, dry gaps, while the steel trestles, built of standard parts, can be constructed to a height of over 60 feet above foundation level and still carry the full load for which the bridge is designed.

76. Fixed bridges.—*a. L. Z. bridge.*—The *L. Z.* (light sectionalized) bridge is normally erected on main lines of communication. It is a through-type sectional truss bridge which can be used for spans up to about 148 feet; it has a track width of 12 feet 2 inches, and will carry wheeled vehicles up to 18 tons or tracked vehicles up to 30 tons (figs. 126 and 127). By a special method of construction, the bridge can be used for light railway traffic over a number of gaps, and as an improvisation it can be built on floating supports. The main trusses consist of rectangular panels, 8 feet 2 inches in length, which are bolted together and resemble the trusses used in the British Bailey bridge. One railway engineer company can assemble and launch a 148-foot bridge in 12 to 15 hours.

Figure 126.—L. Z. bridge over the Meuse River at Maastricht.

Figure 127.—L. Z. bridge completed. (Note the launching nose.)

b. Railway bridges.—Four types of railway bridges are known: the *Roth Wagner, Krupp, Kohn,* and *Ungarn.* None of these is believed to be a recent development, the *Roth Wagner* having been used since World War I. All are believed to be of the unit construction type, built from standard parts which can be used in spans and piers.

c. Improvised bridges.—In the German Army, great emphasis is laid on the construction of improvised bridges, and all engineer companies carry a small supply of timber for this purpose. These bridges vary from light timber footbridges of various types to semipermanent bridges with a capacity of more than 20 tons.

77. Portable tank bridges.—The only known bridge of this type is the *Unger,* a double-track bridge 22 feet long, of timber construction, mounted on wheels, and said to be capable of carrying loads up to 22 tons.

78. Mines.—*a. Antitank mines.*—(1) *Tellermine.*—This is the standard German antitank mine. It is 12.6 inches in diameter and 3.2 inches high, with a convex top and a flat bottom; a carrying handle is provided on one side. The total weight of the mine is 19 pounds, of which 11 pounds is TNT. The ignition assembly is located in the center of the lid and is operated by a direct pressure of from 175 pounds at the edge to 420 pounds at the center. The mine is provided with sockets on the side and base for insertion of additional detonators and igniters; these can be used for connection by means of instantaneous fuzes to other mines, or for detonating the mine by means of trip wires, etc., when it is moved. The mines are normally buried from 2 to 4 inches below the ground surface. When used as hasty obstacles, they may be connected by means of pressure bars to form a continuous obstacle which will detonate under pressure applied to any part of it.

(2) *L. P. Z. antitank mine.*—This is a circular mine, 10.25 inches in diameter, 2.25 inches in height, weighing 9 pounds,

and containing 5 pounds of explosive. It is pressure-operated and has five igniters, equally spaced around a central flash chamber. Specimens were captured from German paratroops in Crete, but nothing further has been heard of the *L. P. Z.* mine. It is assumed that it may have been either an abandoned experimental type or an especially light mine designed to be carried by airborne troops.

(3) *C. V. P. 1 antitank mine.*—This is a Hungarian mine which was used by the Germans in North Africa in September 1942. It is of the same general design as the *Tellermine*, but is smaller, having a diameter of 10 inches and a height of 3 inches. The mine weighs 8 pounds, has an explosive filling of 3.5 pounds, and may be regulated to detonate under pressures varying from 70 pounds to 700 pounds; consequently, it can be used in either an antitank or an antipersonnel role.

(4) *German time-delay railway mine.*—This mine, of special design and construction, is for use by parties of specialists raiding lines of communication; it is reserved for special operations and is not a general issue to the field. The mine is contained in a light wooden box measuring 9 by 9 by 4¼ inches, and contains 8½ pounds of **TNT**. It is usually placed under a railway tie and set for a time-delay of from 1 to 21 days, after which it will detonate when the pressure head is depressed.

b. Antipersonnel traps and mines.—These can be divided into two main types:

(1) *Elementary booby traps.*—These consist of one or more small blocks of explosive and a push or pull igniter, actuated by the usual trip devices, (doors, cupboards, light switches, etc.). Push or pull igniters also may be attached to antitank mines as antilifting devices.

(2) *Shrapnel mine (S-mine).*—This mine is cylindrical in shape, about 4 inches in diameter and 5 inches in height; it

weighs about 9 pounds, contains 1 pound of explosive and 350 ⅜-inch-diameter steel balls, which are packed around the explosive. The mine may be operated by direct pressure on the push igniter in the head, or by a pull on one or more trip wires attached to pull igniters. It is of the bounding type; that is to say, it is projected into the air by a secondary charge before the mine proper explodes and scatters the steel balls. Dummy S-mines are freely used and require careful examination, as they may have booby traps attached.

79. Antitank obstacles.—*a. Antitank mines.*—These are used as follows:

(1) *In mine fields.*—Mine fields are sited in accordance with principles similar to those adopted in the U. S. Army, the mines being spaced at regular intervals. The number of rows is not fixed, but the whole mine field is designed to give a density of at least one mine to every 14 inches of front. Frequent use is made of mine fields consisting of mixed antipersonnel and antitank mines, with the object of impeding the rapid neutralization of the mine field by engineer troops.

(2) *As road and passage blocks.*—These may consist of a number of mines disposed at intervals as in the case of a mine field. Isolated mines may also be used, a board being placed across the top of the mine to increase the contact area.

(3) *In conjunction with other obstacles.*—Antitank and antipersonnel mines are frequently concealed in all types of road blocks and arranged to operate either under pressure or by the pull of a wire when a portion of the obstacle is removed.

(4) *As suspended mines.*—Various devices are used whereby a vehicle running into a wire stretched between trees across a road may cause a mine to explode either underneath the tank or vehicle, or when released from above or pulled from the side.

b. Wire obstacles.—Wire rolls disposed in depth across the road are occasionally used. The spacing between rolls decreases from the front to the rear of the obstacle. Antitank and antipersonnel mines, concealed within the obstacles, are used to increase their effectiveness.

c. *Other antitank obstacles.*—(1) *Dragon's teeth.*—These are composed of from four to eight rows of reinforced concrete blocks of varying heights up to 6 feet. The blocks are broader at the base than at the top, and are cast in rows from front to rear with substantial reinforced connecting sills or foundations. Dragon's teeth are designed to stop a tank through bellying. Continuous rows of these obstacles are constructed in front of prepared positions, usually with the addition, on the enemy side, of a ditch 10 feet wide and a bank. (See par. 124*d* (1), p. 335, and fig. 187, p. 339.)

(2) *Felled trees.*—Trees are felled along forest roads and tied together to form obstacles, which are further strengthened by concealed antipersonnel mines.

(3) *Rails and steel sections.*—These obstacles are employed to form barriers and road blocks. They are usually of varying heights and are spaced at intervals of about 4 feet. Barriers are also formed of special angle-iron frameworks, 6 feet 6 inches high, designed to stop a tank by providing an unscalable slope.

80. Special equipment for use in assault.—*a. Flame-throwers.*—The Germans have three types of portable flame-throwers, two of which resemble those developed in the last war.

(1) *Light-weight Kleif.*—This is operated by a team of two men and throws burning oil or creosote a distance of about 25 yards. Short jets of flame are normally used, but in one continuous jet the duration is about 10 to 12 seconds. The container is carried by one man, who also directs the flame. (See par. 92*b* (10) (*b*), p. 194.)

(2) *New type.*—A new type of pack flame-thrower is characterized by the shape of the fuel and hydrogen containers, which are in the form of concentric rings carried on the back of the operator. The maximum range of this flame-thrower is 25 yards, but the duration of continuous discharge is reduced to 7 or 8

seconds. However, the new type has the advantage of weighing 47 pounds compared with 80 pounds for the *Kleif*. (See par. 92*b* (10) (*b*), p. 194.)

(3) *Medium-weight Grof*.—This is usually operated by three men, the first carrying the fuel and the second the compressed nitrogen cylinder, while the third operates the valves and directs the flame. Additional men may be included in the party to carry added supplies of fuel and nitrogen. The flame is thrown 25 to 30 yards, and in one continuous jet will last about 25 seconds.

b. Bangalore torpedoes (*gestreckte Ladungen*.)—These are used for blowing gaps in barbed-wire entanglements. The standard type consists of 7-foot lengths of steel tubing filled with explosive and connected by bayonet joints. It is fired by a length of instantaneous fuze running the whole length of the torpedo. Torpedoes can also be improvised by securing grenades or standard blocks of TNT to boards or poles.

c. Pole charges (*geballte Ladungen*).—These charges, used for attacking pillboxes and fortified positions, consist of a number of standard explosive slabs fixed to the end of a pole. After being placed, the charge is fired either by a short length of safety fuze or electrically by an exploder operated by a second man.

d. Grenade charge.—This consists of six stick-grenade heads, tied around the head of a seventh that still has its stick. The charge is used against pillboxes and for attacking the tracks and turrets of tanks.

e. Hollow demolition charges (*Hohlladungen*).—These are conical HE charges, designed to perforate cupolas and armor-plating in permanent fortifications. They are supplied in three sizes, weighing, respectively, 12.5 kg (27.5 pounds), 13.5 kg (29.7 pounds), and 50 kg (110 pounds). All are provided with a hemispherical hollow space in the side nearest the target in order to concentrate the force of the explosive on a small surface area. The 13.5-kg charge is fitted with three folding, extensible legs for positioning the charge with relation to the target.

f. Hollow ring charges (Hohlringladungen).—Hollow ring charges, weighing 1.2 kg (2.6 pounds) and 3.2 (7 pounds), consist of pressed TNT in thin annular containers, on the inner side of which is a small hollow space of semicircular cross section. The smaller charge is intended for use in destroying antitank and machine barrels; the larger is intended for use against field guns.

g. Mine-exploding nets (Knallennetze).—These are made of instantaneous fuze and are used for clearing passages through mine fields by detonating the mines. Each net is made up in units 33 feet long and 8 feet wide, with a square 6-inch mesh, and is initiated by a length of safety fuze and a detonator, which can be fixed to any part of the net. Two nets can be rolled up and carried by one man, and are considered sufficient for clearing a passage through most mine fields.

81. Vehicles.—*a. 3-ton truck.*—This is the normal type of heavy six-wheeled truck made by *Henschel*. Both the sides and the ends are let down when tools are carried. A long wooden cupboard, L-shaped in section, is placed along each side of the truck. The men sit on these cupboards, facing inward. When the sides of the truck are let down, the shelves of the cupboards are exposed.

b. Half-track tractor.—This is the normal type of *Krauss-Maffei* tractor and draws the trailers described in *c* and *d* below.

c. Bridge column trailers.—These trailers are large vehicles with four double wheels to carry the bridge column's complement of 9- and 18-ton equipment. There are four types of trailers, each having the same type of chassis but varying arrangements of pins, grooves, and similar parts to fit the different loads.

d. Trailer for motorboat.—This vehicle has a single axle and two double wheels. It includes telescopic launching ways, so that the motorboat can slide off directly into the water.

Section XI
SIGNAL TROOPS

	Paragraph
General	82
Organization	83
Composition and allotment of units	84
Additional communication methods	85
Armament of signal personnel	86
Signal equipment	87
Transportation for signal equipment	88

82. General.—*a. Introduction.*—The German Army attaches the greatest importance to the maintenance of communications among all units of the Armed Forces, and German signal troops are thoroughly trained and equipped to keep vital communication networks in operation. Although signal troops are assigned many varied duties, including the development of new communications equipment, their main task is the establishment and maintenance of communications within the immediate combat zone. In order to reduce the difficulties of supply to a minimum, the Germans have developed simple and practical signal equipment, and, where possible, have concentrated on a few standard types. Thus, for example, many parts in German radio sets, particularly the tubes, are used by two or more arms, facilitating the building up of reserves of spare parts and making it easier to supply signal units in the field.

b. Communications within division.—Within the German division, the division signal battalion establishes lines to the infantry regiments and between the artillery commander and the artillery units operating under his command, in addition to establishing lateral communications to adjoining divisions. When there is a question as to which lines should be built first, artillery connections have priority.

c. Responsibility.—The higher unit is responsible for establishing and maintaining communications with the next lower unit.

Wire communications with neighboring units are always established from left to right, that is, by the unit on the left in each case. This rule does not, however, relieve commanders of the responsibility of maintaining contact with units on their left. The establishment and maintenance of communications between artillery and infantry units is considered of the highest importance. If an artillery unit is under the command of an infantry unit, the latter is responsible for establishing communications. However, if the artillery is supporting the infantry unit but not under its command, the artillery unit is responsible for the communications net. If the artillery unit is unable for some special reason to establish the connection, the infantry unit must undertake the task. Communications with heavy infantry weapon units, such as mortar and infantry howitzers, are the responsibility of the infantry commander concerned.

d. Advance.—In an advance, the division signal battalion constructs and maintains trunk lines along the route over which division headquarters is moving. In friendly territory, existing communications are utilized to the utmost. In enemy territory where such facilities are not available, heavy field wire is strung on poles.

e. Contact with enemy.—Once the enemy is encountered, wire communications with the corps, which were originally established by the corps signal troops, must be maintained at all costs and must be supplemented by radio telegraphy and any other means available.

f. Defense.—In a defensive position, a communications net is established which will meet any situation that may arise. Its extent depends upon the time available to construct it and the period for which the position is to be held. Intercommunications between divisions and other elements are established as described in *b,* above. Several means of communication are always made available between important defensive positions. Wire communication is usually by buried cable. Special communication nets for infantry, artillery, antiaircraft defenses, ground-air communication, Panzer divisions, and similar units are provided. Alarms for gas and air attack are installed, and technical means of intercepting hostile messages are expanded.

g. Recommendations.—The German commander normally issues orders for the employment of his signal units after he has received the recommendations of his signal officer. It is essential, therefore, that the signal officer be given as complete a picture as possible of the general situation, the mission of the troops, etc.

h. Use of radio.—Radio communications are used to duplicate telephone communications and to communicate with highly mobile troops on the move. The Germans employ radically different methods of maintaining radio secrecy in fighting a war of position from those which they use in open warfare. In both cases the strictest secrecy is maintained at all headquarters, from divisions upward. The number of messages is reduced to a minimum and those dispatched are always coded. In stabilized warfare this procedure is followed at all headquarters, whereas in open warfare radio communication is freed from restraint in all units up to and including the regiment. It is the German belief that the advantage of possessing a quick means of communication for smaller units, and from rear to front, far outweighs the disadvantage of having the enemy listen in on radio messages. Hence, with battalions and regiments engaged in open warfare, German radio messages are seldom coded. It is believed that the division commander decides when code restrictions are to be in force and when small units are free to send messages in the clear.

83. Organization.—*a. Signal command.*—The Inspector of Signal Troops (*Inspekteur der Nachrichtentruppen*) supervises the training and technical development of Army signal troops. The same officer also holds the post of Inspector of Armed Forces Communications (*Inspekteur der Wehrmachtverbindungen*), and in this capacity directs that section of the joint staff of the Armed Forces responsible for interservice communications and other similar details of organization and administration. A Signal Troops Commander (*Kommandeur der Nachrichtentruppen*) in each military district (*Wehrkreis*) is responsible for both training and communications within his district. At Army GHQ there is also a Chief of Signal Communications (*Chef des Nachrichtenwesens*), who is a senior officer of the General Staff and is responsible for all signal matters in the field. Similarly there are senior signal officers attached to army group, army, and army corps headquarters.

b. Basic units.—Signal units in the German Army may be divided into two groups: organic units, permanently assigned to divisions or larger units, and units belonging to the GHQ pool.

(1) The organic units are as follows:

(*a*) Army group signal regiment (*Heeresnachrichtenregiment*), one assigned to each army group.

(*b*) Army signal regiment (*Armeenachrichtenregiment*), one assigned to each army.

(*c*) Corps signal battalion (*Korpsnachrichtenabteilung*), one assigned to each corps.

(*d*) Signal battalion (*Nachrichtenabteilung*), one assigned to each division. (In some recently formed divisions the organic signal unit is a company instead of a battalion.)

(2) The GHQ units are as follows:

(*a*) Signal regiment (*Nachrichtenregiment*) and the signal battalion (*Nachrichtenabteilung*), which may be assigned to armies or corps to supplement their organic signal units.

(*b*) Armed Forces GHQ signal regiment (*Führungsnachrichtenregiment*), which is under the direct control of the High Command of the German Armed Forces. It provides and maintains signal communications between Hitler's headquarters and army group and army headquarters, as well as between the three branches of the Armed Forces.

(*c*) Army GHQ signal regiment (*Heeresnachrichtenregiment*), which is under the control of the Army High Command and provides and maintains communications of lesser importance than those handled by the armed forces GHQ signal regiment.

(d) Independent signal companies, which include the following:

1. Telephone construction company (*Fernsprechbaukompanie*).
2. Telephone operating platoon (*Fernsprechbetriebszug*).
3. Teletype company (*Fernschreibkompanie*).
4. Interception company (*Horchkompanie*).
5. Signal reconnaissance company (*Nachrichtenaufklärungskompanie*).
6. Radio supervision company (*Funküberwachungskompanie*).
7. Fortress signal command (*Festungsnachrichtenkommandantur*) and fortress signal command station (*Festungsnachrichtenkommandanturstelle*), which are attached to the staffs of fortress engineer units.

(e) Female signal operations battalion (*Nachrichtenhelferinneneinsatzabteilung*), which consists of women communications operators who work in communications networks, not only in Germany and the occupied countries but also in the communications areas in the immediate rear of the fighting armies.

84. Composition and allotment of units.—*a. Flexibility.*—In all the following descriptions of signal units it should be remembered that the composition and equipment of all such units vary widely according to the mission and circumstances. Thus the data given here must be regarded only as indicating the German method of organizing signal units and not as laying down a set pattern for all such units.

b. Infantry division.—One signal battalion is assigned to each German infantry division and is charged with the construction and maintenance of the division communications net. The work of the battalion is extended and supplemented by personnel with signal training who belong to various subordinate units but are not classified as signal troops. The signal battalion normally includes two companies (one telephone and one radio) and a light signal column. The companies in the infantry division signal battalion are divided into sections performing various specialized duties. Each section corresponds to a large squad or a small section in the U. S. Army. The approximate strength of the battalion in personnel and transport is shown in figure 128.

	O and EM	Mtrcl	Other Mtr vehicles	H-Dr vehicles	Horses
Headquarters group	24	2	5		4
Telephone company	253	14	43	7	52
Radio company	161	11	43		
Light signal column	36	1	13		
TOTAL	474	28	104	7	56

Figure 128.—Composition of the signal battalion in the infantry division.

c. In motorized division.—The signal battalion in the motorized division is ordinarily organized and equipped in the same way as the equivalent unit in the infantry division with the exception that it is fully motorized.

d. In Panzer division.—In North Africa, in order to meet the needs of fluid desert warfare, the German Panzer division signal battalions were equipped with more radio than wire sections. The composition and armament of one type of signal battalion in the Panzer division is shown in figure 129.

	O and EM	Mtrcl	Other Mtr vehicles	LMG
Headquarters group	18	6	4	
Panzer radio company	160	10	37	16
Panzer telephone company [1]	212	10	35	6
Light Panzer signal column	30	1	9	
TOTAL	420	27	85	22

[1] Partly radio and partly telephone.

Figure 129.—Composition and armament of the type of signal battalion in the Panzer division.

RESTRICTED

e. In mountain division.—The signal battalion in the mountain division is believed to be similar to that of the regular infantry division.

f. In corps.—Corps signal battalions are responsible for communications from the corps headquarters to the divisions operating under its command and to corps troops. They may also provide divisions with additional communication facilities when the type of operation or the nature of the terrain so requires. The composition of corps signal battalion is shown in figure 130.

	O and EM	Mtrcl	Other Mtr vehicles
Headquarters corps signal battalion	22	2	5
Three telephone companies	525	33	132
Telephone operating section	52	2	14
Radio company	138	9	37
Light signal company	44	1	19
TOTAL	781	47	207

Figure 130.—Composition of the corps signal battalion.

g. In Panzer corps.—This signal unit differs both in equipment and in personnel from the signal battalion in the conventional type of corps. In particular, it is usually considerably smaller, having fewer telephone units, in view of the relative mobility of the Panzer units. The composition of one type of signal battalion in the Panzer corps is shown in figure 131.

	O and EM	Mtrcl	Other Mtr vehicles
Headquarters, Panzer corps signal battalion	22	2	5
Panzer telephone company	132	11	31
Panzer radio company	161	13	41
Light Panzer signal column	30	1	10
TOTAL	345	27	87

Figure 131.—Composition of one type of signal battalion in the Panzer corps.

h. In army.—Troops of a signal regiment in an army are responsible for communications to corps within the army as well as to specially assigned army troops. They also provide additional communications for subordinate organizations when required. Army signal regiments are wholly motorized. The composition of such units is shown in figure 132.

	O and EM	Mtrcl	Other Mtr vehicles
Headquarters, signal regiment	28	2	4
Headquarters, 1st battalion	24	2	5
Telephone operating company	195	12	35
Radio company	162	11	38
Light signal column	36	1	15
Total, 1st battalion	417	26	93
Headquarters, 2d battalion	24	2	5
Telephone operating company	146	11	37
Telephone company	186	11	52
Two telephone construction companies	456	22	140
Light signal column	50	1	30
Total, 2d battalion	862	47	264
Total, 3d battalion (like the 2d)	862	47	264
TOTAL, regiment	2,169	122	625

Figure 132.—Composition of the army signal regiment.

85. Additional communication methods.—*a. Messengers.*—Messengers are provided in signal units, but only on a limited scale, and they are used only in emergencies.

b. Dogs.—Messenger dogs are still employed with regimental and battalion signal sections, but they are not now included in the higher signal unit organizations.

c. Carrier pigeons.—Carrier pigeons are still employed by signal units and carried in mobile pigeon lofts holding from 100 to 200 pigeons. However, the carrier pigeon is being gradually replaced by other methods of communication.

86. Armament of signal personnel.—Signal personnel are armed with rifles and bayonets or with revolvers, as well as with light machine guns. There is no indication that any signal units have heavy machine guns or other heavier-type weapons. It is to be expected, however, that signal personnel will be equipped with tripods for their machine guns and accompanied by heavily armed troops to act as guards when the need for protecting signal installation is apparent.

87. Signal equipment.—*a. Radio.*—(1) *General.*—German signal troops possess numerous specially designed radio transmitters, receivers, and other radio sets, varying in size from the heavy radios transported by truck or command car to the medium sets carried in armored vehicles and the light portable sets carried by man pack for both ground troops and airborne units. The frequencies of most of the ground communication sets are shown in figure 133.

(2) *Types of radios.*—The Germans use various types of radios, depending on the conditions under which they will have to operate and the performance which is required. For example, in most vehicles of the Panzer division there is a radio set; the commanding general of a Panzer division or brigade communicates by radio with his immediate subordinates and with the air force operating with his headquarters, while in the lower echelons every commanding officer issues his orders, reports to higher officers, and receives his instructions by radio. For the operations on Crete, German airborne attack troops were equipped with several types of radios, but two types were most extensively used: the pack *b.1* and the pack *d.2*. Both of these sets, being very light, are well suited for use by airborne units.

Figure 134 shows the principal German radios used from the forward echelons to the larger communication centers in the rear of the front lines, and the comparable sets used by the Signal Corps of the U. S. Army. In addition, figures 135 to 143 illustrate the principal types of German radios.

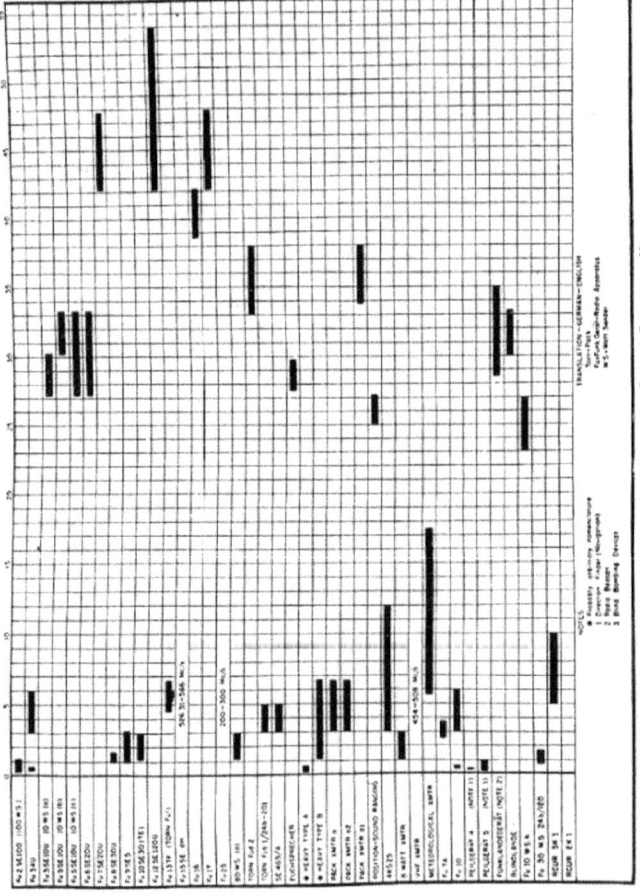

Figure 123.—Frequency coverage (in megacycles) of German radio sets.

Figure 135—Field radio.

Figure 136.—Two-man pack transmitter (14 bands, 950 to 3,150 kilocycles), probably used in the forward echelon for reconnaissance and observation.

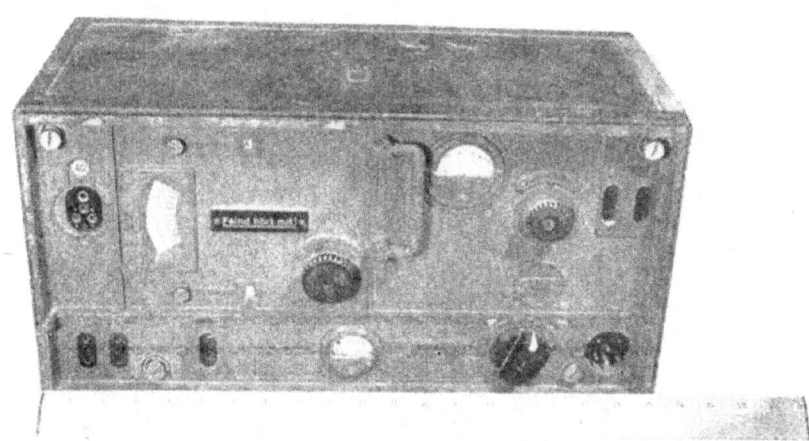

Figure 137.—*20 W.S.d.*, 20-watt transmitter.

Figure 138.—Rear view of *20 W.S.d.*, 20-watt transmitter.

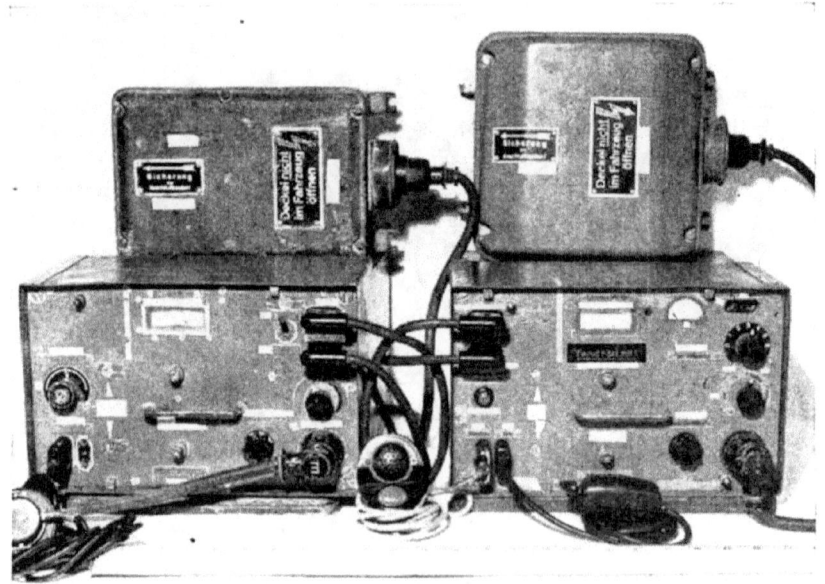

Figure 139.—*Ukw.E.e. 10 W.S.c.*, tank components of *Fu 5-SE 10 U*.

(3) *Interception receivers, direction finders, and ground listening sets.*—Certain German interception receiving equipment can cover all frequencies between 200,000 and 65 kilocycles, but information regarding the sensitivity of these sets is not available. An ingenious ground listening device is known to be in use. It consists of a cylindrical aluminum container, at one end of which are two terminals connected to the end of an internal winding. The other end can pivot around an axis perpendicular to the axis of the cylinder, forming a jaw firmly retained upon its seating by a strong spring. The side of the cylinder carries two openings diametrically opposite, allowing a telephone line to be held therein by the jaw. The inside face of this jaw carries a moving armature of a transformer core made of soft laminated iron. The spring forces the moving armature against the fixed part of the trans-

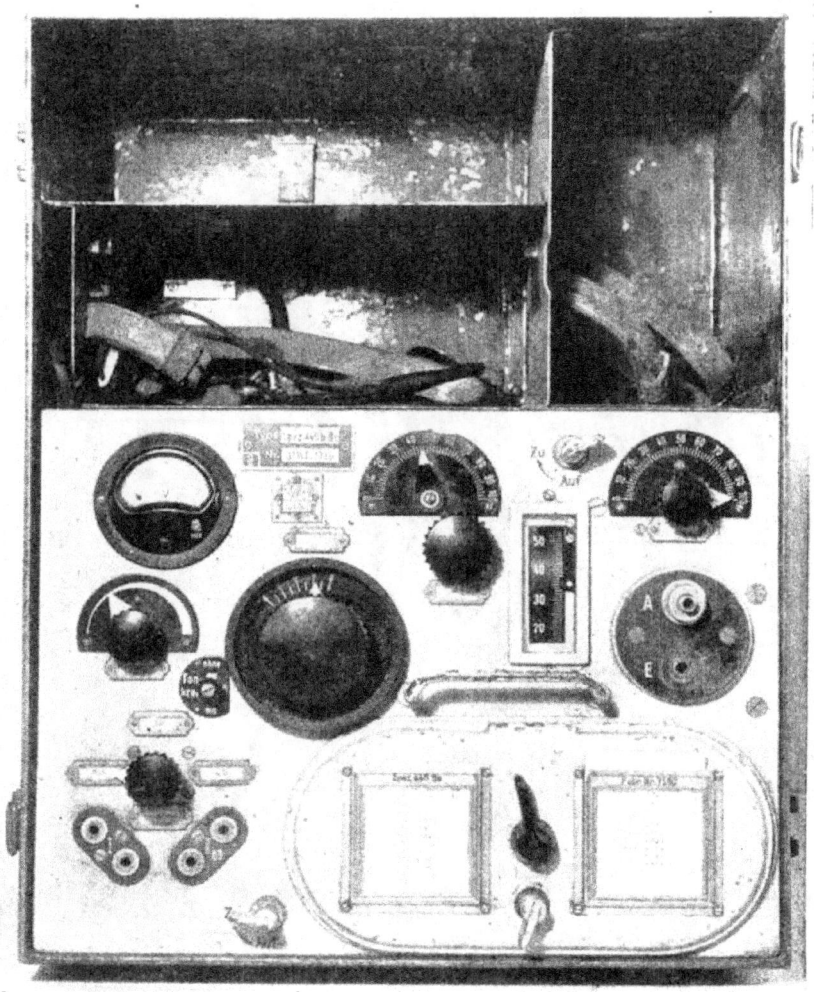

Figure 140.—Man pack receiver, intercept and monitoring type *445BS* (4 bands, 100 to 6,670 kilocycles), used with pack transmitter *TORN Fuf* in the forward echelon.

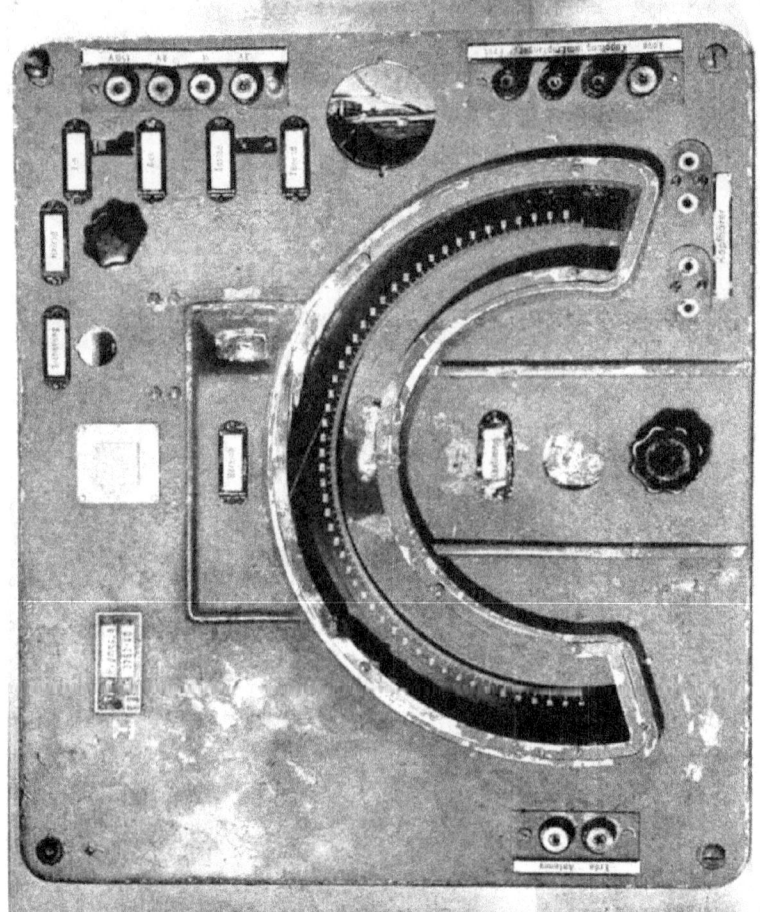

Figure 141.—Receiver, ground intercept and monitoring type (20 bands, 0 to 5 megacycles).

former, thus closing the magnetic circuit. The external terminals are connected by a pair of wires to a low-frequency amplifier. The telephone line, when inserted, acts as the primary of the transformer. The apparatus can be easily put in place, and no indication is given of its presence while it is in place or after it has been removed.

Figure 142.—Airborne transmitter, *FuG 16* (38.5 to 42.3 megacycles), used by single-seat fighters for communication.

(4) *Radio blocking devices.*—Details of radio blocking sets employed by the Germans are not available, but it is known that this type of radio interference is practiced.

b. Telegraph.—Telegraph printers have largely superseded Morse instruments in higher units of the German Army. The Siemens and Halske telegraph printers have been adopted as standard.

c. Switchboards.—The types of exchanges in general use are—

(1) *Two-line switchboard with visual indicator.*—This type consists of a small wooden box, approximately 2 by 6 by 6 inches,

with four terminals, two of which are used for line connection and two for coupling an additional two-line switchboard.

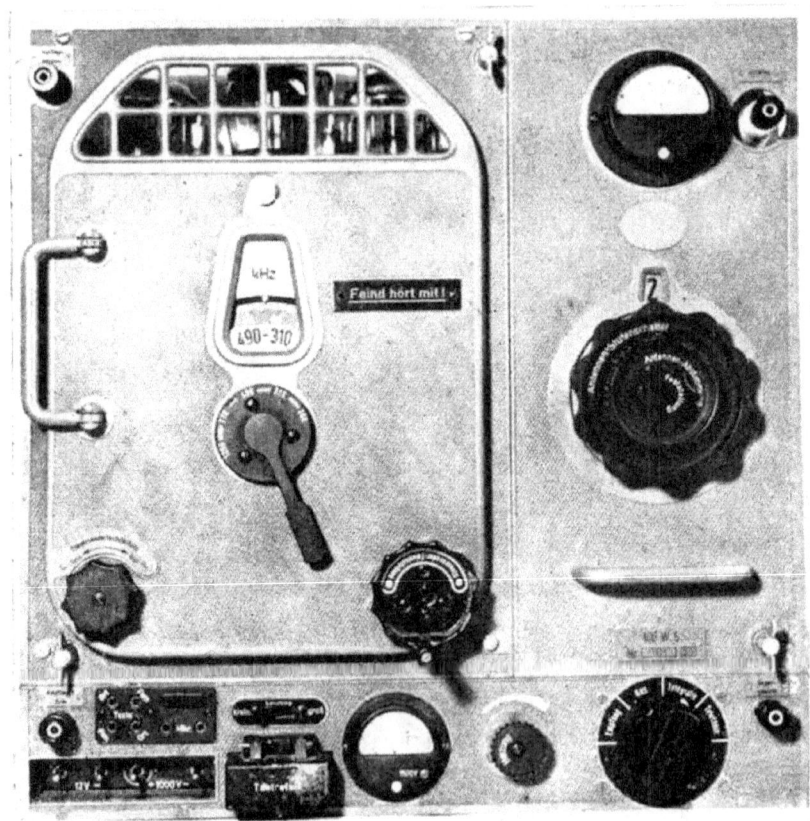

Figure 143.—Mobile transmitter, type *100 WS*, used in the division command net.

(2) *Light ten-line switchboard with shutter indicators.*—Connection in this type is made by the use of plugs and cords. The push-button disks are mounted on the basis of one for each out-

let. The method of calling is to press the required red button, and ring on the exchange operator's telephone. No magneto for ringing is embodied in this switchboard.

(3) *Light ten-line switchboard with plugs and cords.*—In this type the magneto calling device is embodied in the transmitter, and earphones are plugged into the switchboard. The first three jacks on the switchboard are normally used for truck circuits, and there is a special ringing-off indicator. A special battery is normally used for the transmitter circuit, but the standard type can be used if required. The method of calling is the same as above. (See also (4) (c), below.)

(4) *FK 16.*—(a) This heavy switchboard is used where two ten-line switchboards, coupled together, are not sufficient. This is a magneto switchboard made up of one or more thirty-line components. Each thirty-line component consists of three rows of ten-line jacks and indicators; the indicators are of the drop-shutter type. Cross connections are made by the use of plugs and cords.

(b) The *FK 16* switchboard may be adapted for use on a common battery system by the use of an additional component. A breast set and separate headphones are also provided with this type of exchange.

(c) The *FK 16* switchboard, as well as the light ten-line type, may also be used on common battery lines of various systems by the use of an instrument (different in each case) called the *Amtszusatz*, which is connected direct to the switchboard. The method of calling is then similar to the automatic dialing on German post office systems.

d. Telephones.—(1) *No. 26.*—This telephone has a buzzer and magneto generator. The hand-set is supported on a bracket on the side of the instrument and an additional receiver is provided (fig. 144). The buzzer can easily be removed from the instrument, as it is plugged in by means of a five-pin plug. The current is supplied by two cells. The total weight of the instrument is about 14½ pounds. (See (2)(c), below.)

(2) *No. 33.*—(*a*) This is a more modern form of telephone *No. 26*, the casing and hand-set being made of bakelite. A hand generator and bell are provided, but the buzzer is omitted. Current is supplied by one cell. The total weight of the instrument is approximately 12½ pounds.

Figure 144.—Field telephones.

(*b*) The *No. 33* telephone may be used on common battery lines by the use of an adaptor (*Amtsanschliesser 33*). On automatic systems the use of an additional component (*Nummernschreibenkästchen*) containing the automatic dial is necessary. This can be connected to the telephone by plug and cord.

(*c*) The labeling of terminals on telephones *No. 26* and *No. 33* is as follows:

```
La_____ Line terminal.
Lb/E_____ Line or ground terminal.
LB/ZB___ Condenser terminal (only on telephone No. 26).
```

(3) *Table telephone OB 05.*—This is a post-office pattern instrument for use indoors. A peculiarity of this instrument is the presence of magneto handles on each end of the case.

  e. *Cipher equipment.*—The "enigma" cipher machine is part of the equipment of radio telegraph stations in signal units.

  f. *Visual equipment.*—(1) *Signaling lamps.*—Two types of lamps are used. The medium lamp has a range of 3 miles by day and 10 miles by night. It can be attached to a tripod, or to a tree or pole, by a knife blade which protrudes from the bottom of the lamp. Power supply is either by battery (two 4.5 batteries connected in series) or by hand generator. An optical indicator consisting of five small metal tongues is incorporated in the generator box; their oscillations show whether the generator is being turned at the correct speed to produce the requisite current and voltage. The lamp also has a shutter attachment which can be varied to six different apertures, according to the intensity of light required. The small lamp is similar and has a range of 2 miles by day and 3½ miles by night.

  (2) *Infrared-ray telephone.*—This instrument has been introduced for use in forward areas for communication between infantry regimental headquarters and battalions. It is not used, so far as is known, in signal units.

  (3) *Disk signaling equipment.*—Two disks, colored red and white, approximately 4 inches in diameter and mounted on handles, are used for signaling in regimental, battalion, and company signal sections, in accordance with a prescribed code.

  g. *Visual equipment for air cooperation.*—Ground-to-air visual communications are accomplished by flags, colored smoke signals, and panels. During operations in Crete, swastika flags were used to denote German troops. White or yellow ground panels of cloth indicated front lines, while headquarters positions were shown by panels in the form of a cross, and spots where supplies were to be dropped were shown by two X's, side by side. Direction of resistance was indicated by inverted V's with the point in the direction of the resistance. Various other panel designs were similarly employed to convey prearranged messages. Green smoke signals were used to attract the attention of aircraft where supplies were needed; red smoke signals are also believed to be used by the Germans to indicate enemy-defended positions.

h. Light signals.—(1) *Very signal pistol cartridges.*—These are of four or more different colors. They burn for 6 seconds to a height of approximately 250 feet, and can be seen from a radius of about 1 mile.

(2) *Signal grenades.*—These can be fired to a height of 750 feet. They burn for 8 seconds and can be seen from a radius of 1½ to 3 miles by day and 10 miles by night.

(3) *Flares for communication with aircraft.*—These burn for 45 seconds.

i. Message-throwers and projectors.—These are no longer in use.

j. Line construction.—(1) *Open wire.*—The building of open wire lines with light conductors is not considered satisfactory, and the light wire is gradually being replaced by a heavy quad wire. When used, however, the wire is of 2-mm bronze or 3-mm iron, and is built on light posts. The rate of construction of two pairs is 4½ miles per day by a section and 10 miles per day by a company.

(2) *Types of field wire.*—The three main types of field wire in general use are as follows: light insulated wire for use in forward areas (a single conductor); heavy wire similar to U. S. field wire W-110-B; and heavy quad cable, for which the U. S. Army has no equivalent at present.

(3) *Transmission limits.*—The distance for which speech transmission is considered good under favorable circumstances, with light and heavy field wire, is as follows:

	Miles.
Light wire, ground return:	
On poles	8
On ground	2½

SIGNAL TROOPS 87

	Miles
Light wire, metallic return:	
On poles	15
Heavy wire, ground return:	
On poles	30
On ground	8
Heavy wire, metallic return:	
On poles	45

(4) *Methods of laying.*—(*a*) *Light wire.*—The wire is wound on reels in lengths of about 550 yards, and is laid by hand from a carrier supported either on the chest of a man or carried in the hand (fig. 145). A thumb brake is provided to prevent the reel from overspinning. A separate carrier is used for recovery.

Figure 145.—Reeling out field wire.

Collapsible back harness is also provided for the laying of light wire. This consists of a knapsack containing three reels of wire, each of 550-yard lengths, a crookstick, axles for reeling out and in, and various accessories.

(b) *Heavy field wire.*—Heavy field wire is wound on reels, each containing about 1,100 yards of wire. The reel is placed on an axle supported by an iron frame, which can be strapped to the body of a man or laid on the floor of a vehicle. To recover the wire, the reel is revolved by means of a chain attached to a separate reeling-in shaft. As the reeling-in shaft is rotated, a guide, through which the wire is passed, traverses backward and forward, so that the wire can be wound evenly on the reel.

(c) *Heavy quad cable.*—Heavy quad cable is wound on reels. Connection is made by a plug and socket about 2 inches in diameter. A loading coil can be inserted into the connector. Normal simplexing is carried out on this wire.

88. Transportation for signal equipment.—*a. Horse transport.*—Heavy field wire is carried either on a light-telephone limbered wagon or on a single limber. The light-telephone limbered wagon is drawn by two, four, or six horses. The rear half-limber contains the wire and line-construction accessories, 5 miles of heavy wire, and 2½ miles of light wire, while the front half-limber contains telephones, switchboards, men's kits, and two collapsible knapsack-pattern, wire-laying apparatuses. For laying, three reels of heavy wire are mounted on separate axles in the rear half-limber and the wire is drawn off by hand. The poles are carried in iron brackets below the rear half-limber. The infantry signal limber is similar to the light-telephone limbered wagon, but carries equipment for four wire teams and 2 miles of heavy field wire. A collapsible trailer (normally carried on the front half-limber when not in use) can be attached to the rear half-limber for laying the heavy field wire.

b. Motor transport.—The rapid motorization of signal units has led to the introduction of many types of trucks. In addition to the usual types, there are 14 types of special trucks for use by signal units. Five of these are for use in telephone and telegraph operating subsections and 9 in radio subsections. In the majority of cases these special types consist of a standard chassis with a special body.

Section XII

CHEMICAL WARFARE TROOPS

	Paragraph
General	89
Organization and administration	90
Defense	91
Offensive warfare	92

89. General.—The German military organization is thoroughly prepared for chemical warfare. Germany's chemical industry is highly developed, equipment and stocks of war gases in storage and production are ample, and adequate well-trained personnel are available. Offensively or defensively, the German Army is in a position to wage chemical warfare at any time. Unusual activity in research and manufacture has taken place in German chemical plants since the beginning of the present war. From time to time movements of war gases from one area to another have been reported. Conquered countries have been forced to produce additional supplies of chemical agents and antigas equipment for use by the German Army. Military depots are believed to be amply stocked with gas shells of all calibers. Construction of antigas shelters in German cities, issue of gas masks to civilians, and a constant examination and replacement of gas-mask containers have been regularly carried out.

90. Organization and administration.—*a. General.*—German chemical warfare troops (*Nebeltruppen*) have been organized for some years. In 1937 they were removed from the control of the Inspectorate of Artillery and placed under the Inspectorate of Chemical Warfare Troops and Gas Defense (*Inspektion für Nebeltruppen und Gasabwehr*). A troop-training ground near

Münster was reserved for their special training. Formerly restricted to smoke and decontamination operations, chemical warfare troops now function as regular chemical troops, carefully trained in all aspects of chemical warfare, and are equipped to use gas as well as smoke. In addition to 105-mm (4.14-inch) mortars, they are provided with chemical grenades and mines; some are equipped with rocket-type weapons, and others with decontaminating and contaminating devices.

b. Units.—(1) *Regiments.*—(a) *Chemical (smoke) regiment (Werferregiment)*—The chemical (smoke) regiment was formerly known as *Nebelwerferregiment*, but is now designated as *Werferregiment*. This regiment is composed of a regimental headquarters, a signal section, and 3 battalions (*Werferabteilungen*), equipped with 105-mm (4.14-inch) mortars and other weapons. Each battalion consists of a headquarters, signal and meteorological sections, and 3 companies of 2 platoons each. Reports indicate that the total armament of the regiment is 72 mortars. At least 10 such regiments (including 2 experimental regiments) have so far been identified, and 13 independent battalions (including 3 decontamination battalions) are also known. The battalions are trained to shoot gas as well as smoke from their mortars, no adjustment being necessary; thus they could be utilized for chemical warfare at any time.

(b) *Heavy chemical (smoke) regiment (schweres Werferregiment).*—Since the introduction of the sextuple, 150-mm rocket mortar, known as the *Nebelwerfer 41*, now *Werfer 41*, the organization of at least one heavy chemical (smoke) regiment (*schweres Werferregiment*) has been reported. This regiment is said to be organized like the normal chemical (smoke) regiment, except that its total armament consists of 54 six-barreled mortars.

(2) *Other units.*—(a) *General.*—The chemical (smoke) battalion (*Werferabteilung*) and the decontamination battalion (*Entgiftungsabteilung*) exist as independent units in the **GHQ** pool. In addition, it is believed that the road decontamination

battalion (*Strassen-Entgiftungsabteilung*) and motorized decontamination companies also exist as independent units.

(*b*) *Decontamination battalion.*—This unit consists of a headquarters, signal and meteorological sections, and three companies, with nine trucks, each carrying 1.2 tons of bleaching powder. Each company consists of two platoons, each equipped with six medium half-track trucks fitted with hoppers to scatter the bleaching powder. Although the primary function of the decontamination battalion is to clear passages through contaminated areas, it is said to be trained and provided with equipment for contaminating purposes, and thus would be available instantly for offensive chemical warfare. In this role, the unit would be known as *Vergiftungsabteilung* (contamination battalion).

(*c*) *Road decontamination battalion.*—Little is known relative to the organization and duties of this unit.

(*d*) *Motorized decontamination companies.*—These are composed of medical troops attached to the GHQ pool and would be sent wherever high gas casualties had occurred. No details are available concerning the organization of these troops, but they are said to be able to decontaminate and reclothe 150 men per hour.

(*e*) *Attached units.*—Horse-decontamination sections are reported to be attached to each veterinary company and army veterinary hospital. These are motorized and can be sent wherever needed. Their capacity is said to be 10 to 20 horses per hour.

91. Defense.—*a. Organization and training.*—The German Army is on a sound and efficient basis so far as gas defense training is concerned. Army gas defense schools are located in Berlin, Celle, Breloh, and elsewhere; other schools, including one at Anklam, in Pomerania, are also used for training instructors for the Army. Each battalion, or equivalent unit, throughout the Army has an antigas officer assisted by a noncommissioned officer, and each company has an antigas noncommissioned officer. They are charged with instructing their units in proper gas protective measures and with periodical inspection of all gas protective equipment. Six men in each company, or equivalent unit, are trained as gas sentries (*Gasspürer*) and are issued such equipment as gas detectors and alarms. In addition, decontamination or gas protective detachments exist in all higher units.

b. Equipment.—(1) *Gas masks.*—The German Army has had a series of gas masks, the most recent being a model with a rubber-type facepiece (*Gm. 38*) suitable for mass production. The newest canisters for use with gas masks are of the *FE 41* model. Spare gelatin-coated antidimming disks are carried in a compartment on the inside of the lid of the cylindrical metal container, and special spectacle frames with flat-tape sidepieces and antidimming compound for the lenses are provided. A limited number of carbon monoxide masks and oxygen masks are available for land forces, and some pioneer troops have been issued leather helmets having under the front brims a rolled-up piece of rubber, with eyepieces and a flat filter to cover the nose and mouth.

(2) *Protective clothing.*—(*a*) *General.*—Antigas clothing includes raincoats, overcoats, coats, short breeches, dungarees, shirts, trousers, socks, boots, and gloves.

(*b*) *Light clothing.*—Light antigas clothing consists of an overall-type one-piece suit with short legs and open back, knee boots, gloves, and hood; it has a hardened-gelatin inner layer, and when new will resist mustard gas as long as 3 hours.

(*c*) *Heavy clothing.*—Heavy protective clothing consists of a jacket with hood attached, a pair of trousers, and a pair of gloves, all of mercerized cotton fabric, proofed with a substance known as *Oppanol*, a synthetic material similar to rubber and highly resistant to both mustard gas and lewisite.

(*d*) *Parachute clothing.*—It has been reported that some parachute troops have carried suits of protective clothing consisting of an oilskin jacket, shorts tying above the knees, and long boots, the uppers of which were also of oilskin.

(e) *Protective capes.*—The *Gastilt*, a gas protective cape, was introduced into the German Army in 1939, replacing previous types of antigas capes. It consists of a rectangular sheet of rubberized fabric, approximately 6½ feet by 4 feet, treated with *Oppanol*, which is folded and carried in a canvas pouch. It weighs about 2 pounds.

(3) *Antigas paper.*—An aid in crossing contaminated ground is a roll of impregnated paper (*Gasläufer*), 55 yards long by 48 inches wide. It is estimated that 1 to 200 men (in file) can cross it before it becomes unusable.

(4) *Mobile laundries.*—Mobile decontamination plants for the decontamination of clothing and equipment may take the form of motor trucks mounting a water-tube boiler for the rapid generation of steam, as well as a steam chamber and a drying chamber.

(5) *Decontaminating material.*—Bleaching powder is the usual substance for ordinary decontamination work. Troops are issued a pocket flask of decontaminating agent (*Waffenentgiftungsmittel*) for small arms and other equipment. In addition, a decontaminating set, which is packed in a cylindrical container with lid, is issued for use on machine guns and larger weapons.

(6) *Decontamination vehicles.*—(a) *Light decontamination car* (*leichter Entgiftungskraftwagen*).—This is a 5-ton, open, half-track, cross-country vehicle having a three-man crew.

(b) *Medium decontamination car* (*mittlerer Entgiftungskraftwagen*).—This is a 7½-ton vehicle similar to the light model, operated by a three-man crew, and carrying about 1,700 pounds of decontaminating agents.

(c) *Car for decontamination of personnel* (*Mannschaftsentgiftungskraftwagen*).—This is a 10-ton, six-wheeled vehicle operated by a two-man crew. It can decontaminate 150 men per hour.

(d) *Car for decontamination of clothing* (*Bekleidungsentgiftungskraftwagen*).—This is a 10-ton, six-wheeled vehicle.

(7) *Gas protective ointment.*—Each German soldier is equipped with four small bakelite boxes containing tablets of *Losantin*, a high quality, stabilized bleaching powder, which is mixed with water or saliva and applied to the affected parts of the skin.

(8) *Protection of horses.*—The Germans have a horse gas mask of the damp type (model 41). Also, goggles are furnished to protect the eyes, as well as hoof covers, in three sizes, to protect the lower part of the legs. Mobile horse decontamination sections exist and are attached to each veterinary company and to each army horse hospital.

(9) *Gas detectors.*—Gas sentries (*Gasspürer*) are provided with a gas detector set and gas detection powders, consisting of a metal container with five pairs of indicator phials, or test tubes (each containing a different reagent), and a suction pump for drawing air through the tubes. The set weighs about 16 pounds.

(10) *Gas detection car (Gasspürkraftwagen).*—This vehicle is believed to be in use by the Germans. It has a crew of seven men, weighs about 5 tons, and is an open, half-track, cross-country vehicle, intended to carry one or two detection sections and equipment.

(11) *Collective protection.*—Gas protective curtains are probably available in the German Army, and the artillery makes a practice of gasproofing its gun positions. Gasproofing of tanks and armored vehicles has also been mentioned. Many of the fixed fortifications in Germany are reported to be equipped with filtered ventilation.

92. Offensive warfare.—*a. Agents.*—The gases which Germany might use offensively are listed in figure 146. Generally speaking, they have retained their World War I classification, though it is believed that "crosses" have been superseded by the terms "rings" or "bands" for purposes of nomenclature. The Germans favor the combination of gases. Thus a vesicant toxic smoke is a combination of blue-band and yellow-band gases, and

COMMON NAMES	GERMAN NAMES
Blister gases (vesicants)—"Yellow Cross"	
1. Mustard (H)	*Lost; Senf; Gelbkreuz*
2. Lewisite (L)	*Gelbkreuz II (?)*
3. Ethyldichlorarsine (ED)	*Dick; Gelbkreuz III*
4. Nitrogen mustard (HN)	*Stickstofflost*

(Mixtures of mustard gas and Lewisite may be used in cold weather to reduce the freezing point. A 50-percent mixture of mustard and Lewisite is called *Winterlost*. The mustard gas is likely to be an improvement over that of World War I; it is probably more persistent, and possibly more vesicant and more difficult to decontaminate.)

Choking gases (lung irritants)—"Green Cross"	
1. Phosgene (CG)	*D-Stoff; Grünkreuz*
2. Diphosgene (DP)	*K-Stoff; Perstoff; Grünkreuz I, II*
3. Chlorpicrin (PS)	*Klop*
4. Chlorine (Cl)	*Chlor*

(There have been frequent references to mixtures of these choking gases.)

Nose gases (sternutators)—"Blue Cross"	
1. Diphenylchlorarsine (DA)	*Clark I; Blaukreuz*
2. Diphenylcyanarsine (DC)	*Clark II; Cyan Clark*
3. Adamsite (DM)	*D.M. Adamsit.*

(Germany shows a preference for DA and DC. DM was not used during World War I.)

Tear gases (lacrimators)—"White Cross"	
1. Chloracetophenone (CN)	*T-Stoff*
2. Brombenzylcyanide (BBC)	*T-Stoff*

(Neither of these gases was used by the Germans in the last war. They relied upon a number of bromide compounds, which are less powerful than the two substances listed. It is thought that Germany attaches little importance to tear gases alone, but the possible use of other gases camouflaged by tear gases must not be overlooked.)

Figure 146.—List of German war gases.

the nature of the chemical filling would be indicated by two bands of the corresponding colors. Green and yellow bands would indicate a choking gas with vesicant properties. A double yellow band would indicate a vesicant gas of enhanced persistence.

b. Offensive weapons and equipment.—(1) *Aerial spray.*—Since the Germans regard low-altitude spraying (below 1,000 feet) as an effective weapon against personnel and for ground contamination, pure mustard would probably be used for such attacks. For higher altitudes, where temperatures are lower, Lewisite (with its lower freezing point) might be mixed with the mustard. The Germans have carried out considerable experimentation with aerial spray. Two types of gravity-operated spray apparatus (*Chema Fuma L. 9* and *L. 190*), suitable for either smoke or gas, were produced by a Czech firm and are now available to the Germans; their capacities are 23.8 and 50.2 gallons, respectively. There is an apparatus called the *Nebelgerät V. 200*, suitable for both smoke and gas, of 25 to 44 gallons capacity and weighing about 500 to 550 pounds. Still another apparatus, the *Nebelgerät S. 300*, designed primarily for producing smoke curtains, can also be used for cloud emission. A minimum altitude of 90 to 100 feet is necessary, and the length of the cloud wall is reported to be about 10 miles. When filled with its capacity of 60 gallons of liquid, this apparatus has a total weight estimated at 1,400 pounds.

(2) *Chemical aerial bombs.*—The following types of German chemical aerial bombs exist:

(*a*) 1-kg gas bomb with thin-walled container and small bursting charge, described as a break-up bomb.

(*b*) 10-kg fragmentation bomb with high-explosive and toxic smoke effect (blue cross and arsenical gas fillings).

(*c*) 50-kg mustard gas bomb with highly sensitive impact fuze; small burster for ground contamination or larger burster for antipersonnel effect.

(*d*) 250-kg mustard gas bomb with time fuze, to function at about 330 feet above the ground and contaminate an area of about 6,000 square yards.

(e) 500-kg rocket bomb, used mainly as HE for demolition effect on warships, fortifications, etc.; also convertible to gas fillings.

(3) *Projectors.*—(a) *General.*—Two new projectors have made their appearance since the beginning of World War I: the *Nebelwerfer* (smoke projector) and the *schweres Wurfgerät* (heavy throwing apparatus).

(b) *15-cm Nebelwerfer 41 (Werfer).*—Primarily a smoke weapon, this improved version of the *Nebelwerfer "d"* projector (which is also known as the *Do-Gerät*), consists of six barrels, each of 15-cm (5.9-inch) caliber, arranged in a manner similar to the chambers of a revolver (fig. 147). It is mounted on wheels and fitted with a split trail. The barrels are open at both ends, the projectiles being of the rocket type. Firing is electrical and from a distance; initial flame is considerable. Separate barrels fire at intervals of 1 second; including time to reload, a complete series of six rounds can be repeated every 90 seconds. So far, the *Nebelwerfer 41* has been used with HE and possibly irritant smoke, but there seems no doubt that it could be used equally well with gas, especially for heavy concentrations. A 21-cm (8.26-inch) *Nebelwerfer 42* (a larger version of the same weapon) and the 28/32-cm *Nebelwerfer 41* have also been identified.

(c) *Schweres Wurfgerät.*—This projector is known to exist in three types: *schweres Wurfgerät 40*, a static model consisting of a stout wooden frame, or stand, on which four projectors are mounted; *schweres Wurfgerät 41*, similar to the *40* except that the stand is of metal; and *schweres Wurfgerät 40* (mobile), in which six projectors are mounted on a medium half-track armored vehicle and pivoted so that they can be elevated from 5° to 42°.

(4) *Artillery gas shells.*—Although the Germans have always favored the use of HE for artillery shells, they have not overlooked the obvious necessity of being thoroughly prepared with gas and smoke-filled shells. Gas shells are available for German infantry

75-mm and 150-mm guns, for the light and heavy field howitzers of the artillery, and for the 81-mm and 105-mm mortars of chemical warfare troops.

(5) *Mortars.*—In addition to their 81-mm (3.16-inch) and 105-mm (4.14-inch) mortars for the dispersion of gas and smoke (fig.

Figure 117.—150-mm *Nebelwerfer 41* captured in North Africa.

148), the German chemical warfare troops also have a 120-mm (4.72-inch) mortar that is identical with the Finnish 120-mm mortar made by Tampella.

(6) *Gas grenades.*—The Germans have developed special gas grenades for use against tanks and armored vehicles. These com-

Figure 148.—Smoke unit learning to use 105-mm chemical mortars.

prise 2- and 4-inch glass globes filled with hydrogen cyanide, which may have an incendiary action as well as a gas effect.

(7) *Gas mines.*—The German Army has gas mines for defensive purposes, designed to harass landing parties on tidal beaches and to delay armored vehicles and troops. The mines can be laid at the sides of roads, under bridges, in woods, or in other favorable locations, and may be actuated by a time mechanism.

(8) *Bulk contamination.*—Tanks, armored cars, and trucks are generally equipped with apparatus for spraying gas and smoke, and chemical trucks are included in the equipment for the special gas companies. As has already been pointed out, the primary function of the decontamination battalion is to clear passages through contaminated areas, for which purpose it is equipped with special spraying apparatus. But the same equipment is equally well adapted to produce contaminations, so that the so-called decontamination units may be readily used for offensive action (see par. 90 *b* (2) (b), p. 185).

(9) *Toxic generators.*—Generators made by a private firm in Germany containing DA, DC, and diphenylarsenic acid have been found to be very effective, though their storage properties are not good. The French had a large number of arsenical smoke generators which are now presumed to be in German hands. They are large in size, contain DM, and function for about 8 minutes. They are intended to be used in groups of four, arranged to function one after the other and to give a total period of emission of about 30 minutes.

(10) *Flame-throwers.*—(*a*) *General.*—Two types of portable flame-throwers (*Flammenwerfer*) are part of the equipment of the German Army. (See also par. 80*a*, p. 156.)

(*b*) *Light-weight Kleif.*—The lightweight portable type has been changed from the old type to give added advantages (figs. 149 and 150), as may be seen from the following table:

CHEMICAL WARFARE TROOPS

	Old type	New type
Range (maximum)	25 yards	25 yards.
Duration of continuous discharge.	10 to 12 seconds	7 to 8 seconds.
Over-all weight, charged	79.2 pounds	47 pounds.
Over-all weight, empty	57.6 pounds	32.2 pounds.
Weight of projector and hose.	12.6 pounds	12.6 pounds.
Weight of pack	45.2 pounds	19.6 pounds.
Fuel capacity	2.6 gallons	1.5 gallons.
Fuel pressure	370 pounds per square inch.	440 pounds per square inch.
Nitrogen capacity	0.18 cubic feet	0.08 cubic feet.
Hydrogen capacity	0.035 pound per inch	0.300 pound per square inch.
Hydrogen pressure	0.300 pound per inch	0.300 pound per square inch.

(c) *Medium-weight Grof.*—The medium flame-thrower comprises mobile light equipment for two operators, which is carried on a two-wheeled undercarriage with tow straps (fig. 151). Its fuel capacity is 7.8 gallons of oil in a 10½-gallon steel container, with a 2½-gallon charge of compressed gas (nitrogen) at a charging pressure of 440 pounds per square inch. It produces a jet of flames 25 to 30 yards in length, lasting for about 25 seconds. By interruption of the jet, 2 to 50 single blasts of flame can be produced of correspondingly shorter duration. The approximate weight of equipment is as follows:

	Pounds
Undercarriage	73
10½-gallon steel bottle (empty)	61
¼-gallon steel bottle	4
Rapid closing valve with rising pipe	6
Jet pipe with self-closing valve	6
Jet pipe with oxygen hose	6
	156
Oil fill	65
Total weight with oil	221

Figure 149.—Flame-thrower (old type).

(*d*) *Heavy flame-thrower.*—A heavy flame-thrower is used in the following manner:

    1. The flame-thrower unit is made up of a number of vehicles, similar to those used as tractors for 37-mm antitank guns, towing flame-throwers.

196

2. Flame-throwers, mounted on two independent caster-action wheels, weigh about 300 kg (650 lbs). The dimensions of one of these weapons is as follows: width, 3 to 4 feet; length, 6 to 7 feet. A small shield is fitted at the front and provided with two jets. A small, two-wheeled "mechanical horse" (800- to 900-cc engine) assists the crew of four men to handle the flame-thrower in or out of action.

3. A crew totals eight men; of these, four operate the flame-thrower and two are armed with a standard small portable flame-thrower. All eight men are carried on the vehicle or the flame-thrower chassis.

4. Three fuel reservoirs are located on the vehicle. These carry a reserve of about 66 gallons of fuel for the large flame-thrower. These fuel reservoirs are evidently connected by piping to the flame-thrower.

5. The claimed range, 100 yards, is probably exaggerated, but 60 to 80 yards should be obtained with a nozzle about 20-mm. As the system is pressure-operated, intermittent as well as continuous fire is possible.

(e) Flame-thrower tanks (*Flata*) have been mentioned as adapted to carry two short-barreled projectors, one mounted on each front track cover, and three fuel containers within the tank. The range is between 55 and 80 yards, which would require a rate of fuel consumption of from $2\frac{1}{2}$ to 6 or 7 gallons per second. To be effective, a burst of 3 to 5 seconds duration would be required for each target engaged. A Krupp-type *Pz.Kw. I* tank fitted with a flame-thrower was used in North Africa. The flame-thrower, apparently of the 36-kg type, was fitted in place of the left light machine gun. The projector barrel was not fixed in the machine-gun mount, but nearly fitted the hole in the mantlet, and normal traversing and elevating could be carried out.

(11) *Miscellaneous.*—The Germans have a whistling cartridge

(*Pfeifpatrone*) which is used as a gas alarm signal. It is efficient only under quiet conditions and might not be heard during battle.

(12) *Smoke.*—(*a*) *Smoke units and equipment.*—The chemical warfare troops use several types of hand-thrown smoke grenades,

Figure 150.—Small-size one-man flame-thrower.

with a burning time of 1 to 2 minutes; smoke candles, with a burning time up to 7 minutes; smoke projectors similar to the Livens type; and projectors suitable for installation on *Pz.Kw. II, III*, and *IV* tanks. Aircraft apparatus for producing smoke has been identified. The uses to which it may be put include blinding observation and machine-gun posts, obstructing cooperation between enemy infantry and artillery, covering withdrawals, and

Figure 151.—Medium flame-thrower.

screening ship movements as well as other targets from enemy reconnaissance. Aircraft flying below troop-carrying planes can emit a smoke cloud through which parachutists could descend.

There are also colored smokes, known as *Abwurfrauchzeichen*, for signaling from ground forces to friendly planes.

(*b*) *Rear area smoke screens.*—Smoke has also been employed extensively by the Germans outside the combat zone. There are several instances where it has been used to screen rear areas, important industrial cities, bridges, shipyards, and similar aerial targets.

(13) *Incendiaries.*—(*a*) *General.*—The Germans have developed and used incendiary bombs, utilizing magnesium for the lighter weight bombs and steel for the heavier ones.

(*b*) *1-kg explosive-nose bomb.*—This combination antipersonnel and incendiary bomb is based on the 1-kg (2.2-pound) incendiary bomb. The explosive charge has been removed from the tail and a steel extension, containing a much more powerful charge (at first thought to be TNT but later believed to be a picric acid derivative) and a fuze, has been added to the nose. This change was believed due to the perfection of measures for combatting the regular oil, thermite, or magnesium incendiaries.

(*c*) *50-kg high-explosive incendiary.*—Another type of bomb recently developed contains a canister of small incendiary units scattered by a large high-explosive charge. As the bomb bursts, it throws out about 60 metal containers with a thermite-type filling and six preignited firepots of the magnesium-electron type. Immediately thereafter the TNT detonates. The weight of this incendiary bomb (110 pounds) insures penetration, and the explosive charge (16 pounds of TNT) produces a definite demolition effect, wrecking such objects as partitions, doors, ceilings, and flooring.

(*d*) *50-kg phosphorus and oil bomb.*—This bomb, with a filling containing 10 percent rubber and 4 percent phosphorus in an oil base, has been used with questionable success as an incendiary agent, phosphorus burns occasionally being inflicted on personnel.

Section XIII

SUPPLY AND ADMINISTRATIVE SERVICES

	Paragraph
Supply	93
Administrative Service	94
Medical Service	95
Veterinary Service	96
Field Postal Service	97
Military Police	98

93. Supply.—*a. General.*—The highly organized supply services of the German Army have made a substantial contribution to the operations in which German arms have scored successes, not only in western Europe but also in the deserts of North Africa and the vast reaches of the Soviet Union. In the Russian theater, in particular, the efficiency of the rear services has been of tremendous importance in making possible sustained operations on a huge scale. Not only have the supply services successfully overcome great distances, lack of adequate communications, and rigorous climates, but also on many occasions they have continued to function despite harassing attacks by bands of organized Soviet partisans who make the areas behind the lines almost as dangerous as the actual combat zone.

b. Staff control.—In the zone of the interior all supply services are under the control of the commander of the zone of the interior (*Chef der Heeresrüstung und Befehlshaber des Ersatzheeres*), who organizes the procurement of all Army supplies and their storage in suitably placed depots. To each army in the field, he assigns the following: depots from which it can draw directly, a commissary supply section for its rations, and its base area. The commanders of the armies, corps, and divisions conduct supply within their commands in accordance with directives laid down by the Army High Command. For this purpose, they have special General Staff officers as well as officers of the various services at their disposal. The supply of GHQ units in the field is provided for by the commands to which they are attached, such as armies or army groups, or by the Army High Command, if they are retained in the GHQ pool. The staff officers concerned with supply in the Field Army and their duties are as follows:

(1) *At Field Army headquarters, the Generalquartiermeister.*—This officer is directly responsible to the Chief of Staff and is kept constantly informed of the supply situation of the various armies. He regulates passes and permits, the employment as well as the evacuation of prisoners, and the use of communications in the zone of operations. Large stocks of material, including captured material, are under his control.

(2) *At army group headquarters, the second General Staff officer (Ib).*—Army group headquarters, as an operational command, is not in the normal chain of supply, and the army *Ib* intervenes only when a critical situation requires action. Such intervention may be necessary in connection with large troop movements; the apportioning of ammunition, gas defense material, or gasoline and oil, before or during combat; and the relocation of army boundaries. Units attached to army group headquarters are supplied through the army headquarters in the area in which they are located.

(3) *At army headquarters, the Oberquartiermeister (Ib).*—This officer operates in accordance with directives issued by GHQ. He keeps the corresponding staff officers of the subordinate units informed as to the situation of the rear services within the army and advises the army commander on these matters. He deals directly with the *Generalquartiermeister* or the commander of the zone of the interior. He may hold the supplies of the army mobile on railroads, barges, and motor supply columns, or he may establish depots and parks for ammunition, rations, and other supplies. He makes arrangements for the collection and evacuation of weapons, ammunition, and other equipment left on the field of battle. He also reports to the *Generalquartiermeister* all equipment and

supply installations which are in excess of the immediate needs of the army. He advises the chief of the civil administration as to the military requirements to be considered in the administration and exploitation of the army area. He allots zones of communications to the corps and divisions, attaches to them the necessary rear services, and directs the construction and repair of roads, and controls the military police in the army area.

(4) *At corps headquarters, the Quartiermeister (Ib).*—Corps headquarters handles the supply of organic corps troops, but it is not normally a supply echelon for its divisions. The *Quartiermeister* keeps contact with both the army and the division staff supply officers. He makes requisitions on army headquarters, based on reports and requests received, and, if necessary, establishes priorities within the corps. He prescribes the supply roads for the divisions in case they are not laid down in detail by the army. Supply reserves and depots are assigned to the corps only under exceptional circumstances. The corps, however, can be assigned special supply missions: for example, exploitation of areas for commissary supplies.

(5) *At division headquarters, the second General Staff officer (Ib).*—This officer makes his requisitions to the corps supply officer (*Quartiermeister*) on the basis of requisitions and reports of supplies on hand from the troop units. He controls the divisional rear services of supply and provides a systematic supply of reserves of all kinds for the troops. These must be kept mobile on the division transportation.

c. Supply troop commanders.—Each higher echelon staff, from the headquarters of the division up to that of the Field Army, includes a supply officer who commands the organic or attached supply troops. He acts under the orders of the staff officers described above. These supply troop commanders are as follows:

(1) General of Supply Troops (*General der Nachschubtruppen*) on the Field Army staff.

(2) Senior Commander of Supply Troops (*Höherer Kommandeur der Nachschubtruppen*) for each army group.

(3) Commander of Army Supply Troops (*Kommandeur der Armee-Nachschubtruppen*) for each army.

(4) Commander of Corps Supply Troops (*Kommandeur der Korpsnachschubtruppen*) for each corps.

(5) Commander of Division Supply Troops (*Kommandeur der Divisionnachschubtruppen*) for each division.

d. Transportation officers.—(1) *General.*—The employment of railroads, canals, and automobile roads for supply is regulated by the chief of transportation through subordinate transportation officers attached to each army headquarters. These officers, who have full executive power to act in the name of the chief of transportation, control transport headquarters (*Transportkommandanturen*) and forwarding stations (*Weiterleitungsstellen*).

(2) *Duties.*—The transportation officer attached to each army headquarters is the adviser to the army commander on questions concerning the transportation service. He handles all questions concerning the military use of the railroads and waters for the army, and supervises their accomplishment by the transportation service, in accordance with the directive of the chief of transportation. He keeps the army *Oberquartiermeister* informed as to the probable time of arrival of supply trains or larger shipments at the army depots, or at army railheads or stations. If a "call system" (priority system) has been inaugurated, the army transportation officer orders the movement of supply trains from the zone of interior, or forwarding stations, on the basis of the priority list furnished by the *Oberquartiermeister*. He also orders the spotting of the necessary cars and trains for evacuation.

e. Supply service units.—(1) *General.*—The units of the services of supply (*Nachschubdienste*) belong to the rear services of the various higher echelons. They are responsible for the transport to the front of ammunition, weapons, rations, fuel, and combat supplies of all kinds; for the evacuation to the rear of empty cartridge and shell cases, captured weapons, and similar material that might impede the free action of troops; and for the repair of weapons and military supplies. Within a division, supply is normally conducted by the organic supply units of the division, which do not properly belong to the rear supply services.

(2) *Supply columns and their capacities.*—There are four types of supply columns in the German Army, as follows:

(a) *Motorized columns (Kraftwagenkolonnen).*—Motorized columns must, in general, be employed on good roads. They can cover up to 125 miles per day. They are organized into large and small motor transport columns with a capacity of 60 tons and 30 tons, respectively. Motor transport columns are designated in reference to their employment as GHQ, army, corps, or divison motor truck columns.

(b) *Animal-drawn columns (Fahrkolonnen).*—Animal-drawn columns have a capacity of 30 tons, and mountain animal-drawn columns 15 tons. In general, they are equipped with one-team wagons; however, in cavalry units two-team wagons are used. In an emergency, when horses are difficult to obtain, oxen may be used, but only for the movement of heavy loads. Ox-drawn transportation, because of its slower rate of movement, cannot march with horse-drawn trains. According to German training instructions, well-cared-for and trained animals can cover 12 to 15 miles per day, and under favorable conditions up to 20 miles, with a day of rest following.

(c) *Pack trains (Tragtierkolonnen).*—Pack trains, generally consisting of mules or horses, are usually employed in mountainous terrain. A pack train can carry up to 5 tons, but its capacity and speed are dependent on the trails and grades. It can also be employed in other terrain devoid of roads for the supply of combat troops. In level country, pack trains usually march more slowly than foot troops.

(d) *Mountain carrier units (Gebirgsträgereinheiten).*—Mountain carrier battalions and companies use manpower and are employed in terrain where not even pack animals can be used effectively.

(3) *Types of supply units and their duties.*—(a)—*General.*—The various types of units in the supply services may be classified according to their function as transport, labor, storage, and repair units.

(b) *Transport units.*

    1. *GHQ truck columns.*—GHQ truck columns (*Heeresnachschubkolonnen*) are large truck columns composing a GHQ transportation reserve for army supply. They are attached as needed to armies, corps, and divisions.

    2. *Army truck columns.*—Army truck columns (*Armeenachschubkolonnen*) are large truck columns which serve to maintain rolling reserves of ammunition, rations, etc., and assist in stocking parks and depots. They may also be employed in special situations to assist in the supply of corps and divisions.

    3. *Corps truck columns.*—Corps truck columns (*Korpsnachschubkolonnen*) are small truck columns employed to augment the truck columns of divisions assigned to the main effort; when necessary, they are used to supply the corps troops.

    4. *Division truck columns.*—Division truck columns (small), wagon columns, and pack trains (*Divisionsnachschubkolonnen*) carry a portion of the initial supply of ammunition for their division. They also haul supplies from the division railhead and the supply establishments of the army (depots, transloading points) to distributing points. When combat is imminent, two division truck columns loaded with artillery ammunition are assigned to the artillery commander as an artillery ammunition train (*Artillerie-*

Staffel). They haul ammunition to the division ammunition distributing point to be picked up by the battery combat trains, or they haul it directly to the battery positions. Cross-country vehicles are best for this purpose, and these two columns are equipped with such vehicles at the present time.

5. *Mountain carrying company.*—Mountain carrying companies (*Gebirgsträgerkompanien*) are employed to transport supplies in mountainous terrain where supply columns cannot be employed.

6. *Motor fuel columns.*—Motor fuel columns (*Kraftwagenkolonnen für Betriebstoff*) supply fuel and lubricants.

(*c*) *Labor units.*—Supply battalions, companies, and platoons (*Nachschubbataillone, -kompanien,* and *-züge*) furnish the labor in the parks and depots, at railheads, transloading points, distributing points, and equipment collecting points. Their personnel consists of laborers, mechanics, purchasing agents, etc. They may also be given special technical missions such as putting in operation gas, water, or electrical establishments pertinent to army supply. The necessary personnel for these duties is included in the technical platoon of every supply company. Combat troops are not required to furnish labor in rear establishments. Drivers and assistant drivers are not employed for loading and unloading trucks.

(*d*) *Storage units.*—Storage of equipment of all kinds within the Field Army is handled by so-called "parks," or depots. These are usually classified according to arm, as infantry, artillery, chemical warfare, engineer, and signal equipment parks. There is normally one of each type of park attached to an army. The army motor transport parks contain stocks of replacements and parts, tires, and complete vehicles, and can also carry out larger repairs. By utilizing local shops and assigning motor transport shop platoons to operate them, the repair facilities of the army can be greatly increased. Parks also possess the necessary personnel and equipment to tow or haul damaged vehicles. If the park cannot make the necessary repairs, the motor vehicles are sent to transport parks in the zone of the interior. Tires are received in the same way as equipment from the motor transport parks by the supply column and issued to the troops through division equipment collecting points (*Gerätsammelstellen*); or else they are sent forward by way of the gasoline and oil railheads or depots to the distributing points for gasoline and oil.

(*e*) *Repair units.*—These include workshop companies, field workshops, motor maintenance units, and tank maintenance units. They are either organic to divisions or are attached to armies from the GHQ pool. Every equipment park also includes a workshop for maintenance and repair. All parks and repair units having to do with motor vehicles are included in the motor vehicle equipment troops (*Kraftfahrparktruppen*), which is a separate arm. Motor transport workshop sections of the field workshop and tank workshop companies make repair work on all motor vehicles and equipment which cannot be made by the troops. They are usually established in the vicinity of the main supply roads.

f. Flow of general supplies.—Supplies are delivered by the manufacturer or producer to depots in the zone of the interior, where they are stored or prepared for immediate shipment when requisitioned by the forces in the field. From these depots in the zone of the interior they are transported by rail to army railheads, where they are picked up by army supply columns and transported to the depots of the various armies in the field (figs. 152 to 154). Shipments of less than a carload within a railroad division are sent to collecting stations (*Sammelbahnhöfe*) in the zone of the interior, combined into carloads and train shipments, and routed over the forwarding station to distributing stations. Loaded cars and trains for various commands are sent to the forwarding station; unit-loaded trains (such as ammunition or gas and oil trains) destined for one organization

SUPPLY AND ADMINISTRATIVE SERVICES 93

are shipped directly to their destinations without being handled by the forwarding station. The division supply columns receive supplies at the army depots and carry them to the division distribution point, where they are picked up by individual unit supply trains, such as the light infantry column, the light engineer column, etc., and carried forward to the combat units. While this is the usual flow of supply, it may vary widely in

Figure 152.—Railroad motor-truck used for transporting supplies to the front.

different situations, depending upon the type of communications available and the needs of the situation.

g. Ammunition supply.—(1) *Control and flow.*—The Commander of the Field Army (*Oberbefehlshaber des Heeres*) makes all decisions of broad policy concerning ammunition supply. The *Generalquartiermeister* advises the commander of the zone of the interior as to the quantities of ammunition that are to be held on call in depots or loaded as a rolling reserve for

209

Figure 153.—Combat train (horse-drawn).

the Field Army. With approval of the chief of transportation, he designates the area in which the rolling reserve is to be held. In addition, he determines, on a basis of requests, how much ammunition will be made available to the various armies and where it will be delivered. In general, the armies will be allotted only so much ammunition as it is estimated that they will re-

Figure 151.—Loading a transport plane with supplies for the front.

quire for a definite period of combat. Ammunition traveling by railroad is loaded and shipped as follows:

(a) Unit-loaded trains made up for a division.

(b) Ammunition trains made up with caliber units consisting of cars loaded with 15 tons of a single-caliber ammunition.

(c) Single-caliber units (trains loaded with one caliber only). The army *Oberquartiermeister* requisitions the *Generalquartiermeister* for ammunition in tons and types. He sets up his ammunition reserve in such a manner that a portion will be on trains in the army base, or on supply columns, and a portion in depots. Ammunition is issued from trains to trucks only when trains are unit-loaded. The Corps *Quartiermeister* requisitions the army *Oberquartiermeister* for ammunition in tons on the basis of reports of "ammunition on hand" from the divisions and attached units. The allotted ammunition is issued to the division truck columns in accordance with the corps directive. In exceptional cases ammunition can be received by unit trains. The division *Ib* replenishes the ammunition of the troops on the basis of reports indicating the number of rounds on hand. One or more well-camouflaged distributing points are established from the reserves carried on the division truck columns. Distributing points are located out of effective range of the mass of the hostile artillery and if possible on terrain protected from tank attack. Ammunition distributing points are established in accordance with the class (artillery ammunition and other ammunition (small arms)). Depots for the divisions and corps are not usually established. The troops draw ammunition from distributing points with their columns and single combat vehicles at the time ordered by the division. Artillery ammunition is drawn by the artillery from distributing points by columns 7 and 8 from the division trains that are always attached to the artillery regiment when combat is imminent. Ammunition not used, empty shell cases, packing cases, and faulty ammunition must be returned by the troops. The rapid return of this material to the ammunition depots and from there to the zone of communications is considered as important as ammunition supply. Ammunition depots and distributing points are established and administered by the ammunition administrative personnel on order of the various headquarters concerned. In the army, this personnel is on the staff of the supply battalions; in the division, it is on the staff of the division train commander, and consists of the necessary officers and ordnance personnel.

(2) *Ammunition on hand.*—(*a*) *General.*—Each unit has a pre-

scribed amount of ammunition (corresponding to the "day of fire" as used in the U. S. Army), which serves as the basis for computing the ammunition issue. This allowance is based on the number of weapons of each caliber called for in the table of organization of the unit. Each weapon, in turn, has a munitions quota which has nothing to do with the allowable consumption or possible replacement. Two ammunition quotas for all weapons of the division are carried within the division, while a third quota is held by the army on army supply columns or trains. Thus each army has three quotas, or "days of fire," for all weapons of the army.

(b) *Amounts.*—The most recent figures available for the quota for each weapon are as follows:

Rounds	Items
90	For each rifle and carbine of infantry, cavalry, machine-gun, and mortar units.
45	For each rifle of pioneers.
20	For each rifle and carbine of artillery, signal, motor transport, and transport units.
2,500	For each light machine gun of the infantry company, motorcycle company, squadron, armored car, and airplane.
1,000	For each light machine gun of artillery, pioneer, motor transport, and transport troops.
4,500	For each heavy machine gun of the infantry and the light tank battalion.
120	For each light mortar.
30	For each medium mortar.
180	For each field gun of the infantry battery.
200	For each light field howitzer.
300	For each antiaircraft gun (75- and 88-mm).
1,500	For each antiaircraft gun (37-mm).
125	For each heavy field howitzer.
125	For each 105-mm gun.
75	For each 150-mm gun.

(c) *Method of distribution in a division.*—The ammunition quotas within the division are carried as follows:

	Rounds
Infantry regiment (rifle ammunition):	
Carried on men and combat wagons	486,140
Carried on light infantry column (regimental)	81,133
Artillery regiment (rifle ammunition):	
Carried on men and combat wagons	55,500
Carried on light artillery columns (each battalion, 2,811 rounds)	8,433
Artillery regiment (105-mm field howitzer ammunition):	
Carried with guns and caissons within regiment	4,320
Carried on light artillery columns (each battalion, 1,386 rounds)	4,158

h. Ration supply system.—(1) *General.*—Normally, four echelons are concerned with the supply of rations in the German Field Army: zone of the interior, army, division, and troop units. Ration depots (*Ersatzverpflegungsmagazine*) are established in the zone of the interior and supplied from farms, packing houses, mills, dairies, commercial food farms, and slaughter farms. The army ration establishments (*Armeeverpflegungslager*) are located in the army rear areas. These usually consist of two different classes, the forward and the rear. The forward army ration establishments supply divisions at the front, while those in the rear supply reserve units and individual detachments not under divisions, and form a more permanent organization on which to base future military operations. Ration supply within the division is handled through a distributing point (*Verpflegungslagerausgabestelle*). Rations are received daily at this point, and distribution to the division units is similar to that at the U. S. Army division railheads.

SUPPLY AND ADMINISTRATIVE SERVICES 93

(2) *Rations on hand.*—Each man carries 1 day's rations, and 1 day's rations are carried in the unit field kitchen, 2 days' rations in the unit supply transport, and 1 day's rations in the divisional supply columns.

(3) *Amount of rations.*—The following table gives a day's rations for one soldier and for a division, as of June 1941.

(*a*) *Daily rations for one man.*

	Grams
Bread	750
Cold food for evening meal	120
Salt	15
Meat	200
Drink	25
Peas	180
Sugar	40
Cigars	2
Cigarettes	2

(*b*) *Total rations for division.*

	Tons
Bread	12
Meat	2.88
Peas	2.88
Wurst	1.92
Butter	0.80
Salt	0.24
Sugar	0.64
Coffee	0.24
Cigars and cigarettes	64,000

i. Supply of fuel and tires.—(1) *General.*—The commander of the zone of the interior accumulates the supply requirements of gasoline and oil and tires in accordance with the directive from the *Generalquartiermeister*, who determines, with approval of the chief of transportation, what amounts shall be set up as a rolling reserve for GHQ and what amounts shall be delivered to or placed at the disposal of the armies. He handles the requisitions from the armies for gasoline and oil, tires, tanks, and parts. He controls the entire motor transport supply for GHQ troops. He issues, when necessary, orders limiting the use of motor transport. The army, corps, and division *Ib's* handle the requisitions of all units under their control. Specialists from the transport service recommend the employment of establishments and services for motor transport supply as well as regulations covering the use of local (seized or requisitioned) motor equipment, gasoline and oil, tires, and suitable shops.

(2) *Supply of gasoline and oil.*—In reference to administration, GHQ gasoline and oil depots are under the control of the commander of the zone of the interior. The replenishing of their stocks is regulated by him in accordance with the instructions from the *Generalquartiermeister*. Gasoline and oil are delivered from the depots to the field forces in tank car trains. Gasoline and oil are delivered by rail (trains) in tank cars, barrels, or unit containers to the army base and placed at the disposal of the army *Oberquartiermeister*. On instruction from the army *Ib*, unit-loaded trains, consisting of tank cars and cars loaded with barrels, may be made up in order to establish one or more railway filling stations. Trains loaded with unit containers are sent to railheads and there unloaded. The unit containers are placed in gasoline and oil depots.

(3) *Gasoline and oil railheads.*—Gasoline and oil railheads (*Eisenbahntankstellen*) for the corps and divisions are located at railway stations near rail terminals, and, if possible, are separated from railroads. They are operated by personnel and equipment from the motor transport parks.

(4) *Gasoline and oil depots.*—Gasoline and oil depots are established by the motor transport parks, generally in advance of

the railway end points. Gasoline and oil depots and gasoline and oil railway filling stations (railheads) refill the gasoline and oil columns of the armies, corps, and divisions. In case of necessity, tires may also be issued through the motor transport parks.

(5) *Gasoline and oil columns.*—Gasoline and oil columns have a capacity of 50 cubic meters (large columns) or 25 cubic meters (small columns). They bridge the distance between gasoline and oil railheads, or gasoline and oil depots and the gasoline and oil distributing points, at which the gasoline and oil trucks of motorized units receive supplies. Single trucks from the gasoline and oil columns are located as filling stations for the motor vehicles.

(6) *Spare parts.*—Tanks and tank parts and tires are requested by the armies from the *Generalquartiermeister*, who in turn forwards the request to the commander of the zone of interior, while requisitions for all other motor vehicles and motor equipment of all kinds are sent direct to the commander of the zone of interior by the army *Oberquartiermeister*.

94. Administrative Service.—*a. General.*—The Administrative Service of the German Army (*Heeresverwaltungswesen*) controls finance, billeting, rations, clothing and individual equipment, office equipment, and similar supplies. It is supervised by the Army Administration Office (*Heeresverwaltungsamt*), which is one of the branches of the Army High Command. This office is headed by a general, but his assistants, as well as the staff officers for administration in the lower echelons, are civilian officials (*Beamten*).

b. Zone of interior.—In each German military district there is an *Intendant* in charge of the *Wehrkreis* administration who is responsible to the Commander-in-Chief of the Replacement Training Army. His duties include supervision of the administration of replacement and other units in the *Wehrkreis*, as well as control of the replacement installations of the various administrative services, such as buildings and training grounds, finance offices, ration and clothing depots, remount offices, forestry offices, and convalescent hospitals. Subordinate units of the Replacement Training Army have administrative officials similar to those described in *c*, below, for the Field Army.

c. Field Army.—All administrative matters for the armies in the field are controlled by the *Generalquartiermeister* at army headquarters. In lower echelons the staff officer for administration is known as the *IVa* and is actually a civilian official. The army group, corps, and regiments, however, do not normally figure in the chain of administration, so that the army, the division, and the battalion are the usual administrative echelons. The *IVa* section of each battalion or equivalent unit, known as the *Zahlmeisterei* (paymaster establishment), is responsible for administrative details pertaining to finance, ration, clothing, individual equipment, and billeting. The civilian official in charge of this section controls and supervises the administrative work of the following noncommissioned officers in each company: the first sergeant (*Hauptfeldwebel*), the accountant (*Rechnungsführer*), and the mess sergeant (*Verpflegungsunteroffizier*).

95. Medical Service.—*a. General.*—The Medical Service of the German Army (*Sanitätsdienst*) is under the direction of the Army Medical Inspector (*Heeres-Sanitätsinspekteur*), who has his headquarters at the Army High Command in Berlin, and who is a general officer (*Generaloberstabsarzt*). He is responsible for the training and employment of all medical officers, noncommissioned officers, and soldiers. He directs the operation of the medical service both in the field and in the zone of the interior. He has charge of the handling and distribution of wounded among the hospitals in the zone of the interior, as well as of all nursing personnel connected with these and other army medical centers.

b. Organization in Field Army.—The senior medical officers on the staffs of army groups, armies, corps, and divisions are special staff officers (*IVb*) and are in charge of the employment of the medical personnel attached to their various units. They are also responsible for health measures among the civil population and the prisoners of war in their theater of operations. Each division has a medical battalion (*Sanitätsabteilung*) consisting of one or two medical companies, a field hospital detachment, and two or three ambulance platoons. There are also various medical and hospital units, as well as medical equipment parks, attached to armies or under the control of GHQ.

c. Transportation of wounded.—From field assembly points in the combat area, wounded soldiers are taken to their battalion aid stations. Here medical personnel attend to them and provide for their further transport to the rear. The ambulances are kept as near as possible to the battalion aid station to facilitate rapid transport of the wounded. From the aid station the wounded are taken to the field hospital for further treatment, although these stations are equipped to perform all emergency operations. From the field hospital, men who were lightly wounded may return to their units. The more severely wounded are cared for in the field hospital or sent to rear-area hospitals. Hospital trains take those needing lengthy treatment to convalescent hospitals in the zone of the interior. In addition to hospital trains, the Germans have also made use of hospital ships and sometimes even large numbers of transport planes to bring wounded to the rear areas from Norway, North Africa, and parts of the eastern front.

96. Veterinary Service.—*a. General.*—Despite the tremendous strides which the German Army has made since World War I in the development of motor transport, and the vast numbers of motor trucks and vehicles which have been added, the number of horses in the German Army has not decreased since the period 1914–18. The great majority of German divisions still rely principally on horse-drawn transport; a normal infantry division, for example, has more than 4,000 horses. The German Army therefore needs an efficient and well-equipped Veterinary Service, which not only must care for the health of the horses but also must maintain a vast supply of horses for replacements.

b. Organization.—The Veterinary Service of the German Army

(*Veterinärdienst*) is headed by the Inspector of the Veterinary Service (*Veterinärinspekteur*) in the Army High Command, with the rank of general (*Generaloberstabsveterinär*). Army group, army, corps, and division veterinary officers (*IVc*) are in charge of the veterinary services in the commands to which they are assigned. In each division there is a veterinary company charged with caring for sick animals, as well as with performing blacksmith work. Attached to armies or under the control of GHQ are veterinary hospitals, horse parks, veterinary equipment parks, remount depots, and motorized columns for the transport of horses.

97. Field Postal Service.—*a. General.*—During the present war the German Field Postal Service has been very effective in delivering large amounts of mail to all battle fronts, from Norway to North Africa and from the Don steppes to the Pyrenees. The Service handles an average of 15,000,000 pieces of mail daily. Every unit, down to and including the regiment, and every separate unit and staff in the German Armed Forces in the field has a field post number which, for security reasons, is always used on mail instead of the unit or staff designation. For men in the replacement army (*Ersatzheer*), on the other hand, the full address, with unit designation and location, is used. Letters, post cards, and packages up to half a pound are delivered free from civilians to soldiers as well as from soldiers to civilians. Each army in the field has an army field post office (*Armeefeldpostamt*) and army postal stations (*Armeebriefstellen*) for the collection and delivery of mail from and to the units subordinate to it.

b. Mode of operation.—The following example illustrates the operation of the field postal service. When a letter is sent from Germany to the eastern front, it goes first to a field post assembly point near the place of mailing, and thence by train to a larger assembly point in eastern Germany. Here it is transloaded into a field post train which carries it to a rear area station for transfer to the appropriate army by a "front field post train." From the army transloading point it is sent to a railhead in the operations area and then by truck to the proper field postal station, where the mail is sorted out and divided by field post numbers. The transportation personnel of the various fighting units then picks it up and carried it forward for distribution among the troops. Early in 1942 the field post added plane service to the eastern front.

98. Military Police.—*a. General.*—The Military Police (*Feldgendarmerie*) in the zone of operations perform all police functions, such as direction of traffic, security service, and field discipline. In addition, the Military Police establish and guard prisoners of war at collecting points and camps in the zone of operations. The Military Police also check the passes of German soldiers and arrest those absent without leave.

b. Organization.—All higher headquarters, including administrative headquarters (*Feldkommandanturen*) in occupied countries, have Military Police detachments (*Feldgendarmerietruppen*) at their disposal. Each army headquarters is provided with police guard battalions (*Feldgendarmerieabteilungen*), and when necessary other police units can be attached to the various headquarters from the GHQ pool. In all their missions the regular Military Police work in close cooperation with the Field Security Police (*Geheime Feldpolizei*), which are under control of the *SS* (see sec. XIV).

Section XIV

SS, POLICE, AND OTHER MILITARIZED ORGANIZATIONS

	Paragraph
General	99
Elite Guard, or *SS*	100
Police	101
Militarized police	102
Organizations used as Army auxiliaries	103

99. General.—The German police force is a semimilitary organization, trained in the use of such light infantry weapons as carbines, machine pistols, machine guns, hand grenades, and, in some instances, armored cars. Unlike police organizations in the United States, the German police have always played an important part in the political life of the country because the party in power has used it to prevent meetings and demonstrations of opposition groups. During the troubled times following the German defeat in 1918, the German police were a stabilizing influence, preventing large-scale civil disorders and political violence. After Hitler came to power in 1933, the National Socialist Party (*Nationalsozialistische Deutsche Arbeiterpartei*) immediately began to coordinate all local police organizations into a highly centralized instrument to strengthen the hold of the party upon the nation and to prevent the rise of any opposition. Large numbers of trusted Party members were given key positions in the police force, and later Heinrich Himmler, Reich leader of the Elite Guard of the Party (*Schutzstaffeln*, or *SS*), assumed command of all German police forces in 1936, with the title "Chief of the German Police" (*Chef der Deutschen Polizei*).

To speed the process of coordination, Himmler replaced local police chiefs with trusted *SS* officials, or placed *SS* officials over the pre-Nazi police authorities. As a result, the German police lost their separate identity and became a part of the Nazi party machinery, while the *SS*, with its substantial and ever increasing independent military forces (*Waffen-SS*), became the most important organization for the maintenance of the Nazi party in power. The *SS* and regular police are estimated to have a total strength of almost 1,000,000, but with the addition of a number of other special organizations that have either police or semimilitary functions this figure is brought up to about 2,300,000.

100. Elite Guard, or SS.—*a. General organization.*—The headquarters of the *SS* is located in Berlin, where Himmler maintains what is tantamount to a complete ministry, with branches and departments comparable to the main branches of the three armed services for recruiting, training, equipment, and administration. The *SS* administration has divided Germany into 19 districts (*SS Oberabschnitte*) which correspond in most areas to the 17 geographical divisions (*Wehrkreise*) established by the Army for draft and organizational purposes (see par. 23c). Each district is commanded by a senior *SS* and police officer (*Höherer SS und Polizei Führer*). The *SS* also maintains similar headquarters in France, the Low Countries, Norway, Poland, and other occupied areas, with commanders bearing the same title. In all cases, these

Figure 155.—*SS* unit with 37-mm antitank gun.

regional *SS* officials act as Himmler's personal representatives at the headquarters of the corresponding military commanders.

b. *Types of units.*—(1) *General SS* (*Allgemeine SS*) (fig. 155).—The General *SS* is composed of *SS* members who continue their regular employment and serve as "volunteer political soldiers" in their spare time. Only the higher officers and their staffs in the General *SS* are full-time *SS* personnel.

(2) *Waffen-SS.*—The *Waffen-SS* was formed at the outbreak of war from *SS* service troops (*SS-Verfügungstruppen*), which are

under the direct command of Hitler. Also, *SS* Death's Head formations (*Totenkopfverbände*) were organized, primarily to guard concentration camps. The *Waffen-SS* is organized into *SS* divisions which serve in the field like any other combat division. Thus far, the following 14 *SS* divisions have been identified:

(*a*) Panzer divisions:
Leibstandarte "*Adolf Hitler.*"
Das Reich.
Totenkopf.
Wiking.
Hohenstaufen.
No. 10.
Nederland (being formed).

(*b*) Mountain divisions:
Prinz Eugen.
Nord.
Bosnien.

(*c*) Infantry divisions:
Polizei (composed of police regiments).
Lettland (being formed).
Galizien (being formed).

(*d*) Calvary:
Kavallerie (the only cavalry division in the German armed forces) (see par. 16).

These divisions have equipment corresponding to similar types of divisions in the Regular Army, and operate in the field under Army command, but are usually given more or less independent missions. Most of the *SS* divisions have been heavily engaged and have suffered considerable casualties. The growth of the *Waffen-SS* has been so great that it is sometimes regarded as a fourth arm of the services on an equal footing with the Army, the Navy, and the Air Force. Other *Waffen-SS* divisions are believed to be forming.

(3) *Special duty troops.*—In addition to the combat units of the

Leibstandarte "Adolf Hitler" and the *Totenkopf* troops at the front, there are other considerable units of both organizations stationed in Germany, performing the duties for which their units were originally intended.

(4) *SS Security Service (SS-Sicherheitsdienst.)*—The *SS* Security Service is a political intelligence organization, collaborating closely with the Security Police (*Sicherheitspolizei*) and the Secret State Police (*Geheime Staatspolizei*, or *Gestapo*) in combatting domestic and foreign enemies of the Nazi regime.

101. Police.—*a*. The police proper are divided into the following categories:

(1) Regular Police (*Ordnungspolizei*):
 (a) City Police (*Schutzpolizei*).
 (b) Rural Police (*Gendarmerie*).
(2) Security Police (*Sicherheitspolizei*):
 (a) State Police (*Staatspolizei*).
 (b) Criminal Investigation Police (*Kriminalpolizei*).
(3) Other regular police organizations such as the fire protection police, the river police, and the Technical Emergency Corps (see par. 103*d*, p. 226).

b. All police come under the control of Himmler in his capacity as chief of the German police.

102. Militarized police.—The militarized police are particularly important from a military point of view because they are a military force, living in barracks like regular troops and often employed in occupied territory, thereby freeing regular Army units from policing duties. The militarized police are formed into police battalions, either partially or fully motorized. These battalions each consist of about 550 men formed into a headquarters unit and four companies, equipped with rifles, machine guns, antitank guns, and armored cars.

103. Organizations used as Army auxiliaries.—*a. Todt Organization (Organization Todt).*—The Todt Organization formed by the late Dr. Todt in 1938 was first charged with building the German system of defenses in the west known as the West

Wall. Its work now consists in helping Army engineer units in road building, road repairs, bridge construction, and improvement of communications behind the lines of the Army. In addition, the organization is charged with building airfields, permanent fortifications, preparing defensive positions, clearing harbors of wreckage, and improving communications in rear areas. The Todt Organization is organized into battalions, which have a nucleus of German specialists and large numbers of foreign workers. The organization has been under the direction of Dr. Speer since the death of Dr. Todt in February 1942, and has absorbed the similar organization known as the *Baustab Speer*.

b. Reich Labor Service (Reichsarbeitsdienst).—Every German man who is physically fit must serve for a period of 6 months in the *RAD*, before beginning his military career. The labor service is organized in companies with a permanent cadre of commissioned and noncommissioned officers. Labor service units are made available to work on lines of communication and in occupied countries, and in many cases they work with either the Todt Organization or the Army engineers. The strength of the labor service is estimated at something less than 500,000.

c. National Socialist Motor Corps (Nationalsozialistisches Kraftfahrkorps, or NSKK).—Since the outbreak of war at least four motor transport brigades have been assigned to provide motor transport to supplement the transport services of the armed forces. These brigades also provide transport for the Todt Organization in addition to their function of assisting the police in traffic control duties on the line of communications. These brigades are known as *Heer*, *Luftwaffe*, *Speer*, and *Todt*. The *NSKK* maintains motor schools and training units to prepare men for service with the Army's motorized troops. The entire *NSKK* organization has an estimated strength of 250,000.

d. Technical Emergency Corps (Technische Nothilfe, or Teno).—This organization is used in occupied territory or in the actual combat zone for demolition work, removal of unexploded shells and mines, restoration of public utilities, and the reconstruction, maintenance, and guarding of installations of all kinds. Although it is listed as an auxiliary police force and its main work lies in combat areas, it also plays an important role in the German passive air defense within the borders of the Reich. It has an estimated strength of 150,000.

e. Storm Troops (Sturmabteilungen, or SA).—The Storm Troops are now used for many purposes on the home front, including the conduct of premilitary training. Although they are organized in a manner similar to the *SS*, the *SA* have not been called upon to send actual combat units into the field. Their ranks have been greatly depleted by individual enlistment in the Army.

f. National-Socialist Aviation Corps (Nationalsozialistisches Fliegerkorps).—The most important functions of the Aviation Corps in the war thus far have been to train personnel for the Air Force and to develop the use of gliders.

g. Hitler Youth (Hitlerjugend, or HJ).—The Hitler Youth comprises all German youth from the age of 14 to approximately 18. While they are members of the organization, the boys receive considerable premilitary training and indoctrination.

Section XV

GERMAN AIR FORCE

	Paragraph
General	104
Air Force High Command	105
Chain of command	106
Air Force arms and services	107
Army and Navy cooperation	108
Equipment	109
Training	110
Tactics	111

104. General.—The German Air Force (*Luftwaffe*) is one of the three branches of the German Armed Forces and is organized and administered independently of either the Army or the

Navy. Its three main branches are the flying troops, antiaircraft artillery, and air signal troops, and it also includes parachute and airborne troops, air engineers, air medical corps, and air police, and, more recently, a number of special divisions formed of Air Force personnel for service as regular fighting troops. It is organized on a territorial rather than a functional basis, with separate operational and administrative commands. This division of responsibilities has made for a high degree of mobility among the flying units and has thus been responsible for much of the success of the German Air Force.

105. Air Force High Command (see fig. 156).—*a. Commander-in-Chief.*—*Reichsmarschall* Göring serves in the dual capacity of Minister of Aviation (*Reichsminister der Luftfahrt*) and Commander-in-Chief of the Air Force (*Oberbefehlshaber der Luftwaffe*). As Commander-in-Chief he is charged with the administration and operations of the Air Force. As Minister of Aviation he is a member of the Cabinet and is responsible for the coordination and supervision of civil aviation. Since Göring has many other duties in the German government, however, the supreme command is usually exercised by the State Secretary in the Ministry of Aviation and Inspector General of the Air Force, *Generalfeldmarschall* Milch, as Deputy Commander-in-Chief.

b. Air Ministry (*Reichsluftfahrtministerium, or R. L. M.*).—At the Air Ministry—the highest administrative and operational authority of the Air Force—are found the departments which control all Air Force activity. These departments fall into two groups: those of the General Staff and those concerned with administration and supply.

c. General Staff.—The Air Force General Staff (*Generalstab der Luftwaffe*) is divided into six sections:

(1) Operational Staff (*Führungstab*), which is concerned with operational orders and plans, and includes navigation, technical, and meteorological sections. There is also an operational intelligence section.

(2) Organizational Staff (*Organisationsstab*), which is concerned with such matters as the formation of new units and territorial delimitations.

(3) Training Staff (*Ausbildungsstab*), which is concerned with training and the development of tactics.

(4) Supply and Administrative Section under the *Generalquartiermeister*, which is concerned with the supply and administration of operational Air Force units.

(5) Intelligence Section under the Chief of Intelligence (*Chef des Nachrichtenwesens*), which is concerned with nonoperational and long-range intelligence.

(6) Medical Section under the chief medical staff officer (*Chef des Sanitätswesens*).

d. Rear echelon.—The remaining departments of the Air Ministry and Air Force High Command are concerned with static or long-range administrative, supply, and replacement matters similar to those handled by the rear echelon of the Army High Command. These departments are centralized in Berlin under the control of *Generalfeldmarschall* Milch and have regional branches in the various *Luftgaue*. They are organized under five main divisions as follows:

(1) Administrative matters, under the *Chef der Luftwehr*, who controls the following three bureaus:

(*a*) General Air Office (*Allgemeines Luftamt*), for civil aviation, with sections for air traffic, air supervision, meteorological service, and flight security.

(*b*) Air Force Administration Office (*Luftwaffenverwaltungsamt*), with sections for finance, rations, clothing, and billeting.

(*c*) Air Force Personnel Office (*Luftwaffenpersonalamt*), with sections for officers, civilian officials, enlisted personnel, salaried employees, and wage earners.

(2) Supply and procurement matters, under the *Generalluftzeugmeister*, who is in charge of the following bureaus:

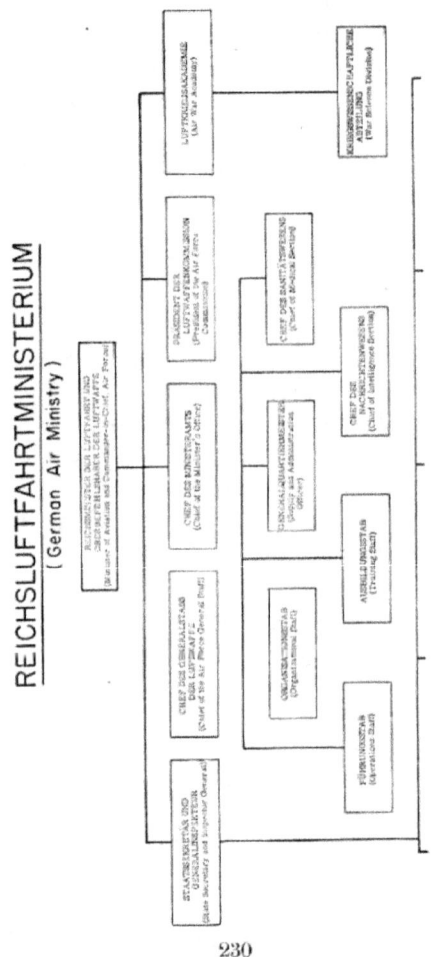

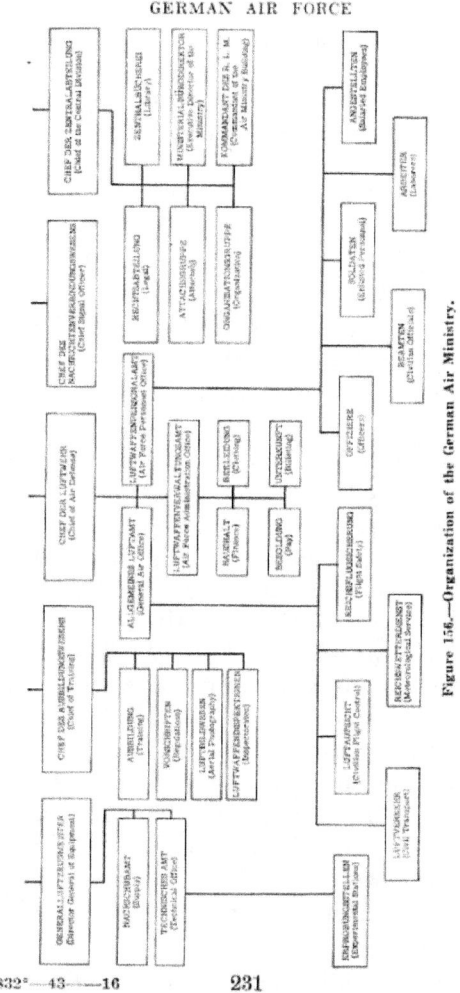

Figure 156.—Organization of the German Air Ministry.

(*a*) Technical Office (*Technischesamt*), with sections for research, procurement, and testing.

(*b*) Supply Office (*Nachschubamt*), with sections for aircraft and aircraft equipment, bombs and ammunition, and other Air Force material.

(3) Training and related matter, under the Chief of Training (*Chef des Ausbildungswesens*), who controls the following sections:

(*a*) Training Section (*Ausbildungs-Abteilung*), controlling all training except that of staff officers in the Air War Academy.

(*b*) Regulations Section (*Vorschriften-Abteilung*), for issuing and amending Air Force regulations.

(*c*) Aerial Photography (*Luftbildwesen*).

(*d*) The 16 Air Force Inspectorates (*Luftwaffeninspektionen*), for the specialized training and development of the various types of flying and ground personnel.

(4) Signal Communications Section, under the Chief Signal Officer (*Chef des Nachrichtenverbindungswesen*).

(5) Ministerial matters, under the Chief of the Central Division (*Chef der Zentral-Abteilung*), who controls the legal department, the air attaché unit, the Air Force library, and the sections for conducting the affairs of the Air Ministry itself.

106. Chain of command.—*a. General.*—The role of the Air Force in the conduct of the war, and to a certain extent in particular operations, is determined by the High Command of the Armed Forces (*Oberkommando der Wehrmacht*). The chain of command is from the Supreme Commander (Hitler), through the *OKW* to the Commander-in-Chief of the Air Force (Göring). The latter directs the actual employment of the Air Force through the Air Ministry and through his subordinate commanders of air combat units. However, when Air Force units are used in conjunction with Army or Navy units, all the forces involved come under a single operational control, in accordance with the German doctrine of unity of command. In such circumstances, a commanding officer is chosen from whichever of the three branches predominates in the operation, and he becomes directly responsible to the *OKW*.

 b. Luftflotte.—All Air Force units are organized into five tactical and territorial air commands known as *Luftflotten*. Each *Luftflotte* is assigned a particular command area, although this assignment is not necessarily permanent, for an entire *Luftflotte* may at any time be moved from one area to another at the direction of the Air Ministry. Within its area, however, each *Luftflotte* not only controls all operations of the flying units, but also supervises the activities of all ground service units. Thus, in addition to a large operations department, each *Luftflotte* has it own adjutant, legal, administration, signal, and supply departments. All commands and formations subordinate to the *Luftflotte* are either essentially operational (*Fliegerkorps, Geschwader, Gruppen,* and *Staffeln*) or administrative (*Luftgaue*). Thus the administrative and operational commands meet at the *Luftflotte* headquarters, where their respective activities are coordinated.

 c. Fliegerkorps.—Operational units within the *Luftflotte* command area are organized into subordinate operational commands known as *Fliegerkorps*. Through these *Fliegerkorps* the *Luftflotten* execute the operational directives received from the Air Ministry. Each *Fliegerkorps* is a composite, mobile command with its own geographical area of control and operations. A *Luftflotte* may command one to three *Fliegerkorps*, depending upon the size of the command area and the nature of operations. A *Fliegerkorps* may be detached at any time for operations in another *Luftflotte* area. The make-up of a *Fliegerkorps* is very elastic, both as to number and type of aircraft, but will normally consist of three to five bomber *Geschwader*, one to four fighter *Geschwader*, in addition to a varying number of short- and long-range reconnaissance *Gruppen*. The most important department of the *Fliegerkorps* command is that of operations. Although the

Fliegerkorps also has adjutant, legal, administration, signal, and supply departments, it depends almost entirely upon the *Luftgaue* for administrative and supply services. The *Fliegerkorps* are numbered nonconsecutively in Roman numerals.

d. *Fliegerdivision.*—All but two of the several *Fliegerdivisionen* which existed prior to the war have now been replaced by *Fliegerkorps*. The two *Divisionen* which continue to exist are the following:

(1) *Fliegerdivision VII.*—This division, a part of *Fliegerkorps XI*, is composed of Air Force parachute troops (see par. 107c, p. 253).

(2) *Lehrdivision.*—This division is unnumbered and is known simply as the *Lehrdivision*. Its primary function is to test the latest types of aircraft, antiaircraft defenses, and air signals equipment from a tactical and operational point of view. *Lehr* units are incorporated directly into the combat commands and function as a part of the command's operational strength. *Lehr* personnel are supposed to have had previous combat experience. This system, by giving the *Lehr* units an operational status, enables them to experiment in actual combat operations rather than under simulated conditions. The *Lehrdivision* is organized into a variety of formations and commands. There are two *Lehrgeschwader* composed of bomber, fighter, and reconnaissance *Lehrgruppen*. There are also two *Lehrregimenter*, one concerned with antiaircraft defenses and the other with signal developments. *Lehr* units are not to be confused with experimental units whose duties are of a technical nature, such as the testing of prototype aircraft.

e. *Geschwader.*—(1) *General.*—The *Geschwader* is the largest mobile, homogeneous formation in the Air Force, and is used for long-range bombers, dive bombers, ground attack units, and both single- and twin-engine fighters. It normally consists of about 100 aircraft organized into three *Gruppen*. Recently a fourth and, in a few instances, a fifth *Gruppe* have been added to several single-engine-fighter *Geschwader*.[1] Apparently the original intention was to have each *Geschwader* operate as a unit by stationing all three *Gruppen* at adjacent airdromes. This plan became impracticable, however, with the constant expansion of the front line; and although all *Gruppen* are now usually found on the same battle front, it is exceptional for all three of them to operate from neighboring fields. In fact, it is not uncommon at present for the Air Force to withdraw one or two *Gruppen* for rest or reequipment and subsequently return them to operations in another theater.

(2) *Command.*—A *Geschwader* is generally commanded by an *Oberst* or *Oberstleutnant* known as the *Geschwaderkommodore*. He has a small staff of officers for the adjutant, operations, organization, technical, signal, navigation, meteorological, and intelligence branches. Some staffs also have a photographic officer. The staff has its own headquarters flight (*Stabs-Schwarm*) of three to six aircraft of the same type as those which make up the *Geschwader*. This *Geschwader* staff is always maintained, even when the subordinate *Gruppen* are separated for operations on different fronts.

(3) *Types.*—There are several types of *Geschwader*, known according to aircraft complement as follows:

German title	Aircraft type	Abbreviation
Kampfgeschwader	Bomber	K. G.
Sturzkampfgeschwader	Dive bomber	St. K. G.
Schnellkampfgeschwader	Ground attack	S. K. G.
Schlachtgeschwader	and antitank	S. G.
Jagdgeschwader	Single-engine fighter	J. G.
Zerstörergeschwader	Twin-engine fighter	Z. G.
Nachtjagdgeschwader	Night fighter	N. J. G.
Lehrgeschwader	Tactical experimental	L. G.

Each *Geschwader* is designated by its abbreviation followed by an Arabic numeral: for example, *K. G. 77*, *N. J. G. 26*, *Z. G. 111*, etc. The numerals are not in consecutive order.

---

[1] These fourth and fifth *Gruppen* are not to be confused with the *Ergänzungsgruppen*, which are devoted to operational training as discussed in paragraph 110, p. 304.

(4) *Equipment.*—Although all *Gruppen* in a *Geschwader* specialize in similar air tactics and are equipped with the same type of plane, the make and model may differ among the *Gruppen*. This variation is most prevalent in fighter *Geschwader*, but also occurs in a few of the bomber *Geschwader*. Thus a *Kampfgeschwader* may have one *Gruppe* equipped with the *Do. 217* and the other two *Gruppen* with the *Heinkel 111, Junkers 88*, or the *Focke-Wulf 200*. Or the entire *Geschwader* may be equipped with the same make of plane, such as the *Messerschmitt 109*, but one *Gruppe* may have the newer model *Me. 109G* while the other *Gruppen* have the earlier *Me. 109F*.

f. Gruppe.—(1) *General.*—The *Gruppe* is the basic combat unit of the Air Force for both administrative and operational purposes. It is a mobile homogeneous unit which is largely self-contained and which may be detached from its parent *Geschwader* for operations in any command area. In fact, directives for the movement of flying units are almost always issued in terms of *Gruppen*. Usually the entire *Gruppe* is based at the same airdrome.

(2) *Command.*—The *Gruppe* is normally commanded by a *Major* or *Hauptmann* known as the *Gruppenkommandeur*. He has a small staff consisting of the adjutant, operations officer, technical officer, and medical officer. Apparently there is no special intelligence officer, since prisoners are sent direct to interrogation centers. Each *Gruppe* also has its own air signals platoon (*Luftnachrichtenzug*) known as a Technical Ground Station (see par. 107b) and a staff flight (*Stabs-Kette*) of three aircraft of the same type as make up the *Gruppe*.

(3) *Equipment.*—The *Gruppen* normally have 27 aircraft each, with another 9 to 10 in reserve for many *Gruppen*. These planes are organized into 3 *Staffeln*. *Gruppen* attached to a *Geschwader* are numbered in Roman numerals in consecutive order. Thus *I/K.G.77, II/K.G.77, and III/K.G.77* are the first, second, and third *Gruppen*, respectively, of long-range bomber *Geschwader 77*.

g. Staffel.—(1) *General.*—The *Staffel* is the smallest Air Force operational unit, and is generally commanded by a *Hauptmann* or *Leutnant* known as the *Staffelkapitän*. One officer serves as adjutant; the signal, technical, and navigation branches are supervised by the flying personnel in their spare time.

(2) *Equipment.*—A *Staffel* consists of nine aircraft. Three additional planes are usually held in immediate reserve. For tactical purposes it may be subdivided into *Schwärme* of five planes, into *Ketten* of three planes, or into *Rotten* of two planes. Each *Staffel* will usually have its own mobile repair shop to do minor repairs in the dispersal areas; other motor vehicles must be drawn from the organization of the parent *Gruppe*.

(3) *Numbering.*—All *Staffeln* in the *Geschwader* are numbered consecutively in Arabic numerals. Thus, in each *Geschwader*, the first, second, and third *Staffeln* constitute *Gruppe I*; the fourth, fifth, and sixth *Staffeln*, *Gruppe II*; and the seventh, eighth, and ninth *Staffeln*, *Gruppe III*. Where a fourth or fifth *Gruppe* exist, the *Staffeln* will be numbered 10, 11, and 12, or 13, 14, and 15, respectively. In unit designations the *Gruppe* numeral is omitted whenever the *Staffel* number is indicated. Thus the fourth *Staffel* of *K.G.77* is known as *4/K.G.77*, and no other reference to its position in *Gruppe II of K.G.77* is necessary.

h. Semiautonomous units.—(1) *General.*—Reconnaissance and Army cooperation aircraft operate and are organized as semiautonomous units, usually as *Staffeln*. Anywhere from two to nine of these *Staffeln* may be loosely organized into a *Gruppe* for administrative purposes, but there is no *Gruppe* headquarters or staff flight. These semiautonomous units fall into three general categories, all of which are numbered nonconsecutively in Arabic numerals of two or three digits.

(2) Long-range reconnaissance aircraft are organized into *Fernaufklärungsgruppen*, which are known as (*F*) units (see par. 108*b* (2), p. 267). Thus *3(F)123* is the third *Staffel* of *Fernaufklärungsgruppe 123*.

(3) Short-range reconnaissance and Army cooperation aircraft are organized into *Nahaufklärungsgruppen*, which are known as (*H*) units (formerly called *Heeresaufklärungsgruppen*) (see par. 108*b* (1), p. 266). The seventh *Staffel* of *Nahaufklärungsgruppe 11* is therefore 7(*H*)11.

(4) Coastal reconnaissance and naval cooperation aircraft are organized into *Küstenfliegergruppen*. These units are abbreviated *K.F. Gr.* Thus 2/*K.F. Gr. 906* is the second *Staffel* of *Küsten Fliegergruppe 906*.

i. Special commands.—(1) *Jagdführer.*—Separate fighter commands known as *Jagdführer*, or more commonly as *Jafü*, have been established in each *Luftflotte* since the outbreak of war. The *Jafü* is directly responsible to the *Luftflotte* commander and has an overriding authority over all fighter units in the *Luftflotte*, including the *Jäger-bomber* (fighter-bomber), or *Jabo*, units. At first *Jafü* was primarily concerned with matters of policy and controlled operations only on specific occasions. However, the two *Jafü* in command on the western front and the one recently in command in Tunisia directed all defensive fighter and *Jabo* operations in that area, and it is believed that the *Jafü* in other *Luftflotten* now exercise similar control over fighter units under their command.

(2) *Fliegerführer.*—(*a*) Highly specialized operations on certain fronts have been put under the control of special commanders known as *Fliegerführer*. These *Fliegerführer* control operations in a particular area only and are directly responsible to the *Luftflotte* commander in whose area they operate. The *Fliegerführer* commands discussed in (*b*), (*c*), and (*d*), below, illustrate the type of operations which a *Fliegerführer* is likely to control.

(*b*) The four *Fliegerführer* in *Luftflotte V*, although primarily concerned with antishipping activities and weather reconnaissance, controlled all types of combat aircraft in their area of operations for example, bombers, fighters, and reconnaissance units. They are known as *Fliegerführer Nord-Ost*, *Flieger-*

führer Nord-Norwegen, *Fliegerführer Lofoten*, and *Fliegerführer Nord-West*.

(*c*) The commander of *Luftflotte III* is known as the *Fliegerführer West* and controls all Air Force units in France and the Lowlands. Subordinated to him is the *Führer der Luft* and the *Fliegerführer Atlantik*, who control all long-range bombers and bomber reconnaissance units engaged in mine-laying, weather reporting, and armed shipping reconnaissance off the coast of France and the Lowlands.

(*d*) Air Force units in North Africa were under the command of a *Fliegerführer Afrika* and, after the opening of hostilities in Northwest Africa, a *Fliegerführer Tunisien* (also known as *Fliegerführer Afrika-West*). The latter was apparently appointed primarily to control torpedo operations against shipping. When forces under the *Fliegerführer Afrika* became available for operations in the Tunisian theater, it is believed that the two commands were combined.

j. Luftgau.—(1) *General.*—The *Luftgaue* are the actual administrative and supply organizations of the *Luftwaffe*. They are stationary or immobile commands whose authority is limited to certain well defined and permanently fixed geographical areas. A *Luftgau* commander is usually a *General der Flieger* or *General der Flakartillerie* and is theoretically responsible to the *Luftflotte* commander within whose command area the *Luftgau* lies. In actual practice, however, the *Luftgau* commanders received most of their instructions direct from the Air Ministry and the *Luftflottenchefs* interfere little with *Luftgau* administration.

(2) *Location.*—Of the 16 *Luftgaue* thus far identified, about one-third are located in occupied territory and function as offshoots of pre-war *Luftgaue* established in Germany proper. These "forward" *Luftgaue* still depend on their parent *Luftgaue* for certain services and are not believed to have undertaken training or recruiting. The *Luftgaue* permanently established in Germany are numbered nonconsecutively by Roman numerals;

those in occupied countries are generally designated by their location: for example, *Luftgau Norwegen*.

(3) *Functions.*—Each *Luftgau* is responsible for the following services within its command area:

(*a*) Administration, supply, and maintenance of all flying units.

(*b*) Active and passive defense against air attack.

(*c*) Operations of signals units.

(*d*) All training other than that of auxiliary units.

(*e*) Recruitment, mobilization, and training of reserve personnel.

(4) *Sections.*—Each *Luftgau* has its own operations, adjutant, legal, administration, signal, and supply sections. It also has a department for prohibited and restricted flying areas which has no known counterpart in the *Luftflotte* or *Fliegerkorps* headquarters. All training within the *Luftgau* area is directed by a Higher Commander of Training. This officer is usually a *Generalmajor* and is subordinate only to the *Luftgau* commander. All other *Luftgau* services are maintained through subordinate section commands which are designated by Arabic numerals preceding the *Luftgau* unit designation. Thus *4/VIII* is the fourth section command in *Luftgau VIII*.

(5) *Airdrome commands.*—The main channels through which the flying units draw on the services of the *Luftgaue* are the airdrome commands. Each *Luftgau* area is divided into about five airdrome regional commands (*Flughafenbereichkommandanturen*). The regional commands are in turn subdivided into five or more operational airdrome commands (*Einsatzhafenkommandanturen*). The regional command is essentially administrative and is not necessarily located at an airfield. The operational airdrome command, however, exists only to serve the flying units at their stations and is thus always found at an airdrome. The manner in which the *Luftgau* has decentralized its authority through these commands is as follows:

(a) The airdrome regional commands are charged with the *Luftgau's* responsibility for supply and maintenance of supplies and equipment within their respective areas; defense of aircraft, equipment, and motor transport against air attack; airdrome development; and air movements. These duties are discharged by specialized units which the *Luftgau* allots to the regional command and which the regional command then redistributes among the operational commands. For example, the Field Works Office (*Feldbauamt*) at the regional command handles airdrome maintenance through its subsidiary Works Superintendent's Offices which are stationed at the airdromes. Similarly, the air signals company at each regional command is divided into platoons which are stationed at the operational commands. A senior technical officer supervises aircraft maintenance in the region through his subordinate technical officers at the operational commands. The airdrome regional command is thus largely self-contained and calls on the *Luftgau* for assistance only when the units already assigned prove inadequate.

(b) The airdrome regional command also acts as the intermediary between the *Luftgau* headquarters and the operational airdrome command. All orders, requests, reports, etc., traveling between the two must pass through the regional command staff. This staff numbers from 50 to 150 officers and enlisted men and is headed by a commandant who usually holds the rank of *Generalmajor*.

(c) The airdrome regional command's primary practical task is that of transporting supplies and equipment from the depots to its subordinate operational commands. For this purpose it is generally assigned a supply company (*Nachschubkompanie*) composed of a supply column staff (*Nachschubkolonnenstab*), some four transport columns (*Transportkolonnen*), and two or three fuel columns (*Flugbetriebsstoffkolonnen*).

(d) The operational airdrome command is primarily concerned with supplying the physical needs of the flying units. Its administrative duties are limited to procuring supplies and equipment for the flying units from the *Luftgau*. The commander of the operational airdrome command normally holds the rank of *Hauptmann*, *Major*, or *Oberstleutnant*. His adjutant handles personnel matters. The personnel complement of an operational command numbers about 350 officers and enlisted men, and the motor transport allotment is between 50 and 100 vehicles.

(*e*) Airdrome maintenance at each operational command is handled by a Works Superintendent's Office (*Bauleitung*) which is subordinate to the Field Works Office at the regional command. The *Bauleitung* has charge of most of the construction done at the airdrome (buildings, dispersal areas, defense works, camouflage, etc.), as well as the laying of runways, extension of landing grounds, and installation of lighting systems. Reports on serviceability and bomb damage are radioed through the regional command to the *Luftgau* and thence to the Air Ministry for broadcast over the Air Force Safety Service network. The *Bauleitung* personnel is composed of civil servants and technical staffs. Any other specialized construction units which may be attached to the airdromes to repair bomb damage or enlarge facilities are also directed by the *Bauleitung*.

(*f*) The operational airdrome command is also responsible for defense against air attack, for which it has both heavy and light Flak units. These guns and other aerial defense units are commanded by the airdrome commander only when there is no flying unit stationed at the field. Otherwise, defense is controlled by the commander of that flying unit which is occupying the airdrome.

(*g*) The telephone, teleprinter, and radio at each operational airdrome command are operated by an air signals platoon (*Fliegerhorst-Luftnachrichtenzug*) (see par. 107*b*) and commanded by a signals officer who is subordinate to the senior signals officer at the airdrome regional command. The signal platoon also transmits the meteorological and airdrome serviceability reports and operates the Air Movements Control. This control directs only nonoperational flying. Signal communications with aircraft in operations are controlled by the tactical ground station attached to the flying unit.

(*h*) Aircraft maintenance at the operational airdrome command—except for servicing and minor repairs which are performed by the ground staff of the flying unit—is the responsibility of a technical officer. This officer not only handles overhauls and major repairs, but also is responsible for maintenance of motor vehicles; for bomb, fuel, and other supply stores; and for equipment stores and the armory. He is subordinate to the senior technical officer at the airdrome regional command.

(*i*) The requests by the operational airdrome command for equipment and spare parts reach the regional command through the technical officer. Requisitions for bombs, fuel, and ammunition are made by the supply section. The operational command also has an administrative section which handles clothing, food, pay, billeting, and other accommodations; a record office; a photographic section; a medical section; and a welfare section.

(5) *Luftgaustäbe z. b. V.*—During campaigns the *Luftgaue* provide the advancing air formations with supplies and services through a system of subordinate commands known as *Luftgaustäbe zur besonderer Verwendung* (*Luftgau* staffs for special duty.) or, simply, *Luftgaustäbe z. b. V.* units. These units may be designated by an Arabic numeral (*Luftgaustab z. b. V. 3*) or by their location (*Luftgaustab Kiev*). They are sent into the forward battle areas by their controlling *Luftgau* and are normally responsible for all services in an area occupied by a *Fliegerkorps*. After conditions have become relatively stabilized—for example, when operational airdrome commands have been established and supply stations and fuel and ammunition field depots have been set up—the *Luftgaustab z. b. V.* unit is withdrawn and the parent *Luftgau* assumes direct command.

107. Air Force arms and services.—*a. Antiaircraft de-*

fenses.—Active defense against air attack in Germany, occupied territory, and the various theaters of war, is the responsibility of the German Air Force. With few exceptions, all aerial defense services are manned by Air Force personnel.

(1) The aerial defense system is a threefold organization as follows:

(*a*) *Aerial defense with the armies.*—Units defending the armies in forward areas are known as mobile units. These units, which are assigned to and operate as a part of the Army and Air Force task forces, are charged with the protection of military establishments and of Army and Air Force units engaged in active operations. Mobile units which function with an army group are organized into a *Flakkorps* with several *Flakregimenter* and *Flakabteilungen* under its command. A *Flakabteilung* may also be allotted to an army or army corps. Flak units are usually controlled by an Air Force officer who is stationed at the army commander's headquarters. All Flak guns with the armies are dual-purpose, carry AP as well as HE ammunition, and provide direct support of the ground forces in antitank fire, assault of fortifications, counterbattery fire, as well as in purely antiaircraft defense.

(*b*) *Aerial defense of Germany and occupied territory.*—All units providing the general air defense of Germany and occupied countries are known as zone of interior units and are attached to the various *Luftgaue*. Each *Luftgau* controls the permanent antiaircraft artillery, balloon barrage units, searchlights, certain fighter units, the Observer Corps (*Flugmeldedienst*), and the Air Defense Service (*Luftschutzdienst*) within its own territory. Antiaircraft guns, balloons, and searchlights are organized into *Flakgruppen*, which are in turn divided into *Flakuntergruppen*. These *Flakgruppen* are controlled by a *Höhere Flakkommandeur* who is directly subordinate to the *Luftgau* commander. The Observer Corps and warning system are the responsobility of a *Luftgau* air signal officer. Fighter aircraft for air defense are lent to the *Luftgau* from the *Luftflotte* within whose command the *Luftgau* lies.

(c) *Aerial defense of vital areas.*—In certain areas of vital military or industrial importance there are special aerial defense commands known as *Luftverteidigungsgebiete.* Under this single command are concentrated all the aerial defense services in the area. Command areas of this type are known to exist for Berlin, Hannover, Hamburg, Saxony, and the Ruhr area (with headquarters at Düsseldorf).

(2) *Flak.*—Antiaircraft artillery, searchlights, and balloons are together known as Flak (*Fliegerabwehrkanonen*—flyer defense cannon). Except for some coastal guns manned by the Navy, and motorized Army antiaircraft artillery units known as *Fla*, all Flak units are manned by Air Force personnel. Flak organization is flexible, and the makeup of the various Flak units, especially the larger ones, is determined by the mission and by the number and importance of objectives to be defended. A Flak unit assigned to a Panzer army will thus be smaller, more flexible, and more mobile than the unit assigned to defend a rear objective such as the Ruhr area.

(a) The largest Flak unit is the *Korps* and usually consists of two or more *Flakbrigaden.* All *Flakkorps* are designated by Roman numerals.

(b) The *Flakbrigade,* or, as it is sometimes known, the *Flakdivision,* normally consists of two or more *Flakregimenter* plus air, signal, and supply units. The brigade is also designated by a Roman numeral.

(c) While the organization of Flak corps and brigades varies with circumstances, that of the *Flakregiment* is fairly standardized. It usually consists of a staff and four *Abteilungen* (battalions). The first two, *Abteilungen I* and *II*, are gun units; *Abteilung III* is a searchlight unit; and the fourth, or *Ersatzabteilung*, is a depot training unit which is usually static at its home station. The regiments are designated by Arabic numerals. The *Abteilung-*

245

en are designated both by their Roman numeral and by the number of the regiment to which they are subordinate: for example, *III/31* signifies the third, or searchlight, *Abteilung* of *Flakregiment 31*. However, the staffs of active *Flakregimenter* do not necessarily operate with their own numbered *Abteilungen;* and there are also several regimental staffs which have no similarly numbered subordinate *Abteilungen*, but which in operations may command three or more active or reserve *Abteilungen*.

(*d*) The *Flakabteilung* is the basic antiaircraft defense tactical unit. The active *Abteilungen I* and *II* and the *Erzsatzabteilung* each contain three heavy and two light *Flakbatterien* (batteries). *Abteilung III* has three searchlight *Batterien*. Both the active and the reserve light *Flakabteilungen* have three searchlight *Batterien*.

(*e*) *Flakbatterien* are numbered consecutively in Arabic numerals throughout the active *Abteilungen*. Thus *Batterien 1* to *5* belong to *Abteilung I*; *Batterien 6* to *10*, to *Abteilung II*; and *Batterein 11, 12*, and *13*, to *Abteilung III*. A heavy *Flakbatterie* usually consists of four heavy (88-mm) guns, with one predictor and two light (20-mm) guns (fig. 157). In the field, the two light guns are truck-mounted and act as antiaircraft defense for the heavy guns. Occasionally a heavy *Batterie* with six 88-mm guns is encountered. A light *Batterie* has either twelve 20 mm guns or nine 37-mm guns (fig. 158) and is also believed to have up to sixteen 60-cm searchlights. A searchlight *Batterie* consists of nine 150-cm lights plus an equal number of sound locators.

(*f*) The *Flakzug* (platoon) is the smallest operational Flak unit. It usually consists of two heavy or three light guns. All *Züge* are denoted by Roman numerals.

(3) *Observer Corps.*—The Observer Corps (or Air Raid Reporting Service) is known as the *Flugmeldedienst*. It is made up of air sentries known as *Flugwachen* who are posted at strategic points throughout Germany and occupied territory. The *Flugwachen* are grouped into air-observation centers, or *Flugwachkommandos*. These centers coordinate the various reports and pass

them on to the *Flugmeldekommandos* (observation commands). The commands then decide which defense authorities shall be warned of the impending attack.

(4) *Air raid warning.*—The air raid warning system is administered by the *Luftschutzwarndienst*, or Air Raid Warning Service. This service also regulates blackouts.

Figure 157.—20-mm AA/AT gun.

(5) *Air raid precautions.*—The air raid precautions services are controlled by a semimilitary organization known as the *Luftschutzdienst*, or Air Defense Service. This association is organized into national air raid defense districts known as *Luftschutzgebiete*. These districts are then subdivided into a series of regional, local, ward, and block groups which finally reach the individual buildings and factories. The association also maintains its own schools

Figure 158.—37-mm antiaircraft gun.

known as *Luftschutzschulen*. These schools are located throughout Germany and train all air raid precautions instructors and leaders.

b. Air Signal Service.—(1) *Function.*—The transmission of all orders and communications necessary for the functioning of the Air Force is the responsibility of its own air signal units. These units are also responsible for the establishment and supervision of navigational aids to aircraft, operation of the aircraft intercept system, manning of the Observer Corps and radio direction finders, and control of the air traffic and air safety services. It is thus difficult to conceive of any flying unit going into operations without the immediate support of air signal units. In fact, so vital is the role of signal units in Air Force operations that this service has had a greater proportionate wartime expansion than any other arm of the Air Force, and now has an estimated strength of some 200,000 officers and enlisted men.

(2) *Organization.*—(*a*) *Small units.*—The basic operational unit in the Air Force air signal organization is the *Truppe*, with a strength of 10 to 20 men. Each *Truppe* specializes in one particular signal activity: for example, telephone, teletype, cable laying, construction, etc. Anywhere from five to ten *Truppen* of the same type or function are organized into a *Zug*, or platoon. The *Züge* have a strength of 80 to 100 men each and are grouped into *Kompanien*, usually three to six *Züge* to each *Kompanie*. The *Kompanie* is generally commanded by a *Hauptmann* and has a strength of some 200 to 300 men. All *Züge* in a *Kompanie* specialize in the same particular branch of signal activity, with the result that each *Kompanies* is a self-contained specialist unit and may operate as an individual unit with the minor administrative or operational commands.

(*b*) *Abteilungen and Regimenter.*—The majority of the signal *Kompanien* are organized into the various signal *Abteilungen* and *Regimenter* which are attached to the major operational and administrative commands. Three to four *Kompanien* usually make up an *Abteilung*, although some *Abteilungen* have been identified with as many as 20 *Kompanien*. The *Abteilung* is commanded by a *Major* and has a staff of 40 to 50 officers and enlisted men; the strength, apart from the staff, depends upon the number and size of the subordinate companies. Of the three to five *Abteilungen* which normally form a *Regiment*, one is reserved for recruiting and training. The remaining *Abteilungen* may consist entirely of companies specializing in a particular signal function, or may include a variety of companies concerned with many signal activities. The composition of a *Regiment* is thus highly variable and is largely determined by the needs of the command to which it is attached. A *Regiment* is usually commanded by an *Oberstleutnant*, and may have a strength of anywhere from 1,500 to 9,000 officers and enlisted men.

(3) The air signal units are allotted to and function with the various operational and administrative commands as follows:

(*a*) The *Oberkommando der Luftwaffe* is allotted two or more signal regiments. The first, *Luftnachrichtenregiment 10*, whose main task is the organization of all Air Force communications, consists of a variety of specialist companies. The one or two additional *Ob. d. L.* regiments are smaller and specialize in telephone and telegraph line construction.

(*b*) Each *Luftflotte* is allotted three or more signal regiments known as *Luftnachrichtenregimenter* which are commanded by a chief signal officer known as the *Höhere Nachrichtenführer*, or *Höhere Nafü*. The primary concern of these regiments is the organization of all communications within the *Luftflotte* command area. They are also responsible, although to a lesser degree, for defense and movement of aircraft within the area.

1. The first signal regiment in each *Luftflotte* is divided into *Abteilungen* which are assigned to aircraft reporting, air safety service, and interception of enemy signals, plus one *Abteilung* devoted to training. Also attached to the regiment is a *Staffel* of signal aircraft. This regiment carries the same number as the *Luftflotte* with which it functions. Thus *L. N. Regt. 5* is the chief signal regiment for *Luftflotte V*.

2. The one or two smaller signal regiments in each *Luftflotte* are concerned only with construction of telephone and telegraph lines. They keep the same terminal number as the *Luftflotte*, but add 10 for the first additional regiment and 20 for the second. Thus *L. N. Regt. 15* and *L. N. Regt. 25* are the first and second additional regiments, respectively, in *Luftflotte V*.

(*c*) Each *Fliegerkorps* is allotted one signal regiment, also known as a *Luftnachrichtenregiment*. This regiment supervises signal activities within the *Fliegerkorps* area and is consequently somewhat smaller than the chief *Luftflotte* regiment. It is commanded by a senior signal officer known as the *Nafü*, who is subordinate to the *Höhere Nafü* at *Luftflotte* headquarters. The *Fliegerkorps* regiment consists of many different specialist companies concerned with telephone and telegraph construction, servicing, aircraft safety, aircraft reporting, and wireless telegraphy. It also has a liaison company which supplies the signal personnel for the *Flivos*.[1] The *Fliegerkorps* regiment also has its own *Staffel* of signal aircraft. The unit designation for a *Luftnachrichtenregiment* attached to a *Fliegerkorps* is achieved by adding 30 to the *Fliegerkorps* number. Thus *L. N. Regt. 34* belongs to *Fliegerkorps IV*, and *L. N. Regt. 42* to *Fliegerkorps XII*.

(*d*) Each *Geschwader* is allotted one signal company known as a *Luftnachrichtenkompanie*, which is responsible for maintaining all tactical communications with aircraft during operations. Each *Kampanie* is broken down into three platoons, or *Züge*, one *Zug* for each *Gruppe*. These *Züge* have some 80 men each and are known as tactical ground stations. They are an integral part of each *Gruppe* and must move with them from airdrome to airdrome. Consequently, most of these *Züge* are motorized to permit their rapid and easy transfer to forward areas and occupied territory. The *Geschwader Kompanie* is commanded by a *Nachrichten Offizier*, or *N. O.*, who is subordinate to the *Nafü* at *Fliegerkorps*

---

[1] *Flivos* are specialist Air Force liaison officers who act as the intermediary between the Army and Air Force for Army cooperation, close support, and tactical reconnaissance (see par. 108).

headquarters. The *Kompanie* takes the same name of the *Geschwader* to which it belongs: for example, *L. N. Kompanie St. K. G. 5.*

(e) Each *Luftgau* is allotted one signal regiment known as the *Luftgaunachrichtenregiment*. The *Abteilungen* which constitute this regiment, except for the one devoted to training, are made up of companies which specialize in aircraft reporting and whose personnel man the Observer Corps stations throughout Germany and occupied territory. *Luftgau* signal units are commanded by a *Nafü*, who is subordinate to the *Höhere Nafü* of the *Luftflotte* commanding the area within which the *Luftgau* lies. The *Luftgaunachrichtenregimenter* take the same number or name as the *Luftgau* with which they operate. Thus *L. G. N. Regt. 8* belongs to *Luftgau VIII*, and *L. G. N. Regt. Norwegen* to *Luftgau Norwegen*.

(f) Each airdrome regional command is allotted one signal company. This *Kompanie* is composed of several *Züge* which are distributed to the various operational airdrome commands within the region. Each airdrome thus has its own signal unit to man the airdrome signal station (*Luftnachrichtenstelle*). This station controls nonoperational flying only; the control of aircraft on combat operations is the responsibility of the tactical ground stations attached to the *Gruppen*. The airdrome regional command signal *Kompanie* has the same number or name as the command and is administered by a senior signal officer, or *Nafü*, who is subordinate to the *Höhere Nafü* at *Luftflotte* headquarters. The operational airdrome command platoons carry the same name as the operational commands to which they are attached. They are commanded by a *Nachrichten Offizier*, or *N. O.*, who is subordinate to the *Nafü* at the controlling regional command.

(g) Each *Flakkorps* or *Flakdivision* is allotted one *Luftnachrichtenabteilung* whose main concern is aircraft reporting and signal servicing. Each *Abteilung* is commanded by a *Nafü* who is subordinate to a *Höhere Nafü* at *Luftflotte* headquarters. *Ab-*

teilungen attached to the *Flakkorps* take the name of the *Korps* with the addition of 100. *Abteilungen* attached to the *Flakdivisionen* add 120 to the division number. Thus *L. N. Abt. 102* operates with *Flakkorps II*, and *L. N. Abt. 135* with *Flakdivision 15*.

(4) There is one experimental air signal regiment known as a *Lehrregiment* which is part of the *Lehrdivision*. This regiment is interested mainly in research into new types of signal equipment and their employment.

(5) Aircraft especially equipped for signal activities have been organized into signal *Staffeln* which are allotted to the various *Luftflotte* and *Fliegerkorps Luftnachrichtenregimenter*. The aircraft are usually *Ju. 52's* and can operate from ground to ground or ground to air. These *Staffeln* have proved particularly useful as advance flying or ground stations in forward areas where the signal platoons have not yet arrived or established themselves.

c. Airborne forces.—German airborne forces consist of parachute troops (fig. 159) and air-landing infantry. Parachute troops are all Air Force personnel and are organized into a command known as *Fliegerdivision VII*. They may be transported in gliders or dropped from transport planes. Air-landing infantry are regular infantry units drawn from the Army for particular operations only, usually for a large-scale operation such as the invasion of Crete. They are actually landed on the ground in transport planes, air transport being merely an alternative to other means of transport. Air-landing Army troops are not trained in parachute jumping. Special equipment has been designed for airborne forces (see fig. 160).

(1) *Fliegerkorps XI.*—For purposes of airborne operations, all parachute and air-landing troops are under the command of *Fliegerkorps XI* headed by *General der Flieger* Student. This command, which is quite unlike the other Air Force *Fliegerkorps*, directs all phases of airborne operations, including the organization of the necessary transport aircraft. It is also charged with the training and administration of parachute troops. Attached

to *Fliegerkorps XI* is an air signal *Abteilung* known as *Luftnachrichtenabteilung 41*. *Kompanie 7* of this *Abteilung* is permanently detached to *Fliegerdivision VII* and has been trained in parachute jumping to permit active cooperation with the parachute troops. The remaining *Kompanien* in *L. N. Abt. 41* con-

Figure 159.—Parachutists receiving last-minute details and orders.

struct and operate the signal network for the *Fliegerkorps in the* area of airborne operations. *Fliegerkorps XI* also has its own air reconnaissance *Staffel* to cover that territory in which airborne operations are to occur.

(2) *Fliegerdivision VII*.—This division comprises the majority of German parachute troops. At the time of the last large-scale airborne operation, the invasion of Crete, *Fliegerdivision VII*

consisted of three parachute rifle regiments. It is now believed to be composed of the following units:

(a) Six parachute rifle regiments known as *Fallschirmjägerregimenter 1 to 6*. Not all of these regiments are fully trained or up to full strength. The remnants of the former *Sturmregiment*

Figure 160.—75-mm recoilless gun *(L. G. 40)* adapted for airborne units.

have been incorporated into *F. J. R. 5*. One or two more rifle regiments are reportedly in the process of organization.

(b) One parachute artillery regiment.

(c) One parachute antitank battalion.

(d) One parachute engineer battalion known as the *Fallschirmpionierbataillon*. The unit is known to have at least four companies, all of which were sent into operations in Tunisia in November 1942. It is entirely possible that additional *Pionier-Kompanien* are undergoing training in Germany at the present time.

(e) A mixed parachute experimental battalion known as the *Lehrbataillon*. This unit is composed of eight companies, of which *Kompanien* 7 and 9 are assault troops known as *Sturmkompanien*.

(f) A parachute rifle depot regiment known as the *Fallschirmjägerergänzungsregiment*. From this regiment are drawn the recruits for the operational rifle regiments.

(g) Divisional supply and medical units.

Thus the number of parachute troops has almost doubled since the invasion of Crete. Despite this expansion, however, there has been no major airborne operation since May 1941. In fact, since the Cretan campaign the parachute troops have been extensively employed as infantry shock troops with Army units.

(3) *Sturmregiment.*—Also attached to *Fliegerkorps XI* during the Crete campaign was the glider-borne assault regiment known as the *Sturmregiment*. This regiment suffered high losses during the invasion of Crete and is no longer believed to exist as a separate organization, the assault units having since been incorporated directly into the parachute rifle regiments.

(4) *Air-landing infantry.*—A special Army division, the 22d Air-Landing Division, is believed to be earmarked for airborne operations. However, infantry units drawn from the Army for airborne operations have not been encountered in operations since the Cretan campaign. The air-landing division used at that time differed from a normal infantry division in the following respects:

(a) The strength was 40 to 60 percent of a normal infantry division.

(b) The percentage of supporting weapons was smaller.

(c) The heaviest artillery was a 75-mm mountain gun.

(d) The supply services were much reduced.

(e) There were no transport vehicles.

(f) The proportion of officers and noncommissioned officers was higher.

d. Air Force fighting units.—Since the outbreak of the war with the Soviet Union, the formation of Air Force fighting divisions (*Luftwaffe-Feld-Divisionen*) has been undertaken by the German Army, and a number of these divisions have already made their appearance on various fighting fronts from the Mediterranean to the Soviet Union. These divisions were at first small improvised units, apparently having only 3,000 to 5,000 men. More recently, however, a number of these units (an estimated 22) have been formed, with Air Force construction battalions, antiaircraft battalions, and similar nonflying units providing the bulk of their personnel. Some of the divisions may have as many as 12,000 men. Little is known of their organization, but it is believed to vary widely among individual divisions.

e. Air transport.—German transport aircraft and gliders are controlled by a General Staff department at the Air Ministry. This department, headed by a *Kommodor und Lufttransportführer*, allocates as well as administers all transport units in the Air Force. The majority of the transport planes consist of the *Ju. 52*. This type, though old, has proved so satisfactory that it has been retained and no newer type specifically designed for transport has been produced in large numbers. There is also evidence that the *He. 111*, which is now obsolescent as a combat type, is being adapted as a freight carrier. This adaption is consistent with the German policy of continuing to produce standard types with modifications rather than changing over to new models. The planes most frequently used for passenger-carrying and liaison work are the *Fieseler Storch* (*Fi. 156*), the *Me. 108*, and the *F. W. 158*. These transport and communications aircraft, which total well over 1,000 planes, are organized for the following services:

(1) *For operational units.*—The Air Force maintains several minor air transport units which are more or less permanently allocated to various commands. These units are not intended to perform any particularly heavy or large-scale transport work, such

as airborne operations or long-term supply. They are rather used for the numerous odd jobs of communications, liaison, and passenger-carrying within the *Luftflotte* area, or between the *Luftflotte* and Air Force headquarters in Germany. These units are distributed among the commands as follows:

(a) The staff of each *Luftflotte* and *Fliegerkorps* is allotted several *Ju. 52's* to be used for transport within Germany proper as well as in forward areas.

(b) Each *Fliegerkorps* is allotted a transport *Staffel* of 10 to 15 *Ju. 52's* in addition to a *Kurier-Staffel* (communications) of lighter planes. The *Fliegerkorps* may then temporarily reallot part or all of the *Ju. 52's* to the subordinate *Geschwader* and *Gruppen* whenever the transport of personnel, equipment, and/or supplies becomes particularly urgent.

(c) Each operational *Gruppe* is allotted several lighter types of communication aircraft. Formerly, each *Gruppe* had at least one *Ju. 52* for transport purposes. Now, however, it is believed that the *Gruppen* must rely on *Ju. 52's* temporarily lent to them by the *Fliegerkorps* headquarters.

(d) Each *Aufklärungsgruppe* (reconnaissance group) has a *Kurier-Staffel* within the *Fliegerkorps* organization which is primarily intended for liaison with army commanders. These aircraft are at the disposal of Army personnel as well as the Air Force reconnaissance officers.

(e) Allotted to each *Flivo* is a *Verbindungs-Staffel* (liaison) of communication aircraft which is used for contact work between Army headquarters and those Air Force units which are providing close or direct support for the Army (see par. 108).

(f) The main air signal regiments of each *Luftflotte* and *Fliegerkorps* have their own *Staffeln* of transport aircraft. Some of these planes are equipped as flying signal stations, but many are used simply for transporting equipment and personnel.

(g) The higher commands, including the *Oberkommando der Wehrmacht*, the *Oberkommando des Heeres*, the *Oberkommando der Marine,* and the *Oberkommando der Luftwaffe,* each have their own *Kurier-Staffel* to carry mail and personnel. These aircraft operate on a fixed schedule over all of Germany and occupied territory. Individual aircraft may also be detailed on special tasks.

(2) *For civil airlines.*—A small number of transports, primarily *Ju. 52's,* are still used on those civil air routes which the *Deutsche Lufthansa A. G.* operated before the war and continues to maintain under military supervision. These civil transports retain their pre-war *D–AGTF* markings. The *Ju. 90's* which were formerly used on these routes are now being used in operational areas.

(3) *For K. G. z. b. V. units.*—(*a*) *General.*—The *Kampfgeschwader zur besonderer Verwendung* (for special duty), known more simply as *K. G. z. b. V.* units, include over two-thirds of the German transport aircraft and are actually the mainstay of the Air Force transport organization. These aircraft are subordinate to and receive their directives from the *Luftflotten* and *Geschwader.* They may be allotted by the Air Ministry to the *Luftflotten* on a fairly permanent basis (for example, to a *Luftflotte* headquarters) or for a specific operation only (for example, an airborne operation). If only one or two units are allotted to a *Luftflotte,* the chief quartermaster department of the *Luftflotte* will handle administration, personnel, and aircraft serviceability. If several units are operating under the *Luftflotte,* however, the Air Ministry will usually detail an air transport officer to the *Luftflotte.* This officer, who normally holds the rank of *Oberst,* is generally assisted by a staff which may include a technical officer, a personnel officer or adjutant, and an operations officer, in addition to a transport officer who apportions the loads.

(*b*) The organization of the *K. G. z. b. V.* units is extremely fluid, and although the original intention apparently was to set up the units in *Geschwader,* the actual strength of most *z. b. V.* units rarely exceeds that of a *Gruppe.* These *Gruppen* normally number 53 aircraft organized into four *Staffeln* of 12 aircraft each plus a *Gruppenstab* of five planes.

(c) For purposes of transporting parachute troops and air-landing infantry in airborne operations, transport aircraft are organized into *z. b. V. Geschwader*. Each such *Geschwader* consists of about 200 aircraft organized into 4 *Gruppen* of 4 *Staffeln* each. Each *Staffel* has 12 aircraft organized into 4 *Ketten* of 3 aircraft each. The organization of the *Kampfgeschwader* thus closely parallels that of the parachute troops which they transport. A *Ju. 52* can carry 10 to 12 fully equipped parachutists. Thus one section of parachutists is carried by one aircraft; a platoon of 36 men is carried by a *z. b. V. Kette*; a company of 120 to 144 men is carried by a *z. b. V. Staffel*; and an entire parachute battalion is carried by a *z. b. V. Gruppe*. Whenever possible, the men are moved by units, that is, a *z. b. V. Kette* carrying a parachute platoon.

(4) *Luftlandegeschwader.*—When the glider-borne *Sturmregiment* was established, a new air transport unit of *Ju. 52's* known as the *Luftlandegeschwader* was organized. This *Geschwader* is organized on lines identical to the *z. b. V. Geschwader*, except that each *Ju. 52* tows one glider instead of transporting parachute troops. The average glider capacity in the Cretan campaign was 10 men, and an assault platoon was carried in 3 gliders towed by a *Luftlandekette* of 3 aircraft. An assault company of 120 men was transported in 12 gliders towed by a *Luftlandestaffel* of 12 aircraft. A *Sturmabteilung* of 480 men was towed in 48 gliders by a *Luftlandegruppe* of 48 aircraft. A *Luftlandegeschwader* of 192 aircraft was thus able to tow the entire *Sturmregiment*. Whether or not this *Luftlandegeschwader* has been dissolved along with the dissolution of the *Sturmregiment* has not been clearly determined.

(5) *Specially equipped transports.*—A number of *Ju. 52's* have been designed for highly specialized transport services. For example, many *Ju. 52's*, a number of which are attached to Air Force medical units, are fitted as ambulance planes with a capacity of 12 stretcher patients and 5 sitting patients. Meat and

other perishable rations can be transported to tropical areas in *Ju. 52's* fitted with refrigerators. Some *Ju. 52's* have been equipped with skis for transporting men and supplies into areas made inaccessible by snow.

(6) *Gliders.*—The Germans are also using towed gliders for air transport. Combining a high load capacity with comparatively small fuel consumption for the towing aircraft, or of the glider itself in the powered version, these gliders have proved increasingly useful as the deployment of the Air Force has spread to all fronts. Towed gliders were first used in the lowlands in 1940. The *D. F. S. 230* and the *Gotha 242* carried troops and supplies from Italy and Sicily to Africa from mid-1941 until the conclusion of the Tunisian campaign. In the fall of 1942, the *Me. 323* powered glider caused wide comment in its operations between Sicily and Tunisia. At the same time it was revealed that each dive-bomber *Staffel* operating from Tunisia had its own *D. F. S. 230* to carry supplies from Sicily to Africa. The *Go. 242* has also helped to relieve the critical supply situation on the Russian front. Thus both the powered and the unpowered gliders may be expected to assume an increasing importance in the German air transport services during the coming months.

f. Sea Rescue Service.—(1) The Air Force Sea Rescue Service (*Seenotdienst*) was first established to take care of airmen shot down over the North Sea area and the English Channel. Its services have now been extended to the Mediterranean, the Black Sea, and the Baltic. The rescue aircraft are seaplanes and were originally painted white with the red cross. Since late 1941, however, they have appeared in the usual German camouflage and are now believed to be used for reconnaisance convoy escort and transport, as well as rescue work. Rescues are normally performed by the service's own aircraft, but where the hazards of water landing are too great, the actual rescue is made by surface craft. These craft may be attached to the service or may be simply lent to it for a particular rescue.

(2) *Seenotdienst* units are organized into 3 sea rescue commands (*Seenotflugkommandos*), each of which is headed by a *Seenotdienstführer* with the rank of *Oberst*. The areas covered by the commands are the North (Norway and Baltic), the West (France, Belgium, and Holland), and the South (Mediterranean and Black Sea). Subordinate to these commands are some 10 regional commands, known as *Bereichkommandos*, which control the various *Staffeln* and detachments. There are now about 8 *Staffeln* organized into 3 *Gruppen*, plus a special *Staffel* for the Black Sea area. The strength of a *Staffel* varies from 5 to 14 aircraft. In addition, there are 20 detachments of 2 to 4 aircraft each for areas of limited need. Also, single rescue planes are often attached to combat units which are operating over water.

(3) All *Seenotdienst* units are operationally subordinate to the *Luftflotte* within whose area they serve. The administration of the service, however, is controlled at the Air Ministry by the Inspector of the *Seenotdienst*. This Inspectorate not only investigates the serviceability of the planes, but also allocates all equipment, appoints personnel, plans sites, and experiments with rescue methods. It also controls the air signal centers (*Seenotzentrale*) at the *Staffel* headquarters. These signal units watch for distress signals and maintain communications between local headquarters and the subsidiary wireless telegraph and sea rescue stations.

g. Meteorological services.—The Air Force Meteorological Service (*Flugwetterdienst*) is controlled by a Chief Meteorological Officer at the Air Ministry under the General Office for Air Communications (*Verwaltungsamt*). The chief responsibility of the *Flugwetterdienst* is to provide all flying units with dependable weather forecasts, since no Air Force aircraft may start on any flight, operational or nonoperational, without a written weather forecast. This office also reports all foreign weather broadcasts to each *Luftflotte*, and prepares all long-term forecasts for strategical planning. The Chief Meteorological Officer has charge of all administration, personnel, and installations of the service. He is further responsible for the scientific development of the service, including the establishment of new bases. Reports and forecasts of the *Flugwetterdienst* are also made available to the Army and Navy during wartime, when the latter are often deprived of their normal sources of information. The two main sources of Air Force meteorological information are weather stations and weather aircraft.

(1) *Weather stations.*—(a) At each airfield there is a relatively small *Wetterstelle* (weather station) which reports on conditions in its immediate vicinity. These reports are collected at regular intervals (usually hourly) by a *Wetterberatungszentral* (weather reporting center) which then coordinates the reports of all the *Wetterstellen* within its area and prepares maps for the flying units. A center usually serves an area covered by a *Fliegerkorps* and is frequently motorized. Some centers carry a *Luftgau* unit designation such as *W. Z. B./XIII*. The chain of command from the airfield to Air Ministry is completed through meteorological officers stationed at *Luftgau*, *Fliegerkorps*, and *Luftflotte* headquarters.

(b) In the forward areas where the standard Air Force services have not been set up, weather conditions are reported by motorized *Wetterstellen*. These stations are usually found at advance airdromes serving short-range flying units. There are also special meteorological stations attached to several *Geschwader*.

(2) *Weather aircraft.*—(a) Attached to each *Luftflotte* is a *Wetterkündigungstaffel* (weather reconnaissance squadron), commonly known as a *Westa* unit. These units normally have 9 to 12 aircraft equipped with automatic recording instruments. The crews include a meteorological officer and a specially trained wireless operator. In the early stages of the war the *Westa* units worked very closely with the *Luftflotte* with which they were identified. With the wide deployment of Air Force units, however, and the establishment of forward *Luftflotte* headquarters, the *Westa* units have become less closely associated with their *Luft*-

flotte headquarters. It is now common for a *Westa* to report directly to the Air Ministry, which then distributes the information to the *Luftflotten* concerned.

(*b*) Combat aircraft are often detailed to report on weather conditions encountered during their operations. The outstanding example of this type of reporting is that of the long-range bomber units operating from Bordeaux and Norway. Weather reconnaissance performed by these units has become almost as important as their antishipping reconnaissance.

108. Army and Navy cooperation.—*a. Army cooperation.*— Air Force cooperation with the Army is divided into two distinct types—direct or close support and indirect support. This division is so fundamental that it forms the basis for the organization and employment of all German Army cooperation units. Both types of support are provided by the ordinary bomber, fighter, and ground-attack units attached to the *Fliegerkorps*. These same units are used for strategic missions when not actively engaged in supporting the Army.

(1) *Close support.*—(*a*) Close support is usually confined to the actual battle front. It includes bombing and strafing enemy ground forces, tanks, artillery, antitank positions, forward dumps, batteries, antiaircraft defenses, and field defense works. It also attempts to prevent enemy aerial reconnaissance and army cooperation. Dive bombers, fighter-bombers, and ground-attack planes are used as highly mobile artillery in direct support of advancing ground forces. Fighters are used to escort bombers and to prevent enemy attacks on German ground forces. Long-range bombers are used for direct support when the situation requires that all offensive units of a *Fliegerkorps* be concentrated on the enemy's forward area.

(*b*) The manner in which the Air Force units directly support the Army is highly elastic and depends largely upon the nature of operations. However, the general relationship of units to the *Fliegerkorps*, and the liaison arrangements between the Army and

Air Forces, are fairly uniform. A *Fliegerkorps* is alloted a geographical area within which it supports the Army for a specific operation or operational period. The Army and *Fliegerkorps* commanders together draw up the general plans for close support, but the *Fliegerkorps* retains control over all flying units. All units required for close support are then grouped into a composite command known as a *Nahkampfgruppe* (close-support group). Each *Gruppe* is under the tactical control of an Air Force commander known as the *Nahkampfführer*. This officer is directly subordinate to the *Fliegerkorps* commander and is responsible for the execution of the general plans for close support. Tactical details are worked out with the Army commander and submitted to the *Fliegerkorps* commander for a daily check.

(c) The organization of the *Nahkampfgruppen* is extremely flexible. A close-support group may consist of anywhere from one to three dive-bomber *Gruppen*, one to four fighter *Gruppen*, and two to three *Staffeln* of heavily armored ground-attack planes. A short-range tactical reconnaissance *Staffel* is sometimes included to take care of vital reconnaissance. The *Gruppe* also has special air signal units for liaison between the Air Force and the Army and among the flying units themselves. On rare occasions a long-range bomber *Gruppe* or *Staffel* may be added, although the diversion of long-range units for direct support is generally brief.

(d) It must also be remembered that the *Nahkampfgruppen* are not permanent fixtures in the *Fliegerkorps* organization. They exist only where direct support of the Army is required of the *Fliegerkorps*, and an entire *Nahkampfgruppe* or part thereof may be moved from one *Fliegerkorps* to another. Normally, however, there is one *Nahkampfgruppe* in each *Fliegerkorps*, and a second has been allotted when the situation required it. Each *Gruppe* generally supports an army or a Panzer army, or both. *Gruppen* are frequently designated by the names of their commanders.

(2) *Indirect support.*—Air Force indirect support involves attacks on targets beyond the battle area such as rear maintenance

and supply depots; road, rail, and sea communications leading to the battle area; and enemy airfields. Indirect support missions are generally undertaken by long-range bombers. Sometimes units which are normally engaged in direct support are diverted to attack airfields and lines of communication, but such diversion is rarely protracted and is employed only to meet critical situations. Long-range bomber units are not believed to be specially reserved for indirect support in the manner in which certain short-range units are confined to direct support, and there is no known organization for indirect support within the *Fliegerkorps*, which is analagous to the *Nahkampfgruppen* organization for close support.

b. Tactical reconnaissance.—Both short- and long-range tactical reconnaissance and artillery spotting for the Army and Air Force are the responsibility of special Air Force *Aufklärungs* (reconnaissance) units. These units are within the normal *Luftflotte-Fliegerkorps* organization and are represented at the Air Ministry by a *General der Luftwaffe beim OKH und General der Aufklärungsflieger* (Air Force General at the High Command of the Army and General of Air Reconnaissance). The units themselves are organized into short- and long-range reconnaissance *Gruppen* as follows:

(1) *Short-range reconnaissance.*—(*a*) Short-range reconnaissance and artillery spotting units are organized into (*H*) *Staffeln* of 9 to 12 aircraft each. These *Staffeln* are then organized for operations into *Nahaufklärungsgruppen* (close-reconnaissance groups) under the command of an Air Force officer known as the *Gruppenführer der Flieger*, abbreviated *Grufl* (commander of reconnaissance units). Normally one *Nahaufklärungsgruppe* is attached to each *Fliegerkorps* and supports an army or Panzer army. An (*H*) *Staffel* is then allotted to each army corps or Panzer corps. Occasionally one *Nahaufklärungsgruppe* is allocated to two armies.

(*b*) An (*H*) *Staffel* is normally responsible for reconnoitering the area occupied by the army corps with which it is cooperating.

Reconnaissance by an (*H*) unit will include reporting on enemy troops, guns, tanks, field defenses, and motor transport. It also involves watching the activities of enemy air forces, as well as the position of its ground forces and its antiaircraft defenses. (*H*) units must also be on the lookout for any vulnerable point in the enemy's flank. If operations are near a coastal area, (*H*) *Staffeln* may even be sent out to reconnoiter shipping, both in ports and off the coast. Reconnaissance with tanks requires a special technique, and those (*H*) units which have been specially trained for Panzer operations are used almost exclusively for this purpose. Artillery spotting and reconnaissance over areas of limited activity is generally undertaken by the *Hs. 126*, the *B.V. 141*, and the *F.W. 189*. Well-defended and active areas are now reconnoitered by single- and twin-engine fighters, most of which are obsolescent as combat fighters and have been modified for reconnaissance.

(2) *Long-range reconnaissance.*—(*a*) Long-range tactical reconnaissance units are organized into (*F*) *Staffeln* of 9 to 12 aircraft each. Two or more (*F*) *Staffeln* are organized into a *Fernaufklärungsgruppe* (long-range reconnaissance group) under the command of a *Gruppenführer der Flieger*, or *Grufl*. (*F*) units are operationally subordinate to the *Luftflotte* instead of the *Fliegerkorps*, and the *Grufl* is directly under the *Luftflotte* commander. Usually one *Fernaufklärungsgruppe* is assigned to each *Luftflotte* and reconnoiters for that army group which the *Luftflotte* is supporting. The *Staffeln* cooperate with the various armies. This arrangement has probably been adopted because the *Luftflotten*, rather than the *Fliegerkorps*, have liaison with army groups to whom the results of long-range reconnaissance are most useful.

(*b*) An (*F*) *Staffeln* is usually responsible for an area 150 miles or more over the front line and up to 300 miles in breadth. Long-range tactical reconnaissance involves reporting on movements on railroads and roads; field defenses and battery positions; enemy airfield and general air activity; the conditions of bridges and roads; and weather conditions. When operations are near the sea coast, one or more *Staffeln* may be reserved for shipping reconnaissance. Types of airplanes used for long-range reconnaissance are the *He. 111*, the *Do. 17*, the *Ju. 88*, and the *Me. 110*.

(3) At the present time both (*H*) and (*F*) *Staffeln*, because of their equipment, are capable of reconnoitering much the same areas, and there are increasing instances of some (*F*) *Staffeln* being reclassified as short-range (*H*) units. This tendency was particularly evident in Africa, where both (*H*) and (*F*) *Staffeln* were organized into an *Aufklärungsgruppe Afrika* under the command of a *Führer der Aufklärer*. This assimilation has enabled bomber reconnaissance planes to collaborate with the tactical reconnaissance units, and permits a certain interchangeability of units to overcome shortages or to meet extended requirements.

c. Liaison.—(1) *Flivos.*—Liaison between the Army and Air Force for both Army cooperation (direct and indirect support) and short- and long-range tactical reconnaissance is provided by specially trained Air Force liaison officers known as *Flivos* (*Fliegerverbindungsoffiziere*). Although the primary task of the *Flivo* is to forward to Air Force headquarters the Army's requests for aerial support, he must also keep the Air Force informed of the front line of the army unit which is receiving air support, the safety bombing line, message dropping points, and the situation at army headquarters. He functions with the army units as follows:

(*a*) The *Luftflotte* appoints a *Flivo* to each army group and to each army or Panzer army. This *Flivo* transmits the army's requests for long-range reconnaissance and indirect support to the *Luftflotte* commander. Orders for long-range reconnaissance are then passed on to and executed by the *Fernaufklärungsgruppe*.

(*b*) Each *Fliegerkorps* also appoints a *Flivo* to each army corps and Panzer corps and, occasionally, to a division. This *Flivo* forwards the army's requests for close-support and short-range reconnaissance to the *Fliegerkorps* commander. The commander then orders the *Nahkampfgruppe* or the *Nahaufklärungsgruppe*, respectively, to provide the support or reconnaissance requested.

(2) *Communications and liaison aircraft.*—(*a*) Each *Fern-* and *Nahaufklärungsgruppe* has its own *Kurier-Staffel* (communications) of short-range aircraft to be used by Army and Air Force Staff officers and for delivering photographs, reports, etc. One aircraft of this *Staffel* is normally reserved for the special use of the army commander, both for traveling behind the lines and for any forward reconnaissance which he may make personally.

(*b*) Attached to the *Nahkampfgruppen* are *Verbindungs-Staffeln* (liaison) for the use of the *Flivo*, the *Nahkampfführer*, the flying units, and the army commands to which support is being given. One plane of the *Verbindungs-Staffel*, usually a *Fieseler Storch*, is reserved for the *Flivo*.

d. Navy cooperation.—The Air Force meets all naval and coastal air requirements, including all coastal and carrier-borne aircraft, through the *Luftflotte* operating in that area. Navy requirements are met in a manner similar to Army requests, that is, by alloting the required aircraft for general naval support and for particular naval operations from regular Air Force combat units.

109. Equipment.—*a. Aircraft.*—German aircraft (fig. 161) were apparently designed for a short war where the sheer weight of numbers would count. For this reason, the Air Force standardized the plane types to permit quantity production. As the war was prolonged, however, improvements became necessary. To prevent these changes from interfering seriously with production schedules, and particularly to avoid change-overs to entirely new types, almost all the improvements consisted of modernizations and adaptations of existing types rather than the creation of completely new models. The most favored improvement was the installation of more powerful engines. If this did achieve the desired end, the plane's structure was changed. One of the outstanding weaknesses of early German planes—their lack of defensive armament and protective armor—has received increased attention and in many cases has been adequately remedied. Nevertheless, after an aircraft has undergone a certain number of improvements, it must be entirely redesigned or else superseded by an altogether new type. Since the Air Force is still reluctant to introduce new types (only four new types have appeared since mid-1941), German aircraft in almost every theater of combat are now suffering from a qualitative inferiority which seems likely to increase rather than decrease.

(1) *Single-engine fighters.*—(a) *General.*—The German single-engine fighter force is made up of only two plane types—the *Messerschmitt 109* and the *Focke-Wulf 190*. Both types are produced in several versions and series, but the basic design of each has remained unchanged. Improvements have been achieved mainly by the installation of more highly powered engines. The principal developments in these fighters have been the introduction of special high-altitude versions and the conversion of both types into fighter-bombers. German fighters evidently will be even more definitely divided. Medium-altitude planes will probably tend toward high speeds and heavier armament, while the high-altitude machines will most likely have reduced armor and armament and be designed for maximum performance at about 30,000 feet and above. An all-around improvement in German single-engine fighters is to be expected, for this plane type has been the subject of an expanded research program and is at the top of the Air Force's future building list.

(b) *Messerschmitt 109.*—This plane has been the standard single-engine fighter since the beginning of the war. The older version, the *Me. 109E*, has been largely superseded as a first-line combat plane by the newer *F* (fig. 162) and *G* series. However, a certain proportion of the combat strength is still equipped with the *E*, mainly for advanced operational training and photographic reconnaissance. The *F* series is being used both as fighters and fighter-bombers, but in decreasing numbers. The newest series, the *Me. 109G*, now comprises the majority of German single-engine fighters. The *G*, which made its appearance in operations in 1942 in both the Russian and the African theaters, has a more powerful engine and slightly more armor than the *F*. Armament has also been improved since the model was introduced. However, several crashed *G's* have been found without self-sealing fuel tanks. A high-altitude series of the *G* with a sealed cockpit and full pressurizing equipment has been developed, as well as a tropical version

Figure 162.—*Messerschmitt 109F*, the standard German single-engine fighter. This type of plane is also used as a fighter-bomber. Note the rounded wing tips and the cantilever tail.)

with a special air cleaner. A still further improved *G* with a more powerful engine is reported to be undergoing development and may be introduced in 1943.

(*c*) *Focke-Wulf 190*.—The *F. W. 190* (fig. 163) did not appear in operations until 1942, but now forms about one-third of the German single-engine fighter force. It is the first single-engine fighter in the Air Force to use an air-cooled, radial engine. Of a

introduction for almost a year. Thus, except for a brief appearance on the Russian Front in the latter part of 1941, the *Me. 210* did not become operational until late 1942, and then only in small numbers. Meanwhile, the Air Force adapted two of its long-range bombers as twin-engine fighters, the *Ju. 88* and the *Do. 217*. The fighter version of the *Ju. 88*, the *C*, appeared in 1941, and this type has since been used in increasing numbers and now constitutes almost half of the German twin-engine fighter force. The *Do. 217* fighter is used primarily for night fighting, but has not achieved the success of the *Ju. 88*. All of these twin-engine fighters will continue to specialize as long-range and night fighters. Further developments may be an increased service ceiling for some types and the introduction of a special version with a sealed cabin for high-altitude intruder work.

(*b*) *Messerschmitt 110*.—The *Me. 110* (fig. 164), a small, fast, long-range fighter, carrying a crew of two, was designed primarily as a ground-controlled defensive night fighter and long-range day fighter. It can be easily converted for bombing and is consequently being used in increasing numbers as a light bomber and ground-attack plane. In this latter role it carries a crew of three and is capable of considerable overloads. It is highly maneuverable. Armor protection is provided for the crew only. The latest version, the *Me. 110F*, became operational in mid-1942.

(*c*) *Messerschmitt 210*.—The *Me. 210* (fig. 165) is an entirely new design and bears little resemblance to the *Me. 110*. Although designed as a long-range and night fighter, it has become better known as a speedy light bomber, dive bomber, and ground-attack plane. It is also used for reconnaissance. The armor, which protects both the crew of two and the liquid-cooled engines, is very extensive. Unlike most fighters, it is fitted with dive brakes. Its unique feature is the armament: on each side of the fuselage is a blister carrying two 13-mm rearward firing guns which are remotely controlled by the radio operator. Thus the *Me. 210* incorporates the first known attempt at power-controlled armament in a German fighter.

Figure 164.—*Messerschmitt 110* (twin-engine long-range fighter).

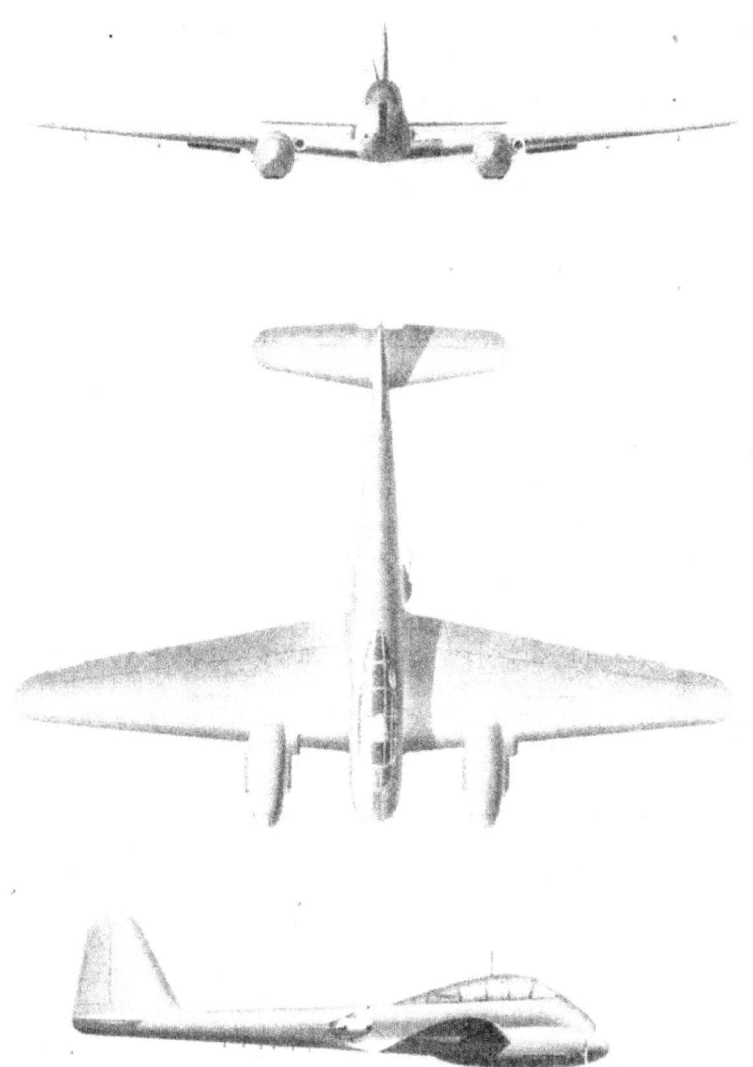

Figure 165.—*Messerschmitt 210* (twin-engine fighter, light bomber, and ground-attack plane).

(d) *Junkers 88C*.—The *Ju. 88C* (fig. 166) is encountered mostly as a night fighter and intruder. It is similar to the bomber version (see (6) (c), below) except for the transparent nose, the absence of dive brakes, and the modified armor and armament. Also, it carries a crew of three instead of four. Pending the introduction of a new version with more powerful engines and pending the wider use of the *Me. 210*, the *Ju. 88C* is expected to become increasingly prominent in night fighting.

(3) *Dive bombers*.—The *Junkers 87* (*Stuka*) dive bomber (fig. 167) became famous in the early days of the war and is still the standard Air Force dive bomber. Its active and close support of the Army has insured the success of many German ground operations. Except for a slight increase in armor and armament, minor modifications to the airframe, strengthening of the undercarriage for heavier bomb loads, installation of a new engine, and introduction of a tropical version, the *Ju. 87D* in current use is little different from the *B* and *R* series which appeared in 1939 and 1940. The angle of dive and the well-known *Stuka* "screaming" device which seemed so formidable in 1939 no longer compensate for the relative lack of speed, armor, and armament which today makes the *Ju. 87* a vulnerable aircraft. This drawback, plus the growing strength of the Allied fighter force, now makes it necessary that the *Ju. 87* be provided with a sizeable fighter protection to insure its success in large-scale operations. Considering the manifold demands made upon the German fighter force today, it is not hard to understand why the *Stuka* has become too costly and is being replaced by newer types (*Hs. 129*) or by twin-engine fighters and bombers modified for dive-bombing (*Me. 210* and *Ju. 88*).

(4) *Transport planes*.—Although a pre-war model, the Junkers *52* (fig. 168) is the standard freight- and troop-carrying transport of the Air Force. It is also used extensively for carrying and dropping parachute troops and has seen service as a glider tug. The *Ju. 52* is a three-engine, low-wing monoplane using the regular

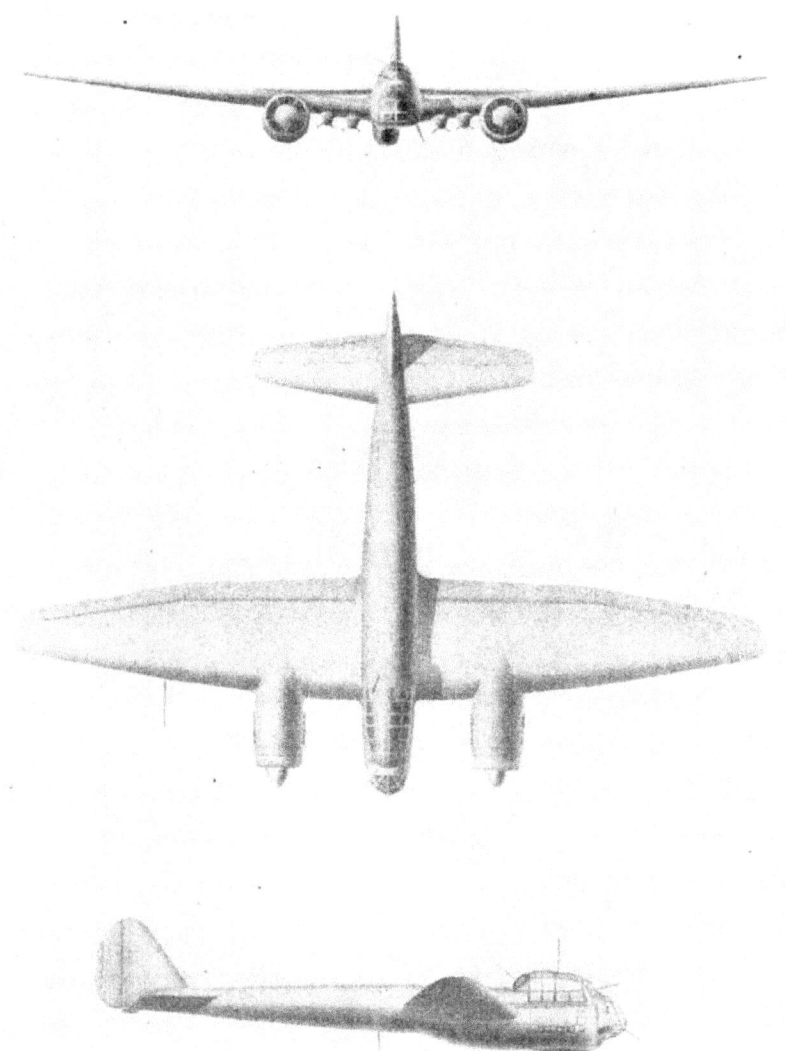

Figure 166.—*Junkers 88C* (twin-engine night fighter and bomber).

Figure 167.—*Junkers 87* (famous *Stuka* dive bomber).

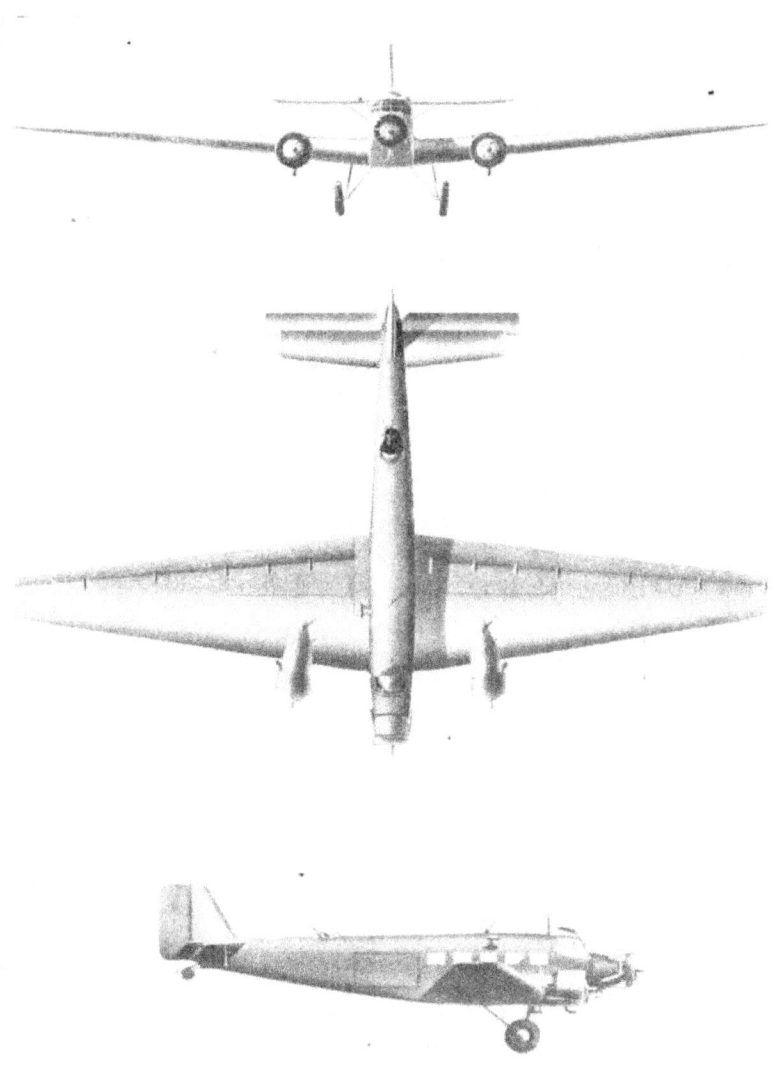

Figure 168.—*Junkers 52* (standard three-engine troop transport and cargo plane.) (This type of plane is also used as a glider.)

Junkers "double wing" wherein the inner portion varies the camber of the wing while the outer sections also "droop" but act differently as ailerons. The plane has a fixed landing gear and a single vertical fin and rudder. A notable feature of this airplane is the corrugated fuselage and wing covering.

(5) *Ground-attack planes.*—In 1941 the Air Force undertook the development of a specialized ground-attack type of plane which, because of heavier armor or greater speed and maneuverability, would require less fighter protection than the *Ju. 87*. These developments produced the *Henschel 129* (fig. 169) and the bomber version of the *Messerschmitt 210* (see (2) (c), above). The *Hs. 129* is a single-seater and was designed especially for close cooperation with the Army. It is primarily a ground-attack plane and only secondarily a dive bomber. It has a completely armored cabin, as well as armor protection for the oil coolers and the air-cooled radial engines. A 30-mm cannon may be installed under the fuselage for use against tanks and armored vehicles. With the cannon removed, about 550 pounds of bombs can be carried. The *Hs. 129* was produced in series during the latter part of 1941 and was first used in Russia. A tropical version appeared in Africa in 1942. However, the *Hs. 129* has not completely lived up to expectations, and has yet to prove itself to be a really successful specialized ground-attack plane. Consequently, it has become necessary to drawn on another arm of the Air Force— the single-engine fighters—in order to find the speed and maneuverability demanded by ground-attack operations. Thus some of Germany's most successful ground-attack planes today are simply the *Me. 109* and the *F.W. 190* carrying bombs and known as fighter-bombers.

(6) *Long-range bombers.*—(*a*) *General.*—German bombers in the early days of the war relied on their superior speed, maneuverability, and bomb capacity to compensate for their lack of armor and armament. Their primary defense was to be provided by accompanying fighters. This fighter protection, however, did not

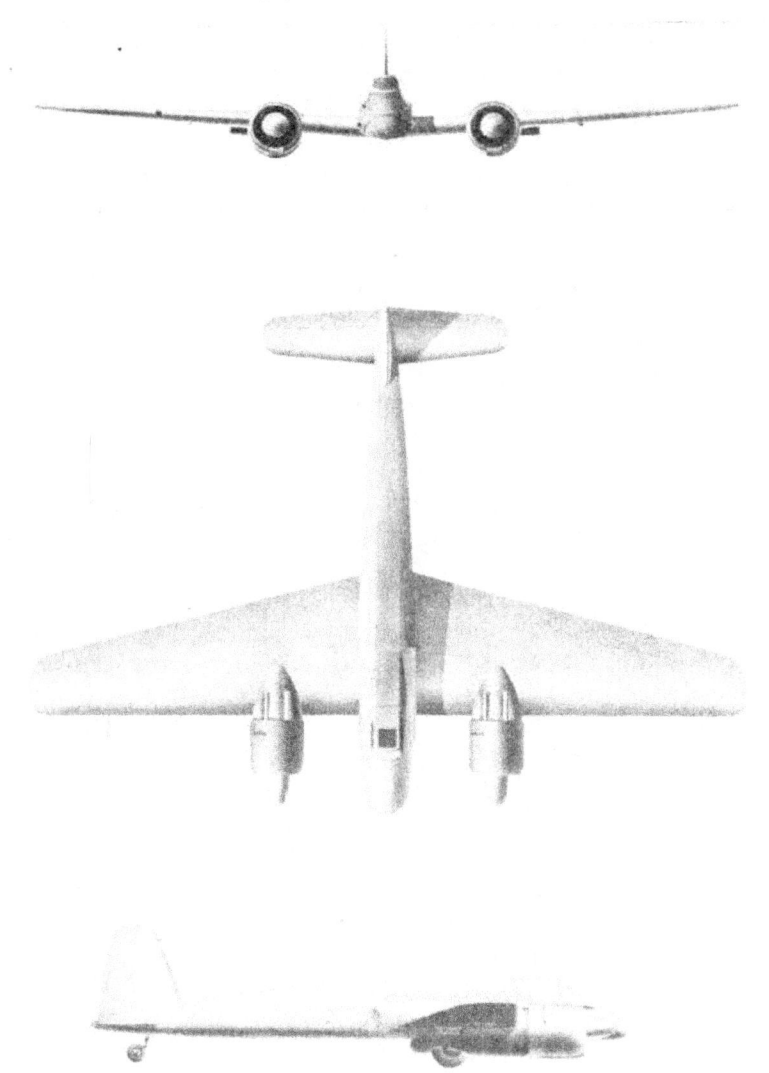

Figure 169.—*Henschel 129* (new ground-attack, low-level, and dive bomber, used primarily against tanks).

prove entirely adequate, and the Air Force soon found it necessary to increase the armor and armament of their bombers at the expense of load and speed. This increased protection is largely of the makeshift variety, and not until the *Do. 217* appeared in mid-1941 was there any power-operated armament on a German bomber. Meanwhile, the *He. 111* and the *Ju. 88* have suffered all the disadvantages of manually operated free guns. The present tendency in German bombers is toward greater loads, longer range, increased armor protection, limited adoption of powered armament, higher wing loadings, maximum speed at medium altitudes, and versatility. This last feature—versatility—has made German bombers readily adaptable for specialized duties such as dive-bombing, mine-laying, reconnaissance, ground attack, and even night fighting. Consequently, the German aircraft industry has been required to produce only three main bomber types—the *He. 111*, the *Ju. 88* (with which the Air Force started the war), and the *Do. 217* (designed to replace the *Do. 17Z*, which was operational in the early days of the war and is now obsolescent). Two other long-range bombers should be mentioned, both of which are four-engine types. One is the *F.W. 200K*, which forms only a small part of the German bomber strength. The other is the *He. 177*, which is just now coming into service after several years of experimentation.

(*b*) *Heinkel 111.*—The twin-engine *He. 111* (fig. 170) was one of the first modern long-range bombers in the Air Force. It normally operates with a crew of five, although it has been known to carry six. It has been continually modified since its introduction and was undergoing further developments as late as 1942. Most of the improvements have been in armor and armament, although high overloads have also been obtained and assisted take-off is used operationally. However, the *He. 111* is now considered to have reached its load limits, and further improvements or refitting with a new engine would involve so many structural modifications that they are not likely to occur. Until early 1942, the *He. 111* was used almost entirely as a night bomber. Since then it has been used

Figure 170.—*Heinkel 111* (twin-engine medium bomber).

for armed shipping reconnaissance, usually with an aerial torpedo under each wing, and mine-laying as well as bombing. It has also been used as a transport, both in the Russian and Mediterranean theaters, and as a tow plane for gliders. The *He. 111* is now practically obsolescent for first-line operations, and although it still constitutes a large part of the Air Force long-range bomber force, it is expected gradually to disappear from service as it is replaced by more modern types.

(*c*) *Junkers 88.*—The *Ju. 88* is probably the most versatile plane in the Air Force and is certainly the mainstay of the bomber force. Originally designed and introduced in 1939 as a level bomber, the *Ju. 88* has been successfully modified for all types of bombing, torpedo-carrying, reconnaissance, night fighting, assisted take-off, etc. The original *Ju. 88 A–1* was developed into the *A–5* level bomber which was used extensively from 1940 through 1941. This series was further developed into the *A–4* level and dive bomber which is today the principal German bomber. Other series of the *Ju. 88* are the *A–6* dive bomber; the *A–11* tropical version; the *A–13* ground-attack plane; the *A–14* torpedo bomber; the *D–1* reconnaissance bomber of which the *D–3* is the tropical version; and the *C–5* and *C–6* night fighters. The bomber version of the *Ju. 88* normally carries a crew of four. Armament was increased during 1942 and it is now reported that the *Ju. 88* is to be refitted with a more powerful radial engine. There is also the possibility that the *Ju. 88* may be superseded by a quite different and far more advanced model. Pending these developments, however, the *Ju. 88* will undoubtedly continue to be the most widely used bomber in the Air Force for many months to come.

(*d*) *Dornier 217.*—The *Do. 217* (fig. 171) is the most modern German bomber in current operations. Actually it is a scaled-up and improved version of the now obsolescent *Do. 17Z*. When the *Do. 217* was introduced in mid-1941, its speed and performance were both superior to that of the *He. 111* and *Ju. 88* and its bomb load was at least their equal; it was also the first German operational

Figure 171.—*Dornier 217* (twin-engine heavy bomber). (This was the first German operational bomber with a power-operated gun turret.)

bomber to incorporate a power-operated gun turret. It was therefore believed that the *Do. 217* would soon replace most of the other bombers in service. This expansion has not developed, however, and the *Do. 217* today forms only a very small part of the German bomber force. Nevertheless, the plane has undergone numerous improvements since its introduction. The unique type of umbrella dive brake in the tail with which the *Do. 217* was originally fitted did not prove satisfactory and has now been replaced by wing dive brakes. Auxiliary fuel tanks can be added for long-range general or anti-shipping reconnaissance. The *Do. 217* can also be used for mine-laying and torpedo-carrying. A night-fighter version with increased armament and a crew of three instead of the usual four has also been introduced. The *Do. 217* thus has a variety of uses besides the level bombing for which it was designed, and were it not for production difficulties, it might be used far more widely than it is today.

(*e*) *Focke-Wulf 200 Kurier*.—This plane (fig. 172) is the military version of the civil *F.W. 200 Condor* transport. The first planes of this type to be used operationally were converted commercial machines, slightly strengthened for mounting guns and stressed to withstand the concentrated weight of bombs. The newer *Kurier* is specifically constructed for military purposes. It has more powerful engines and several built-in modifications, such as bomb racks in the wings, manually operated gun turrets, and a gun tunnel beneath the fuselage. The overloading is still a problem, however, and the armor protection is particularly weak. The *Kurier* thus remains a vulnerable plane with a low safety factor, and although it can be used as a level or torpedo bomber, most of its operations now consist of reconnaissance against armed shipping and cooperation with U-boats.

(*f*) *Heinkel 177* (fig. 173).—This plane, which has been undergoing constant experimentation since its prototype appeared in 1940, has been encountered only rarely in operations, and although it is not believed to be quite ready for introduction into first-line

Figure 172.—*Focke-Wulf 200 Kurier* (four-engine heavy bomber, used for long-range bombing and attacks on Allied convoys).

Figure 173.—*Heinkel 177* (new twin-engine heavy bomber, used for long-range attacks).

service, the Air Force has been so persistent in its development that *He. 177* cannot be lightly dismissed. It was apparently designed for long-range antiblockade use, but may be used for medium-range bombing and dive bombing as well. A high-altitude version may also appear. The most interesting feature of the plane is the mounting in each wing of two engines geared to the same propellor shaft. This feature creates the appearance of a twin-engine plane, although the *He. 177* is actually classified as a four-engine bomber. Increased use of armor and armament are also evident, with indications that the guns are of a heavier caliber than heretofore encountered in German bombers. Despite the difficulties which have been connected with the *He. 177*, it is believed to have been in series production in 1942 and is expected to appear in service in the near future.

(7) *Army cooperation.*—(*a*) *General.*—The standard Army cooperation types of planes, of which the *Hs. 126* is the best example, are small, slow, and lightly armed planes which not only are vulnerable to antiaircraft artillery and small-arms ground fire, but are no match for the modern fighter. This vulnerability has imposed definite restrictions on their employment, particularly in any well defended area, and there is today little future for a plane such as the *Hs. 126* for short-range reconnaissance. It has thus been necessary for the Air Force to develop a fast, maneuverable, well-armed plane which can undertake short-range reconnaissance without fighter protection. But instead of developing an altogether new type of Army cooperation plane, the Germans have found it more expedient to convert their obsolescent fighters for this purpose. This conversion usually amounts to replacing some of the armament with cameras. The *Me. 109E*, the *Me. 109F*, the *Me. 110* and the *F.W. 190* have appeared in this role on all fronts and are now the standard equipment for many Army cooperation units. As a reconnaissance plane, the converted fighter is handicapped by its high landing speed. Also, the fact that many are single-seaters means that the pilot must also act as observer. However, their

higher speed, greater maneuverability, and heavier armament afford distinct advantages and more than compensate for the disruption which the German aircraft industry would have suffered had it been obliged to produce an entirely new model. The older Army cooperation types will still be useful, however, but mostly for delivering messages and urgent supplies over short distances behind the line.

(b) *Henschel 126*.—The *Hs. 126* (fig. 174), two-seater, has been the standard Air Force artillery spotting plane since the beginning of the war. It is a slow, lightly armed, parasol-wing monoplane. No further improvements are expected and the plane can now be considered as obsolescent. It will continue to be used in first-line Army cooperation units, however, but in decreasing numbers.

(c) *Focke-Wulf 189*.—The *F.W. 189* (fig. 175), which is also a specialized short-range reconnaissance type, was introduced in 1941 and now forms a substantial part of the Air Force Army cooperation units. It has twin tail booms between which is carried the cabin nacelle. This cabin is almost entirely glass-enclosed and affords excellent visibility, both because of its construction and because of its position. But like the other standard Army cooperation types, the *F.W. 189* is functionally vulnerable because of its low speed and light armament. Nevertheless, it has performed well in operations and is expected to remain in service for some time.

(d) *Fieseler Storch 156*.—This plane (fig. 176) has proved to be one of the most versatile short-range reconnaissance planes in the Air Force. The transparent cabin and roof provide excellent visibility for artillery spotting and observation. The plane is inherently stable with a low flying speed, and can consequently be flown by pilots of comparatively little training and experience. Also, it is able to operate from any small, open, and reasonably level area because of its low landing speed and short take-off run. It is thus an ideal plane for use in the forward zone of operations, particularly for liaison and courier service, command observation, and limited artillery spotting.

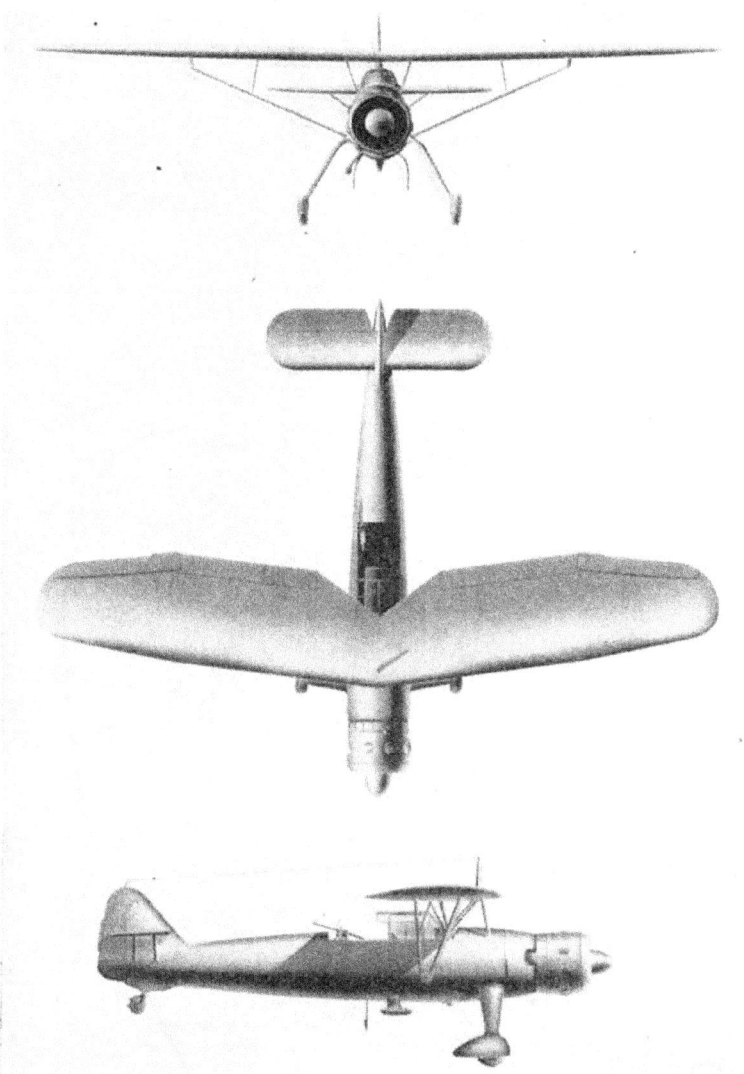

Figure 174.—*Henschel 126* (standard Army cooperation plane, used for tactical reconnaissance and artillery spotting).

Figure 175.—*Focke-Wulf 189* (twin-engine short-range reconnaissance plane for Army cooperation).

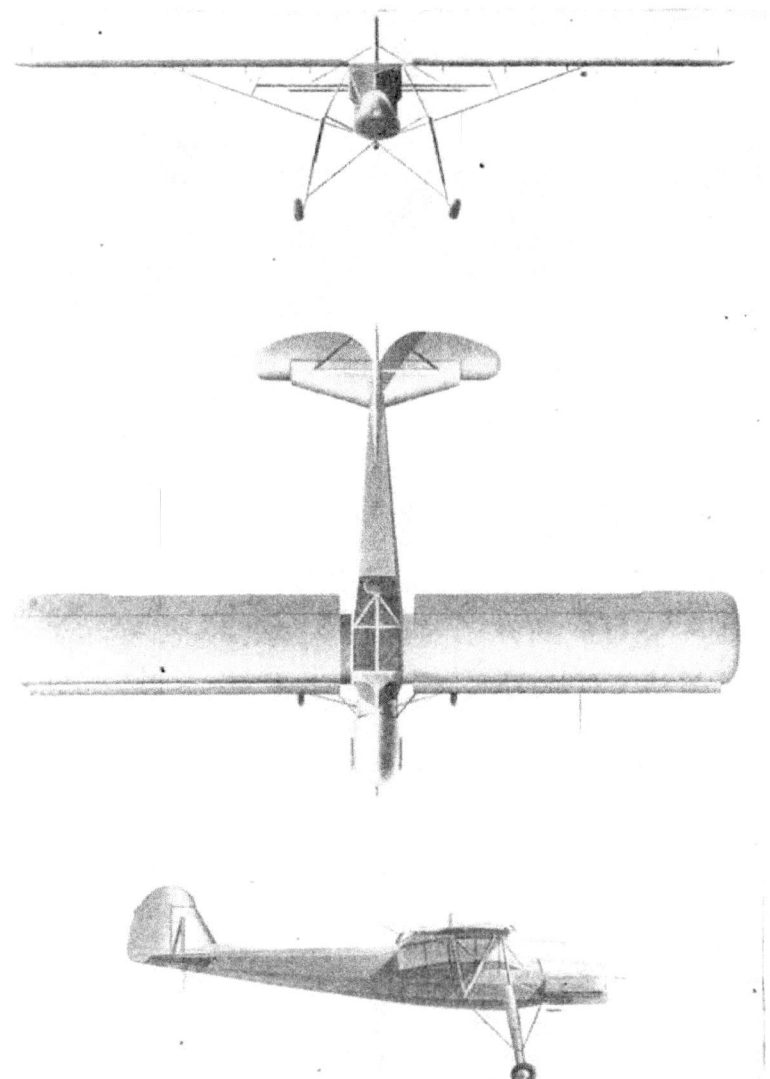

Figure 176.—*Fieseler Storch 156* (single-engine short-range observation plane for Army cooperation).

(8) *Coastal*.—The equipment of Air Force coastal units is limited almost entirely to two types. One is the *Arado 196*, which is the standard catapult plane used aboard German ships and which may be equipped with single or twin floats. It is normally employed as a fighter, but is also widely used for reconnaissance and occasionally used for light bombing. The other coastal type is the *Blohm-Voss 138* flying boat. This plane, armed with bombs or torpedoes, was designed primarily for long-range coastal reconnaissance, but has also been used for freight transport and submarine supply. The *B.V. 138* is probably the most important coastal plane in the Air Force today.

  b. *Gliders*.—(1) *General*.—The Germans have greatly increased the efficiency of their transport organization by the use of towed gliders. Unlike the conventional soaring plane, tow gliders resemble a sturdily built monoplane without the motor or conventional landing gear. Wheels are usually used for take-off; then they either are retracted into the fuselage or are jettisoned after the craft is airborne, in which case the glider lands on a spring-loaded central skid. Tow gliders are also equipped with landing flaps, dive brakes, and both navigation and landing lights. The advantages of these gliders are numerous. They are relatively easy and cheap to produce, and the use of a tug allows a greatly increased load. Furthermore, gliders can use a small landing ground and are excellent for operations in forward areas. Of the three types of gliders now in service, only one, the *D.F.S. 230*, has been used with *Fliegerkorps XI* for air-landing operations.

  (2) *D.F.S. 230*.—This glider (fig. 177), which is the product of the *Deutsche Forschungsanstalt für Segelflug*, was for a long time the standard troop-carrying glider of the Air Force and was used for air-landing operations in the capture of Fort Eben Emael in Belgium and used also in Crete. Its normal load is 10 men (including the pilot) with full battle equipment. Up to three of these gliders can be towed at one time by one *Ju. 52*, although only one has been towed at a time in actual operations. The *D.F.S. 230* can also be towed by the *Hs. 126*, the *Ju. 87*, and other smaller aircraft,

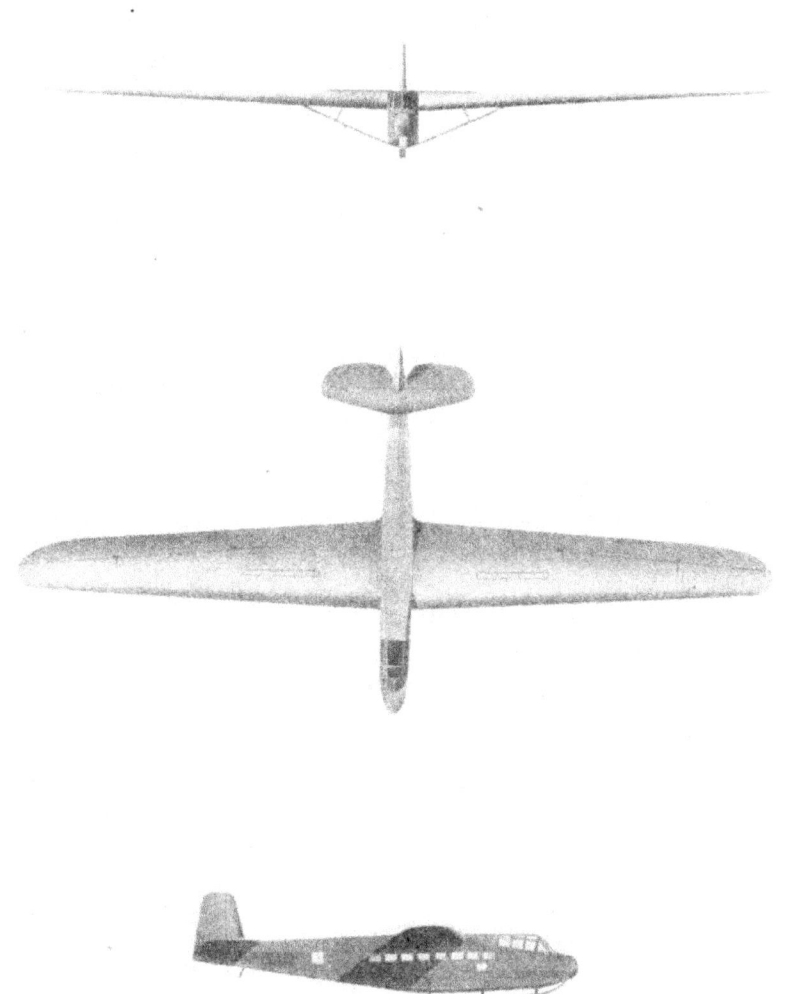

Figure 177.—*D.F.S. 230* (standard glider, designed to carry 10 men with full battle equipment).

and it is with such tugs that it has been encountered most recently transporting personnel, equipment, and supplies in Russia and the Mediterranean.

(2) *Gotha 242 and 244.*—This twin-boom glider (figs. 178 and 179) with its useful load of 5,500 pounds became the standard freight-carrying glider of the Air Force during the spring of 1941. It can alternately carry 23 men (including a crew of 2) or a 3-ton tank, and the rear part of the fuselage is hinged at the top to permit the loading of bulky materials. Armament consists of 2 machine guns. Armor protection is provided for the pilot. The *Go. 242* can be towed by a *Ju. 52* or a *He. 111* and has been used regularly in both the Russian and Mediterranean theaters.

(3) *Messerschmitt 323.*—This plane is the powered version of the large tow glider which was identified on the Merseburg airfield in mid-1941 and known for some time as the *Merseburg* glider. It is now known as the *Gigant*, or *Me. 321*. Apparently this tow version which required 2 large or 3 small aircraft as tugs either proved uneconomical or involved too many technical difficulties. The 6-engine powered version known as the *Me. 323* was then developed and introduced in late 1942 in the Mediterranean theater. The *Me. 323* can carry over 100 troops in its 2-deck fuselage; or motor vehicles or small tanks can be loaded through the large curved doors in the nose. Armament includes 6 machine guns. The fixed undercarriage consists of 10 wheels arranged in 2 rows of 5 each in tandem. The *Me. 323* should prove one of the most useful transports now available to the Air Force.

c. Engines.—The trend in German aeronautical engine development has been toward an increase in power at rated altitudes. The recent development of twin-row radial engines suggests that the Air Force is seriously interested in air-cooled engines and that an increasing proportion of German aircraft will be powered by such units. It is expected that the use of direct fuel injection will continue and that designers will not revert to the carburetor system formerly used. The three main German aero engines are the

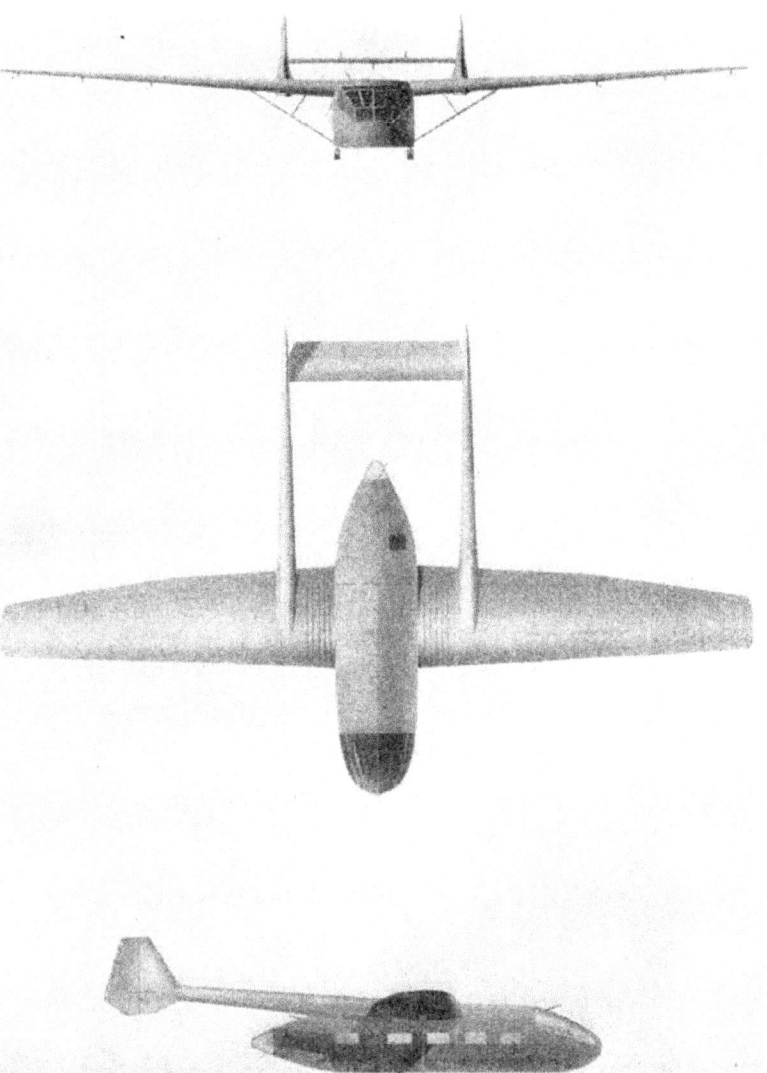

Figure 178.—*Gotha 242* (standard freight-carrying glider, with a useful load of 5,500 pounds).

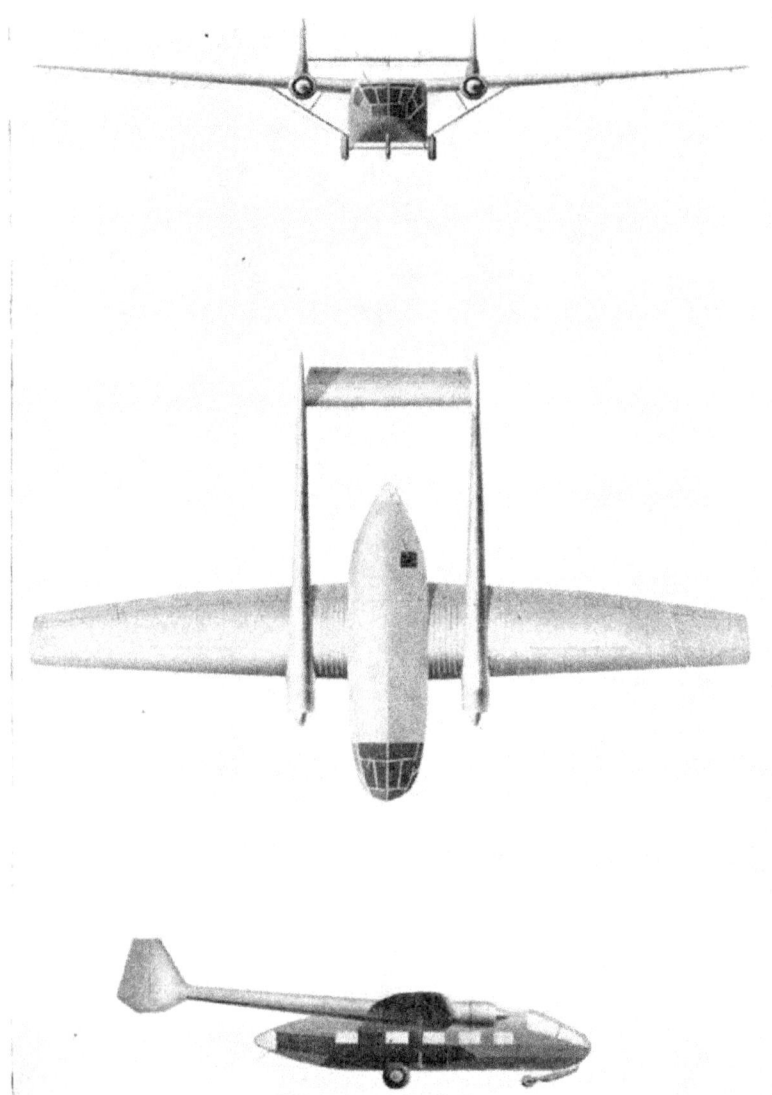

Figure 179.—*Gotha 244* (troop-carrying glider, similar to the *Gotha 242*).

Daimler-Benz (D.B.), the *Bayerische Motoren Werke (B.M.W.)*, and the *Junkers (Jumo)*. Engines used in Air Force combat planes in mid-1943 were the following:

(1) *Argus 410.*—This 12-cylinder, air-cooled, inverted V engine with its single-speed supercharger is rated at 450 horsepower for take-off. It was designed for light communications aircraft and trainers, but is now also used in some Army cooperation types (*F.W. 189*) and ground-attack planes (*Hs. 129*).

(2) *F.M.W. 132.*—Older and comparatively slow transports, seaplanes, and some Army cooperation types are now the only operational planes which use this 9-cylinder, air-cooled, radial engine. The older version of the *F.M.W. 132* is fitted with a carburetor, but the newer models have direct fuel injection. There are thus several different rated altitudes for the engine. The maximum power rating is 800 horsepower at about 10,000 feet.

(3) *B.M.W. 801.*—This 14-cylinder, twin-row, air-cooled, radial engine is comparatively new to the Air Force and is the first engine of its type to be produced in series. The models in service have a single-stage, two-speed supercharger and direct fuel injection. A novel feature is the engine-driven cooling fan mounted immediately behind the propeller. This fan is used primarily to cool the engine during taxying and take-off. The *B.M.W. 801* has several subtypes designed to use fuels of different octane rating. It is now installed in the *F.W. 190* and *Do. 217*, and is also expected to replace the engines currently used in other types, such as the *Ju. 88*. The power output has been raised from the original 1,480 horsepower to about 1,600 horsepower or more.

(4) *D.B. 601.*—Since the beginning of the war the *D.B. 601* in its several versions has powered most of the German single- and twin-engine fighters (except the *F.W. 190*). The original *D.B. 601 A* and *B* series which were used in 1940 are now obsolescent and have been superseded by the newer *N*, *E*, and *F* series. All are 12-cylinder, inverted V. liquid-cooled types with direct fuel injection. The majority are fitted with an automatically controlled, hy-

draulic-coupled supercharger. Each new series has further increased the power output, either by increasing the compression ratio as in the *N* series, or by improving the induction system and introducing cylinder scavenging as in the *E* series. The *F* series is believed to have an improved reduction gear ratio. The maximum emergency rating obtained from the *E* and *F* series has been in the neighborhood of 1,400 horsepower at about 14,000 feet. Further development of the engine is expected to increase the power output as well as the rated altitude.

(5) *D.B. 605.*—This engine, which appears to be an improved version of the *D.B. 601E*, is one of the newest Air Force engines to come into service. It is a 12-cylinder, inverted V, liquid-cooled unit with a somewhat larger bore than the *D.B. 601E*. The *D.B. 605* has been identified only on the *Me. 109G* to date, but is expected to appear before long in the *Me. 110* and *Me. 210* twin-engine fighters.

(6) *D.B. 606.*—This 24-cylinder, inverted V, liquid-cooled engine is composed of two *D.B. 601* units driving a single reduction gear. The engines are coupled by a clutch which enables the pilot to cut out one of the 12-cylinder units in case of damage to one unit or to conserve fuel. Thus far, this engine has been identified on only one plane type, the *He. 177*. It is believed to produce a maximum of 2,600 horsepower at around 15,000 feet.

(7) *Jumo 207.*—This *Junkers* Diesel engine is a development of the earlier *Jumo 205*, which was the first successful opposed-piston engine to be flown. The *Jumo 207* is a two-stroke, opposed-piston, liquid-cooled engine with compression ignition. It uses an engine-driven blower for scavenging, and an exhaust-driven, turbo-supercharger for take-off and high-altitude operations. The *Jumo 207* is installed in the high-altitude *Ju. 86P* bomber and reconnaissance planes.

(8) *Jumo 211.*—Since 1939 this engine has been the most widely used type for bombers and is fitted in both the *He. 111* and the *Ju. 88*. As with the *D.B. 601*, the basic design of the *Jumo 211* is

well known and has changed very little during the course of the war. It is a 12-cylinder, inverted V, liquid-cooled unit. The most notable improvements have been the fitting of induction air coolers and a new supercharger. The B and D series were used in 1940 and are now obsolescent. The G and H series are similar to the earlier models except for a modified fuel pump. The newest series are the F and J. The F has a higher compression ratio and develops almost 1,100 horsepower at about 13,000 feet. The J has the new induction air cooler and develops almost 200 horsepower more than the F at approximately the same altitude.

d. Armament.—The Germans started the war with relatively few types of aircraft armament, in order to standardize manufacture and achieve large-scale production. As the war progressed, however, improvements became imperative, and, beginning with 1942, noticeable changes have appeared. The main trends have been toward a more rapid rate of fire, greater muzzle velocity, and larger calibers. Other innovations have been electro-magnetic cocking and firing, and electric detonation. Armament used in German operational aircraft in mid-1943 consisted of the following:

(1) *M.G. 15.*—Since the beginning of the war this 7.9-mm drum-fed gun has been the standard Air Force rifle-caliber free gun for all types of aircraft except single-engine fighters. It has undergone no material alteration during its service and is now being largely superseded by the newer *M.G. 81.*

(2) *M.G. 17.*—This fixed-gun version of the *M.G. 15* is of 7.9-mm bore, but is belt-fed. The *M.G. 17* also has been in use since the beginning of the war and is still the standard rifle-caliber fixed gun on all single- and twin-engine fighters, on the fighter versions of twin-engine bombers, on dive bombers, on ground-attack planes, and on the *He. 111.*

(3) *M.G. 81.*—This 7.9-mm belt-fed gun is the newest Air Force rifle-caliber free gun. It is of very compact construction and light weight, and has a very rapid rate of fire. It is the first air-

craft gun to be used in a twin mount and is installed as such in both the *Ju. 88* and the new *Ju. 87*. The *M.G. 81* has already replaced the *M.G. 15* in many planes and is expected to become the standard free gun of this caliber.

(4) *M.G. 131.*—Mounted singly or as a twin gun in turrets, this 13-mm belt-fed *Mauser* gun appeared in early 1942 and is rapidly becoming the standard defense weapon on German multi-seat aircraft, particularly the *Do. 217*. It is also used in four-engine bombers and for the novel rear defense in the *Me. 210*. Not only is the *M.G. 131* light in weight and of compact design, but also it incorporates one of the newest German features in aircraft armament, electro-magnetic firing and electric detonation.

(5) *Oerlikon FF.*—This German version of the Swiss 20-mm explosive-shell cannon has been used without substantial alteration since the beginning of the war. Until the *M.G. 151* was introduced, the *Oerlikon FF* was the standard fixed or engine gun of this caliber in all single-engine fighters. It is still used as a fixed gun in the *Me. 110* and some *F.W. 190's*, and as a free gun in most of the German bombers. It is either drum- or clip-fed and has a much lower rate of fire than the *M.G. 151*.

(6) *M.G. 151.*—This belt-fed Mauser cannon has two versions, one of 15-mm (fig. 180) and the other of 20-mm caliber (fig. 181). These versions are not the same gun with interchangeable barrels, as is sometimes reported, but are two distinctly different guns with several variations in design. The 15-mm version is installed as a fixed gun in the nose of the *Do. 217* and *Hs. 129*, and as a single or twin gun in the turrets of several flying boats. It has been superseded in several other types, particularly single-engine fighters, by the 20-mm version, which is easily synchronized with the propellor because of its electro-magnetic loading and firing mechanism. In fact, the *M.G. 151* is rapidly becoming the standard armament of this caliber on practically all German single-engine fighters.

(7) *M.K. 101.*—This 30-mm gun is the largest caliber armament to be used operationally on German aircraft up to mid-1943. It

GERMAN AIR FORCE

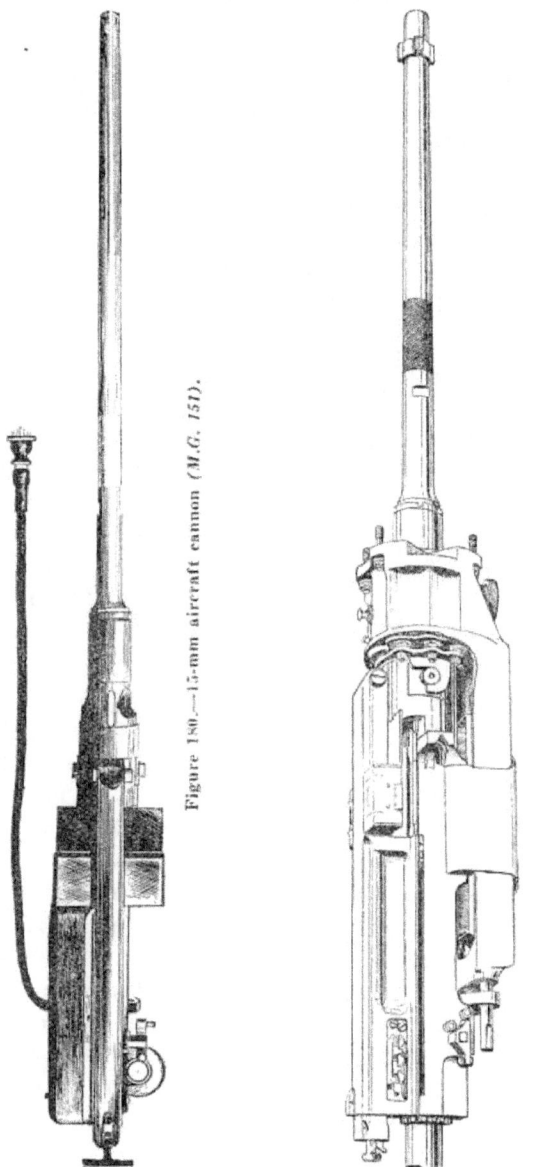

Figure 180.—15-mm aircraft cannon (M.G. 151).

Figure 181.—20-mm aircraft cannon (M.G. 151).

appeared in late .1942 on the *Hs. 129* ground-attack plane as an alternative to the bomb load and was intended primarily for antitank use. It may also be used on the *Me. 110* and a *Do. 217* subseries, and may possibly appear as an antishipping gun on the *He. 177*.

e. Armor.—The armor protection in German planes varies in thickness from 4 to 13 mm. The total weight per plane may be less than 100 pounds for some Army cooperation types to over 1,000 pounds for a ground-attack plane. The present tendency is to increase the total weight of armor per plane with particular emphasis on providing protection for accessories as well as for the crew. Armor protection for the engines was almost nonexistent in German planes in the early days of the war. In 1942, however, a policy was adopted of protecting the engines of fighters against attack from ahead and the engines on bombers against attack from astern. More recently coolant and oil radiators have also received armor protection. Crews, as a rule, are amply protected. The pilot usually has a plate on his seat and another fitted to his back and curved over the top of his head. Gunners, bombardiers, and observers are normally protected by plates on the sides and floor of the plane.

110. Training.—*a. General.*—Air Force training is the responsibility of the Air Ministry Training Inspectorate headed by *General der Flieger* Kuhl. Representatives of an executive body known as the Higher Training Command (*Höhres Ausbildungskommando*) control training activities in each *Luftflotte*. Each *Luftgau* is then responsible for the administration of training within its area. At the individual flying schools all training, both theoretical and practical, is under the control of a *Lehrgangsleiter*, who is also responsible for the maintenance of training planes.

b. Recruit training.—All men who join the Air Force go directly to a *Fl.A.R.* (*Fliegerausbildungsregiment*) where they receive their initial training as soldiers and their preliminary mechanical training in aviation. This recruit course was shortened from 12 to 5 months prior to the war, and was further shortened to 2 months shortly after war was declared. In 1942, however, the course was lengthened again to 3 or 4 months to permit more actual battle training instead of the former simple infantry drill.

c. Pilot training.—(1) *General.*—All pilot candidates are sent from the *Fl.A.R.* to a pool known as the *Fluganwärterkompanie*, where they await their assignment to a flying school. Although this pool provides a certain amount of physical training, military drill, and aviation background, it primary purpose is to regulate the flow of personnel to the elementary flying schools. Thus the length of the course actually depends upon the rate at which the flying schools can absorb new students. The average time spent at the *Fluganwärterkompanie* thus far has been about 2 months.

(2) The actual Air Force flight training begins at the elementary flying schools known as *Flugzeugführerschulen A/B*, or *F.Z.S.A./B*, where students receive the so-called *A/B* training. *A* training consists of dual and some solo flying and lasts about 3 months. *B* training is divided into the *B1* and *B2* courses. Training in the *B1* school is on the more advanced types of single-engine ships. At the *B2* course students receive their advanced training in navigation and are introduced to twin-engine types. At some time during the *A/B* course pilots take a *K1* (*Kunstflug*) course in elementary aerobatics. The total flying time at *A/B* schools averages 100 to 200 hours and takes about 6 to 9 months. Prospective fighter pilots normally receive more flying time than bomber candidates. Upon completion of the *A/B* course the pilots receive their Air Force pilot certificates and are ready to start their specialized training on the particular aircraft types to which they are assigned.

(3) Pilots who have been selected to fly bombers, twin-engine fighters, and bomber reconnaissance planes go from the *A/B* school to an advanced training school known as the *Flugzeugführerschule C*, or *F.Z.S.C.* This school specializes in multiple-engine types and provides a course which is commonly known as the *C* training. This course lasts from 2 to 6 months and includes 50

to 70 hours of flying. Pilots begin on the *Ju. 52* and obsolescent combat types and gradually advance to the operational types on which they are to specialize. Bomber candidates work up to the *Ju. 88* and *He. 111*. All pilots at the *C* school also receive some training in instrument flying, learn to use the direction-finder apparatus, and are given their first few hours on the *Link* trainer.

(4) Bomber pilots then proceed from the *C* school to a blind flying school known as the *Blindflugschule*. The course here lasts from 4 to 6 weeks and includes 10 hours on the *Link* trainer plus some 35 to 60 hours of flying. This course is also given to wireless telegraph operators who are to fly.

(5) Bomber pilots, upon completion of their blind flying course, usually go to an advanced bomber school known as the *Grosskampffliegerschule*, where they meet the other members of their crews. These crews are usually kept together for their training and are eventually stationed with the same operational unit. The 3 months spent at this school are devoted to crew training and include 40 to 60 hours of flying. Upon completion of the course the pilot with his crew is posted to an *Ergänzungsgruppe*. The total bomber pilot training thus amounts to 12 to 22 months with some 240 to 300 hours of flying.

(6) Single-engine fighter pilots go directly from the *A/B* school to a fighter specialist school known as a *Jagdfliegerschule*, or *J.F.S.* The course here lasts 3 to 4 months and includes an average of 50 flying hours on types leading up to the *Me. 109*. Gunnery and formation flying receive special attention. Upon completion of the *J.F.S.*, pilots go to a fighter operational training pool. When the *Jagdfliegerschulen* are too full to take on new students, pilots are sent from the *A/B* school to an intermediate school known as the *Jagdfliegervorschule* to await an opening. This intermediate course is primarily designed to care for the overflow of pilots destined for the *J.F.S.*, but it does sometimes offer a maximum of some 15 hours of flying. Thus, by the time the single-engine fighter pilot has completed the *J.F.S.* training, he

has had 9 to 13 months of training with 180 to 250 hours of flying.

(7) Twin-engine fighter pilots are sent from the *C* school to a specialized twin-engine fighter school known as the *Zerstörerschule*. The training here lasts 2 to 3 months and concentrates on gunnery and target flights. Here also the pilot meets his wireless telegraph operator with whom he does most of his training. If the *Zerstörerschulen* are full, the pilots and their operators are sent to a *Jagdfliegervorschule* until there is an opening. After completing the *Zerstörer* training, each crew (pilot and wireless operator) is sent to a *Blindflugschule* for the 4-week blind flying course and is then posted to a twin-engine fighter operational training pool.

(8) Dive-bomber pilots proceed from the *A/B* schools to the *Sturzkampffliegerschule*, which is a specialized dive-bomber school. Diving practice is started almost immediately at some schools, but is not permitted in others until the student has had 100 or more hours of formation flying and aerobatics. Most of the training is devoted to accuracy of bombing in the dive approach, but also includes some navigation and theory. The course usually lasts 4 months, after which the pilot and his operator are posted to the *Ergänzungsgruppe* of some operational unit.

(9) Long-range reconnaissance pilots are sent from the *A/B* school to the *C* course and thence to the *Blindflugschule* for 4 to 6 weeks of blind flight training. From here they go to a specialized reconnaissance school known as the *Fernaufklärerschule* which is their equivalent of the specialized advanced bomber or fighter schools. Upon completion of the *Fernaufklärerschule* the students are posted to an *Ergänzungs-Fernaufklärungsgruppe*.

(10) Army cooperation and short-range reconnaissance pilots are not believed to receive any specialized training after completing the *A/B* course.

c. Observer training.—Observer candidates are sent from the *Fl.A.R.* depot to a specialized observer school known as an *Aufklärungschule*, or *A.K.S.*, for a 9- to 12-month specialist course. Training includes navigation, map making and reading, photography, bombing, gunnery, and tactics. Students thus learn a little of the work of each member of the crew, including some actual flying, in order that they may replace a wounded crew mate. After completing this course the observer is sent to a *Grosskampffliegerschule*, where he meets the remainder of his crew for crew training.

d. Wireless operator training.—Prospective wireless telegraph operators proceed directly from the *Fl. A. R.* to a *Luftnachrichtenschule* for 9 months of specialist training in ground wireless receiving and transmitting. The student is supposed here to attain a speed of 100 letters a minute, become familiar with the use of instruments, and learn some elementary navigation. Those operators who are to become members of an aircrew are then sent to another school for actual flight practice and training in navigation, map reading, and radio direction finding. The operator is then ready for his crew training and a gunnery course at the *Grosskampffliegerschule*.

e. Air gunner training.—Air gunner candidates are sent from the *Fl.A.R.* to a *Fliegerschützenschule*, which is a specialist school in air gunnery. This 5-month course includes ground firing practice with small arms and machine guns, elementary navigation, camera gun practice on a trainer plane, air-to-air firing practice with machine guns, and elementary instruction in aircraft engines. The air gunner is then transferred to a *Grosskampffliegerschule* as a member of a crew. Air gunners are also recruited from the wastage of the *A/B* schools and from ground personnel.

f. Flight engineer training.—Flight mechanics go from the *Fl. A. R.* to a technical school known as a *Fliegertechnischeschule*. Here they receive some theoretical training on the gasoline engine and elementary aerodynamics, followed by practical work on engines. The students are sometimes sent to a nearby airplane factory for this practical training. After completing this course the prospective flight engineer goes to a *Grosskampffliegerschule* for his crew training, a gunnery course, and possibly some elementary wireless telegraphy instruction.

g. Crew training.—As has been mentioned above, the various members of the bomber crews meet at the specialist bomber school (*Grosskampffliegerschule*) for their crew training. Personnel is divided into several companies, each of which is subdivided into crews consisting of a pilot, an observer, a wireless operator, and a flight engineer. Training here amounts to 40 to 60 hours on first-line types and usually lasts 3 months. In several recent instances the functions of the *Grosskampffliegerschulen* have been taken over by the *Ergänzungsgruppen*.

h. Operational training schools.—Upon completion of the course at the bomber, fighter, or reconnaissance specialist school, personnel are usually sent to an operational training school to await posting to an operational unit. These schools are a part of the Air Force training system and are not attached to a particular operational unit. A pilot's training at the school is merely a continuance of his instruction on his special aircraft type and may last anywhere from a few days to several weeks, depending upon the requirements of the operational units. The schools thus amount to a pool of personnel receiving further instruction as they await assignment to a combat unit. In 1940, when there was superfluity of pilots, many of the schools were replaced by the *Ergänzungsgruppen* (see *i*, below). More recently, however, as the supply of flying personnel has dwindled, some of the specialist schools have not been turning out enough trained pilots to keep the *Ergänzungsgruppen* full. There has therefore been a reversion to the operational training school system for certain types, particularly single-engine fighters, and pilots are posted direct from the school to the operational unit without any intermediate training in an *Ergänzungsgruppe*.

i. Ergänzungsgruppe (*Reserve Training Unit*).—In the early part of 1940, when pilot output was exceeding pilot losses by a wide margin, the operational training school system could not entirely accommodate the large numbers of personnel awaiting assignment to a combat unit. Each *Geschwader* was therefore ordered to form its own operational training unit to be known as an *Ergänzungstaffel* from which replacements for the *Geschwader* could be drawn. This *Staffel* was to be in the rear of the *Geschwader* and provide the pilots and crews with training under conditions that were as identical as possible to actual combat conditions. The *Staffel* was also to offer instruction in the particular tactics in which the *Geschwader* specialized. The amount of time to be spent in the *Staffel* would depend on the replacement requirements of the operational *Gruppen*. As the supply of pilots continued to increase, the *Staffel* soon expanded to the size of a *Gruppe* and became known as an *Ergänzungsgruppe* (or *Gruppe IV* of the *Geschwader*). Each *Ergänzungsgruppe* consisted of two to three *Staffeln*. Each *Staffel* is supposed to have nine crews undergoing training and three experienced instructor crews known as *Lehrbesatzungen*. These instructor crews are members of the regular combat personnel of the *Geschwader* and are only temporarily assigned to instructing as a relief from the strain of combat duty. As mentioned in the foregoing paragraphs, these *Ergänzungsgruppen* soon replaced many of the operational training schools and, except for the single-engine fighter pilots, still do. Furthermore, in long-range bomber training, which has become somewhat disorganized because of a fuel shortage for training purposes and the withdrawal of bombers for transport use, the functions of the *Grosskampffliegerschulen* have also been taken over by some of the *Ergänzungsgruppen*.

111. Tactics.—*a. General.*—The German air war doctrine is predicated on close cooperation with the Army and Navy in order to expedite and increase the effectiveness of combined land-sea-air operations. Thus, to quote the Supreme General Staff, "The Air Force, as an independent arm, is not called upon to conduct an independent war apart from the Army and Navy. * * * The Air Force, Army, and Navy form a single unit within the framework of the conduct of total war." Air Force tactics have been evolved with this doctrine in mind.

b. Level bombing. Although the Air Force has probably created the greater sensation through its dive bombing, it has not failed to realize the many possibilities of level bombing, that is, the release of bombs while the plane is in level flight. Air Force tactics for level bombing have undergone considerable change during the course of the war, and in mid-1943 consisted mainly of the following:

(1) *In formation.*—The usual tactics employed for level bombing in formation is to send up a *Staffel* of 9 aircraft flying in a large **V** composed of 3 *Ketten*. The 3 aircraft of each *Kette* are also in **V** formation. Sometimes the *Staffel* numbers 12 planes, in which case the fourth *Kette* flies behind and in line with the leading *Kette* and thereby creates a diamond-shaped formation. When operations involve an entire *Gruppe* of 27 to 36 planes, the 3 *Staffeln* usually fly in a **V** with some 200 to 300 yards between each *Staffel*. Although the close formation is usually preferred for the *Gruppe*, each *Staffel* will occasionally form a **V** of 9 planes and the *Gruppe* formation then takes the shape of 3 large stepped-up **V**'s. In formation level bombing, the rank and file of the formation do not aim individually, but release their bombs at a signal from the leader of the formation. Planes generally approach at 10,000 to 13,000 feet and take continuous evasive action by changing course and altitude. If the attack is being made at night, 2 or 3 planes are sent ahead to drop flares on the target. This type of formation attack is usually undertaken only by long-range bombers and is now almost entirely confined to night operations, particularly over Britain.

(2) *Singly.*—(*a*) The isolated "hit-and-run," or "pirate," attack is assuming increasing importance in German level-bombing tactics. In these attacks the planes approach the target individually, and the time, altitude, and direction of approach are left to the discretion of the pilot. Most of the attacks are made from a low level,

The lone raiders are usually sent out in a steady stream against widely scattered targets, with rarely more than three planes being dispatched against the same objective. Both long-range bombers and single-engine fighters carrying bombs are used for isolated raids, but with somewhat different tactics.

(*b*) Long-range bombers, when sent on individual raids, usually operate in daylight and are sent against a specific target. These targets are selected well in advance of the raid and are generally isolated and lightly defended. The favorite targets have been railways, airfields, and factories. Experienced crews are used, and the routes are carefully worked out to avoid, as far as possible, any hills or other natural or artificial obstructions. Approach is generally made under cloud cover, and the pilot waits until the target is reached before dropping to a low level and releasing the bombs. By thus coming out of the clouds only long enough to make a short run to the target, the planes are less likely to be engaged by antiaircraft artillery. Single long-range bombers are also being used against shipping. Tactics for antishipping attacks are to fly at a low level, using cloud cover, if possible, or along the coast with land as a protective background until the target is reached. The beam approach is preferred for attacks against unescorted ships, while attacks against a convoy are usually along the length of the ship or from the quarter.

(*c*) Single-engine fighters acting as bombers have been responsible for most of the "pirate" attacks during recent months. These raids usually occur during daylight and are almost always conducted at extremely low altitudes. In small attacks the fighters operate in pairs. The rear plane acts as cover and no other escort is provided. When larger formations, or five to eight planes, are used, however, fighter protection is necessary. This escort normally flies at 3,000 to 4,000 feet to draw off ground fire and fighter opposition, while the fighter-bombers continue at ground level. These tactics have been best defined in operations over Britain. Here the planes cross the Channel at sea level to avoid radio interception, and continue at low altitudes to the target. After releasing their bombs, they strafe any object which may appear. The favorite primary targets for these raiders have been railways, power stations, gas works, and service installations. Frequently, however, the pilots are not dispatched to any specific objective, but are merely instructed to bomb and strafe anything which might terrorize the people. Night attacks of fighter-bombers by moonlight were introduced over Britain in the spring of 1943. In these raids visual navigation was used, and the planes operated in pairs, making their approach and bomb-release at 20,000 feet or higher.

(c) *Dive bombing.*—(1) The Air Force is not believed to have a sufficiently accurate bombsight to permit extensive high-altitude level precision bombing, and has therefore used dive bombing (that is, the release of bombs while the plane is in a dive or steep glide) against those targets where accuracy is of primary importance. Dive bombing has been particularly valuable from a tactical point of view when used in the close support of ground troops to strike the first heavy blows at troop columns, lines of communications, road crossings, bridges, bunkers, tanks, forts, etc. Almost as important tactically has been its employment against enemy airdromes (especially buildings and hangars), shipping, ports and harbors, and small industrial or concentrated targets.

(2) Dive-bombing raids are generally concentrated on a single objective, with methods of attack varying with the type and accessibility of the target. Targets are usually located within 100 miles of the base airport, and since the dive bomber rarely operates beyond the range of its fighter protection, the maximum distance flown per sortie seldom exceeds 200 to 250 miles. Each pilot is generally assigned an individual target.

(3) The basic unit of the dive attack is the *Kette* of 3 planes in V formation, or 4 planes flying in 2 pairs (*Rotten*). The latter formation provides greater protection against enemy fighters and is usually employed in small raids where fighter protection is lacking. The basic units may then be formed into larger *Gruppe*

formations of 30 to 40 planes with 10 or more single-engine fighter escorts 1,000 to 2,000 feet above. The bombers usually approach from the sun at 14,000 to 17,000 feet and descend when near the target to 6,000 feet. Upon reaching the target they "peel off" from the formation one by one, line up the targets in their sights, and make the actual attack individually.

(4) In dive-bombing attacks against shipping the approach is made at between 5,000 and 15,000 feet, but usually at about 8,000 feet. The planes generally dive in flights of three "in line ahead" and attack alternate ships up or down a column of the convoy. Succeeding waves of bombers then concentrate on the column farther ahead or astern.

(5) The two planes used most frequently as dive bombers are the *Ju. 87*, which was designed as a dive bomber, and the *Ju. 88*, which can be easily modified for dive bombing. The *Ju. 87* dives at 70 to 80 degrees, and the *Ju. 88* at 50 to 60 degrees.

d. Torpedo bombing.—At the beginning of the war, Air Force coastal units were organized and equipped for antishipping torpedo operations, but these operations were subordinated to coastal reconnaissance and became increasingly limited during 1940. In 1941, however, the Air Force began equipping landplanes for torpedo carrying and started an expansion in the German aerial torpedo force and the torpedo pilot training program. At this time aerial torpedo attacks were delivered by single planes. Since then the Air Force torpedo tactics have received increased attention and development and have taken the following form:

(1) The tactical feature on which the Air Force now places the greatest emphasis in torpedo bombing is the mass attack in formation, especially on convoys and escorted capital ships, on the theory that if enough torpedoes are released at one time, some are bound to strike home. A *Fühlungshalter* plane, which is sent out 20 to 30 minutes ahead of the main striking force, locates the convoy and then guides the bombers to the target by means of the direction-finder apparatus. The preferred time for torpedo at-

tacks is bright moonlight, or dawn, or dusk. The formation used is very similar to that employed by low-level bombers, that is, a small, tight **V** of about 30 planes.

(2) The formations generally approach the targets at sea level and rise to about 150 feet for the actual release. Usually the planes fly on a parallel or reciprocal course to the ships, at a range of a mile or more, until they have a favorable bearing on the bow or beam. They then turn in to make the final approach. Most attacks are delivered in a steady level approach from the beam or broad on the bow. The average height of torpedo release is between 40 to 150 feet, depending upon the type of torpedo. The average range for the actual release is about 900 yards.

(3) Aerial torpedo attacks are also being used in conjunction with level and dive bombing. These attacks are carefully synchronized and the torpedo attack follows the bombing by a matter of minutes. The low-level or dive bombing is intended to confuse and distract the defenses. The torpedo planes then come in head-on at sea level, usually from the same direction as the bombers, to deliver the attack.

e. Fighters.—(1) *General.*—Almost all Air Force fighter tactics are based on the *Rotte* formation, that is, two planes flying one behind the other and slightly offside. This formation allows the leader to concentrate on the attack while the second plane acts as cover and protects the rear. Two *Rotten* may be combined to form a fighter *Schwarm* of four planes. Larger formations are then composed of a series of *Rotten*, and although each *Rotte* always stays intact, the over-all formation is not a rigid one. Thus when aerial combat develops, the mass formation can quickly break up into *Rotten* with each pair operating as a unit.

(2) As a rule, German fighters enter combat only when the advantage is with the Germans—either in numbers, altitude, or direction of attack. Their characteristic tactics are to "shadow" their targets from above and at a distance and then dive down on them when conditions are favorable. The preferred attack is from

the sun. The fast rate of climb and high service ceiling of German fighters have made this method of attack very effective, and, consequently, German fighters rarely attack from the same altitude as their opposition. The favored maneuver in a mass attack is to send the main body of fighters over the enemy and leave a *Schwarm* or *Staffel* to attack from above and behind. After diving on the opposition this section climbs back to rejoin the main formation. Another maneuver frequently encountered is the use of decoy tactics to lure opposing planes out of formation. The decoy is usually a *Rotte* flying beneath and at right angles to the line of flight of the enemy. When the enemy turns to attack, he is in turn attacked from behind by the main German force which was flying above.

(3) German fighters employed as bomber escort may fly either as a direct escort or as a "distant" protection. The direct escort is made up of four groups of fighters which fly, respectively, on both sides of the bombers, above them, and behind and below. This distribution permits the escort group which is between the bombers and the attackers to turn and engage the opposition while one of the other escort groups moves over and takes the place of the first group. The usual ratio for the direct escort is two or three fighters per bomber. "Distant" escorts fly ahead and frequently out of sight of the bomber formation in order to divert any attackers before they can reach the bombers in force. The fighter escort for dive bombers, as at Malta, usually splits into two groups. One group remains at a high altitude as a protective cover and the other dives with the bombers. This maneuver provides protection for the bombers during the pull-out from the dive, which is the moment of greatest vulnerability for a dive bomber.

(4) In single-engine-fighter attacks on ground forces (as distinct from *Jabo* attacks) the planes usually fly at extremely low altitudes until the target is sighted. They then climb to around 1,500 feet and make a dive attack along the troop or transport columns. Tanks are attacked in shallow dives, preferably from

the rear. Twin-engine fighters, however, generally approach at about 1,000 feet in a wide **V** formation and break into an irregular circle outside the perimeter of the target. The actual attack is then made at low altitudes by individual planes or by small groups of two or three planes which break away from the others, machine-gun the targets, and then return to the formation.

f. Airborne troops.—German parachute and air-landing troops were used as early as May 1940 in the Flanders Campaign. Parachutists were used again in April 1941 on the Isthmus of Corinth. But the German combined attack on Crete in May 1941 was the first airborne invasion and capture of strongly defended enemy territory across a body of water. It also defined the German tactics for airborne combat along the following lines:

(1) Airborne attacks are preceded by short, intensive low-level bombing, dive bombing, and machine-gunning of enemy antiaircraft guns, airdrome defenses, and troop positions. This action ceases in the areas which have been selected for the descent of airborne troops as soon as the troops arrive, but continues in those areas surrounding the objective which are still held by enemy forces.

(2) Glider-borne shock troops are the first to be landed. These troops disrupt communications and silence batteries and antiaircraft positions in preparation for the landing of parachutists. In Crete the gliders preceded the parachutists by 15 minutes. Shock troops normally operate in companies. They are able to go into action almost immediately, since they carry their arms with them in their gliders and do not become dispersed in landing.

(3) Parachute troops are next dropped to capture an airdrome or landing ground in preparation for the air-landing troops. Parachutists are dropped in depth around the area selected for attack instead of on the site itself. The transport planes fly in *Ketten* of three aircraft each in tight **V** formation. Troops are released from 300 to 500 feet altitude. Descents are usually made at several points from 1 to 20 miles apart. The time for descent averages 10

seconds. The troops then need another 10 to 15 minutes to collect equipment and assemble themselves before they are ready for action. Companies promptly contact their battalions and regiments and then operate as a normal infantry unit. In Crete the parachute troops were dropped at a density of one battalion per square mile during the first day of attack.

(4) Air-landing troops are finally landed in their transport planes at a spot as near as possible to their final objective. Although they are usually landed on a captured airdrome, air-landing troops may be expected to descend on any reasonably flat area within 3 miles of the objective. The infantry and engineers are usually landed first, and the heavier units with the antitank and antiaircraft artillery follow. The first move of air-landing troops is to contact and reinforce the parachute and shock troops. The command of all operations is usually assumed by the commanders of the air-landing Army units, and the entire airborne force sets out to block the approach of enemy reserves, block defenses from the rear, seize and clear a harboring area for their own armored formation, and draw off reserves.

(5) The Germans have also dropped parachutists and landed glider-borne troops in conjunction with land operations. Any number from a platoon to a battalion of parachute troops may be landed behind enemy lines to disrupt communications and to seize key points such as railroads, roadheads, bridges, power stations, ammunition dumps, etc. They also do a good deal of sabotage. Parachutists employed on these missions are generally expected to hold their positions for a few hours only—or a day at the most—before they are relieved by their advancing ground forces. This technique has been demonstrated in Russia, where parachutists have been dropped from 5 to 15 miles in advance of oncoming tanks to entrench themselves in a village or hilltop and prepare the way for the armored units. In using glider-borne troops, one to three *D.F.S. 230* gliders are sometimes sent over enemy lines and landed in isolated spots. The troops leave the gliders as soon

as possible, and, after conducting their sabotage (generally, destruction of bridges or railheads), try to work their way back to their own lines.

Section XVI

TACTICS

	Paragraph
Doctrine	112
Reconnaissance	113
Marches	114
Meeting engagement	115
Preparations for attack	116
Attack	117
Pursuit	118
Defense	119
Delaying actions	120
Breaking off combat	121
Withdrawal	122

112. Doctrine.—*a. General.*—German tactical doctrine is based on a well-trained Officer Corps, a thoroughly disciplined enlisted personnel, and years of aggressive philosophy. The German always sees the solution of his tactical problem in attack. When the situation is not clear, he usually attacks, for he believes that hostile weaknesses are disclosed in such actions, upon which the commander may capitalize and which he may then exploit.

b. Fortifications.—Although their main tactical policy is centered on their century-old doctrine of the offensive, Germany's military leaders are fully aware of the powers of modern defense by virtue of automatic firepower, long-range artillery, and steel and concrete fortifications. In their construction of the vast system of defense along the northwestern coast of Europe and in Norway, as well as by their earlier construction of the West Wall, they have fully exploited the advantages of defense.

c. Responsibility.—German tactical doctrine stresses the responsibility and the initiative of subordinates. The German Army is no machine where "military thinking" is confined to **GHQ** and where every move of a battalion or platoon is regulated by written orders of superiors. Recent German military history is full of examples where subordinate commanders have seized opportunities to exploit situations on their own responsibility. It is recognized that there are dangers in permitting subordinates so much independence, but these dangers are accepted as a price worth paying in order to obtain an offensive spirit in the Army. The Germans believe that the offensive alone can bring about decisive success; the old-time myth of the machine-like woodenness of the German Army is one that soldiers of the United Nations cannot afford to hold. An aggressive, daring leadership which carefully weighs the situation and executes a bold decision has played and will play the dominant role in German warfare. When the leadership was excellent, Germany triumphed; when it was only mediocre, Germany was decisively beaten.

d. Principles of tactics.—The following paragraphs contain the basic principles on which all German tactics are based. Their application may be slightly modified to suit varying situations, such as night fighting, fighting in wooded areas, river crossings, or similar operations, as well as to fit the various arms, such as infantry, artillery, Panzer units, or engineers.

113. Reconnaissance.—*a. Types.*—The terms which the Germans use to indicate the different types of reconnaissance are slightly different from those which are employed in the U. S. Army, but the principles involved are identical. The Germans classify reconnaissance as operational, tactical, and combat. In carrying out reconnaissance missions, German air and ground units pay special attention to terrain, noting carefully the road net, the number of roads and their condition, roadblocks, mines and demolitions, and similar features which will round out the reconnaissance picture.

(1) *Operational.*—Operational reconnaissance penetrates over a large area in great depth and provides the basis for strategic planning and action. This type of reconnaissance is intended to

determine where the enemy forces are located. It is carried out by Air Force reconnaissance squadrons and by motorized reconnaissance battalions. Photographic and direct observation is maintained over march and transport movements of large forces on roads, railroads, and waterways; over the assembly and transfer of large bodies of troops; and over the construction and improvement of fortifications, positions, and other military installations and repairs on military buildings and the traffic network.

(2) *Tactical.*—Tactical reconnaissance is carried out in the narrow area behind the operational reconnaissance. The direction and mission of the tactical reconnaissance is often dependent upon the results of the operational reconnaissance. Air Force reconnaissance squadrons and motorized battalions are also used for tactical reconnaissance. Their mission is to discover from which direction the enemy is approaching and where contact with the enemy will be established, as well as to determine the organization, disposition, strength, and flanks of the enemy deployment. This information provides the basis for the commitment of troops. In tactical reconnaissance, photographic and direct observation is maintained over assemblies and march movements of the enemy before contact is established, as well as over the main concentration (*Schwerpunkt*) and deployment of enemy forces. Similar observation is maintained on enemy preparations and the activities of enemy air-force units. Reconnaissance of advance terrain by ground units is coordinated with these tasks. Divisional reconnaissance battalions seldom operate more than 1 day's march (18 miles) in front of the division. The reconnaissance is carried out by means of small reconnaissance detachments or patrols (*Spähtruppen*). These reconnaissance detachments of the motorized units are not allowed to operate more than 1 hour's distance (20 miles) away from their units.

(3) *Combat reconnaissance.*—All troops participating directly in battle carry out combat reconnaissance through patrols, artillery observation posts, observation battalions, and air reconnaissance

squadrons. The information obtained on the organization and strength of the enemy provides the basis for the conduct of the battle. This reconnaissance is supplemented by interrogation of prisoners, reports of agents, signal reconnaissance (interception of enemy radio messages and bearings from enemy transmitters), and captured maps and documents.

b. Units.—There are five specialized types of reconnaissance units in the German Army: the reconnaissance battalion of the infantry division; the reconnaissance battalion of the motorized division; the reconnaissance battalion of the Panzer division; the reconnaissance battalion of the mountain division; and the mounted platoon of the infantry regiment. (Detailed organization and composition of these units will be found in secs. V, Infantry, p. 51; VI, Cavalry and Reconnaissance Units, p. 61; and IX, Panzer Troops, p. 103.) In addition to the above, Air Force Reconnaissance units are attached in war to all larger German units to conduct reconnaissance missions.

114. Marches.—*a. General.*—Where possible, marches are preceded by a careful reconnaissance of the routes to be followed. The march is undertaken on one road or on several roads simultaneously, depending upon the road net and the tactical situation. Motorized units, with the exception of those employed on reconnaissance or security missions, are organized into one or more motorized detachments and follow the march column, advancing by bounds, or else move as a motorized march column along a separate road.

b. Security.—March columns are divided into the advance guard and the main body, in order to protect them against attack. Although the size and composition of the advance guard is determined by the commander on the basis of the tactical situation, it usually consists of from one-third to one-sixth of the infantry of the marching force, with additional units attached from the engineer, antitank, and artillery components of the column. A column may also have flank guards and a rear guard.

c. Missions.—It is the mission of the advance guard to overcome enemy resistance speedily, to clear the road for the main body, and at times to render possible the entrance of the main body into combat. Flank guards are organized when scouting patrols are not sufficient; they are formed in a manner similar to the advance guard. A rear guard protects withdrawals, retiring by bounds and thus insuring a systematic disengagement of the main body from the enemy. As a rule, the rear guard in a withdrawal is stronger than the advance guard in a forward movement because it cannot rely upon the support of the main body.

d. Defense against air attack.—In the event of an air attack from great heights, the column continues to march. Only when the column is attacked by low-flying aircraft, do the troops take cover and organize a defense. Night marches are interrupted only when flares are dropped. Air-defense safety intervals are maintained between the platoons of marching troops and between the vehicles of motorized troops in areas where they might be threatened by air attack.

e. March preparations.—The equipment of motorized and horse-drawn troops is made ready for movement 2 hours before the start of the march. Rest periods of about 2 hours are provided for food, adjustment of harnesses and saddles, and feeding and watering of horses so as to conserve their effectiveness.

f. Contact during march.—Runners, or in exceptional cases officers, maintain contact between sections of the march column. The division signal battalion advances along the road, installs the main trunk line, and marks the call stations by flags. Construction of the line is kept abreast of the advance party.

g. Road distances.—The following road space is necessary for each of the several German units:

	Yards
Rifle company	130
Machine-gun company	290
Infantry battalion	760

	Yards
Infantry regiment	2,815
Infantry howitzer company	435
Bicycle company	290
Battery	325
Light artillery battalion	1,085

115. Meeting engagement.—The Germans believe that the obscurity and vagueness of the given situation will usually require decisions and actions which must take into account all factors of uncertainty. The meeting engagement may take any of several courses, depending upon the tactical situation which develops upon first contact. German tacticians state that the first contact of the most advanced sections with the enemy has a strong influence on the development and progress of the battle. When both adversaries attack immediately from march columns, the decisive factors are the initiative of the junior officers and the calmness and efficiency of the troops. In the meeting engagement the advantage lies with the side which succeeds first in making effective preparations for the attack and thereby deprives the enemy of his freedom of action. The senior commander must quickly coordinate the various independent actions undertaken by his junior officers, while the advance guard secures for him freedom of action and the opportunity for a speedy deployment of his artillery and infantry. Once the advance guard has completed this mission, it merges with the main body. If the commander decides not to wait until he has deployed his main forces, but to attack directly from march columns, his order to attack will dissolve the march disposition of the main body. Troops employed from the rear must immediately reconnoiter the situation in the sector immediately to their front and their flanks to prevent surprise by the enemy.

116. Preparation for attack.—*a. The order.*—The German order for an attack generally contains the objectives of the attack, the disposition of the infantry, the zones of action and boundaries, the dispositions and support missions of the artillery, the reserves and their locations, and the time of attack. The order is not drawn up in accordance with any stereotyped form, but usually assumes the following pattern:

(1) Position of the enemy.

(2) Own objectives, adjacent units, and the time of attack.

(3) Instructions for rear services (medical service and ammunition replacement).

(4) Location of the command post.

b. Neutralization of enemy artillery.—Before the beginning of the attack, the previously reconnoitered enemy artillery should be neutralized or destroyed by German artillery. Immediately before the advance of the infantry, the artillery fire is shifted to the enemy infantry lines. In the course of this action, newly discovered batteries are fired upon.

c. Deployment of troops.—The movement of troops into action consists of two phases: the first, where they are deployed tactically, with the platoons remaining together organized in depth; and the second, the development of the attack, in which they are formed into lines of skirmishers.

117. Attack.—*a. General.*—German infantry works itself forward close to the enemy, avoiding open terrain with a careful coordination of fire and movement (figs. 182 and 183) and with support from artillery fire and heavy infantry weapons. When the infantry reaches a point close to the enemy lines, the fire of the supporting weapons is lifted to more distant targets. Fire is concentrated on points of resistance the location of which has been established in advance, in order to destroy them. The breakthrough may be executed uniformly on a wide front, or at single penetration points. The attack finally culminates in the penetration of enemy lines. Since a rolling barrage closely follows the penetration of the infantry, advanced firing positions are established or at least reconnoitered before the attack. The attack is carried through as a penetration until enemy artillery positions are reached. Once these have been overrun, the German reserves that follow the first waves turn to the task of rolling up the enemy front. Enemy units which escape encirclement must be pursued, though if German forces in the area are not adequate for this task, they take up defensive positions in the newly conquered area.

b. Frontage.—The width of the front which infantry units must cover depends upon the probable strength of the enemy forces as

Figure 182.—Light machine-gun team, using the 7.92-mm machine gun *(M.G. 34)* with drum magazine, in typical attack tactics.

well as the mission, the combat strength of the unit, the supporting fire, and the terrain. An infantry battalion supported on both sides usually attacks on a front between 400 and 1,000 yards wide, while a division attacks on a front from 4,000 to 5,000 yards wide. Against a strongly fortified position, however, a division cannot attack on a front more than 3,000 yards wide. Zones of action are prescribed to eliminate overlapping of units and prevent them from being impeded by each other when they deploy. These zones are separated from adjacent zones by boundary lines.

c. Attack from assembly area.—When it appears to German commanders that the enemy has decided to defend his position or that he has a considerable advantage in his preparation for combat, German troops are first deployed and made ready for the attack. Terrain for the assembly of the infantry is considered favorable

Figure 183.—37-mm antitank gun with crew in position during street fighting in the Russian Ukraine sector.

when there is cover and concealment and when it can be assumed that the infantry, under the protection of heavy supporting weapons, will advance easily. The Germans believe that terrain which is suitable either for development or for observation posts must be seized as soon as it moves into its assembly position. German infantry must undertake reconnaissance missions. While the infantry is deploying, the artillery is brought up. Observation posts and firing positions are chosen with the idea of possible future concentration of fire against decisive targets. The infantry must communicate all details of the attack to the artillery so that the artillery may be prepared to give the advancing units full support. The initial assembly must be accomplished in such a manner that the various missions which arise during the attack will be fulfilled from the first positions occupied.

d. Attack on position.—(1) In attacking an enemy position frontally, the Germans believe the execution of the assault should depend upon how the attacker can employ his forces and supplies in regard to time and space. Thus if his resources are insufficient for a penetration, the objective must be limited. The requirement for such an attack will depend upon the nature and strength of the enemy defenses. In order to make sure that the main weight of the attack is directed against those points of the enemy lines where possession will be a determining factor in the battle, the Germans stress the necessity for careful and complete reconnaissance before the action begins. The mass of attacking infantry must remain outside the range of enemy artillery.

(2) Strong forces of infantry are concentrated against the most important points in the enemy's lines. The Germans believe that points of penetration should not be too narrow, in order that their troops may not be exposed to too concentrated a fire by enemy forces. The stronger the enemy is, the more the action must be divided into several successive attacks with limited objectives. Since enemy artillery is already in place and ready to fire, the initial assembly of German artillery is undertaken with the greatest care.

(3) The German commander's plan of attack provides the basis for the detailed use of the support weapons. The firing charts for both the artillery weapons and the infantry support weapons must be coordinated, and one of the most important features is the consideration of all known obstacles blocking the attack. Such obstacles, as well as any new obstacle, revealing themselves during

the course of the attack must be overcome. German tactical doctrine emphasizes that in the course of attacks against positions, artillery and infantry will almost always alternate. Germans use combat engineers during assaults for the destruction of obstacles, including the removal of mines. The closest contact is maintained with the retreating enemy, and combat engineers and artillery are brought forward at once to exploit any successes which may be achieved.

e. Development of attack.—According to German training regulations, once the attack has been undertaken, either from a meeting engagement or out of an assembly area, it may assume one of the five following forms:

(1) *Frontal attack.*—The frontal attack is directed against an enemy front line and is the most frequent form of attack. It usually leads to hard fighting and almost always requires considerable superiority.

(2) *Penetration.*—A successfully conducted frontal attack produces a penetration. Through rupture of the enemy front after a complete break-through, it may lead to great success.

(3) *Enveloping attack.*—An enveloping attack is directed against the wings and flanks of the enemy. The deeper the attack against the flanks or the rear of the enemy is carried, the greater are the possibilities of destroying him. The envelopment of both wings requires considerable superiority.

(4) *Flanking attack.*—The flanking attack develops either from the direction of the approach march or through a turning movement. The enemy must be surprised and deceived. Under unusual circumstances, an attack from the rear may result from the approach march or the turning movement. Such an attack, if launched as a surprise and with strong forces, may be even more effective than the flanking attack.

(5) *Limited objective attack.*—The attack with a limited objective strives to bring about a success of limited extent in a particular area. Its execution is not different from that of other forms of attack.

118. Pursuit.—*a. General.*—German tactical doctrine stresses the necessity for boldness, ruthlessness, and frequently complete independence of action, even by junior officers, in carrying out pursuit missions. In order to win complete success, German commanders are taught to start pursuit immediately, even if their troops are exhausted. In pursuit, particular attention is paid to reconnaissance so that the commander may be informed at all times of the situation at the most advanced lines. Special emphasis is placed upon keeping the commander informed as to the commitment of supporting artillery and air units. Fast-moving troops, preferably motorized units, are used in pursuit wherever possible.

b. Missions of units in pursuit.—The infantry scatters the enemy, outflanks strongpoints, and leaves their final destruction to units following in the rear. Part of the artillery pounds all avenues of escape, while other guns are advanced to a point where they can effectively shell enemy rear areas. Combat engineers who are not used to block roads which the enemy is using to escape are employed to repair damaged roads and speed the arrival of fresh troops, ammunition, matériel, and rations. The signal battalion extends the trunk lines up to the area immediately behind the most advanced front lines in order that the commander may conduct operations according to plan. Crossing of boundary lines between units should not halt the pursuit; it can be halted only on the express orders of the task force commander.

119. Defense.—*a. Main position.*—The Germans call the area in which troops defend themselves the position (*Stellung*), while the section of the front in width is called the sector (*Abschnitt*). The main part of the position is known as the main zone of resistance (*Hauptkampffeld*), which is limited toward the front by the most important part of the defensive position, namely, the main line of resistance (*Hauptkampflinie*, or *HKL*). German troops have orders to hold this line until they are overrun and destroyed or until they receive specific orders to retreat. The defense of the main zone of resistance is secured by the organization in depth of all committed troops so that the enemy will not be able to overcome their firepower by concentrating his own on massed targets. Although the sectors vary in width, the Germans believe that the width of the sector occupied by troops in defense should be about twice the width which the same troops would occupy if they were attacking.

b. Forward defensive positions.—The Germans organize the forward part of the positions into two sections: the combat outposts (*Gefechtsvorposten*) immediately in front of the *HKL*, and the forward position (*forgeschobene Stellung*) beyond it. The area in front of this last position is known as the forward area (*Vorfeld*).

c. Organization of positions.—The *HKL* is strongly fortified with trenches, barbed-wire entanglements, and obstacles distributed in depth. The most advanced installations of the main zone of resistance must be well in advance of the observation posts of the heavy infantry weapons, and of the artillery, and must be situated in such a manner that they surprise the attacking enemy. German advance positions are planned to prevent the seizure by the enemy of important terrain features and at the same time to provide good observation points for artillery. They are intended to deceive the enemy as to the location of the *HKL*. In order to make the enemy deploy his forces prematurely, German advance positions are equipped with heavy machine guns, armor-piercing weapons, and light field guns. Such outposts must hold up the enemy long enough to give the troops manning the *HKL* time to prepare for action. In order to confuse the enemy as to the disposition and strength of the artillery in defensive positions, use is made of dummy batteries, slight fire activity, and mobile batteries. Particular stress is laid upon keeping the artillery mobile.

120. Delaying actions.—*a. General.*—The Germans make extensive use of the delaying action (*hinhaltender Widerstand*).

They organize their defensive positions in great depth whenever possible and fall back slowly from forward positions, making the enemy pay the highest possible price for each individual nest of resistance which they overrun, so that if they finally reach positions which the Germans have previously prepared or which are naturally strong, they are so weakened that they may not be able to storm them. Such defense is strengthened by strongpoints on the flanks of the successive defensive lines, equipped with light artillery or heavy machine guns and known as *Aufnahmestellungen* (rallying points).

b. Counterattacks.—The Germans believe in continual counterattacks to slow down the progress of advancing enemy forces, and these are usually delivered against the flanks of hostile troops.

121. Breaking off combat.—In engagements where the Germans break off combat in order to withdraw, they make great use of delaying positions in order to facilitate the movement of the main body of their forces, particularly if the latter are involved in heavy fighting. The Germans often engage in brief actions in order to cover such withdrawals, thereby winning the freedom of action which they regard as vital for such an operation. They also often withdraw during the night so that their movements can be covered by darkness.

122. Withdrawal.—*a. General.*—German commanders withdraw only when they feel that every possible chance of success has been exploited, or when the cost of holding a certain area is out of all proportion to the possible advantages. In order to facilitate withdrawals, the Germans enforce absolute march discipline on the retiring columns. They also use their mobile troops, particularly antitank units, to keep the enemy from pressing them too hard. Traffic on roads is controlled by specially detailed traffic officers, while radio traffic is reduced to a minimum in order to hinder the enemy from intercepting orders which would give him a clue as to troop movements.

b. Disengagement.—After the infantry has been disengaged on a wide front, it takes advantage of the road net and the protection of artillery fire to retire. The heavy batteries are withdrawn first, while the light batteries are the last to go. The rear guard covers the disengagement of the main body, feigning the occupation of former positions. Once this mission has been fulfilled, the rear guard withdraws to the delaying positions.

Section XVII

PERMANENT FORTIFICATIONS

	Paragraph
Basic principles	123
West Wall	124
Beach defenses	125

123. Basic principles.—*a. General.*—An integral element in Germany's concept of warfare is the provision of strong permanent fortifications. The German doctrine, however, has always emphasized that these fortifications are in fact offensive rather than defensive in character, since they make it possible to concentrate a relatively large proportion of the field forces for action at any given point.

b. Organization of terrain.—The fundamental principle upon which German permanent fortifications are designed is organization of the terrain in great depth. This includes extensive use of obstacles, covering the terrain by fire from fortified works, employment of additional artillery fire from open emplacements, and provision for antiaircraft defense. A comparison with the French Maginot Line shows that the German permanent fortifications are organized in much greater depth and generally use a larger number of smaller works. In any German system of fortifications the obstacles are unusually formidable and much of the fire is delivered from fortified works. Carefully planned counterattacks by battalions, regiments, or larger units from concealed, shellproof shelters are considered an important element of the defense.

124. West Wall.—*a. General.*—The classic example of the German system of permanent fortifications is the West Wall. However, fortifications similar to those of the West Wall have on occasion been constructed on a smaller scale in other localities, as, for example, along the former German-Polish border. Construction of the West Wall itself was begun in 1938 and was almost completed within a period of 1 year. This rapid construction was made possible both by a concentration of all the construction resources of Germany and by the fact that the Wall itself consists of relatively small individual works.

b. Defensive belts.—The West Wall protects Germany's western frontier from about the point where the Rhine River flows into Holland to the Swiss frontier. The total depth of the fortified area varies from 8 to 15 miles. The "air defense zone," in which are located the antiaircraft defenses, includes the first and second fortified belts and extends to the rear an additional 10 to 30 miles. Considered from front to rear, the Wall consists in general of the following defensive belts:

(1) An area of field fortifications, including trenches, barbed-wire entanglements, machine-gun emplacements, observation posts, and artillery emplacements. (See figs. 184 and 185.)

(2) A fortified belt from 2,000 to 4,000 yards deep, consisting of fortified works and artillery emplacements. In general, this belt of fortified works is from 5 to 8 miles to the rear of the field fortifications.

(3) Another fortified belt similar to, but in general not so strong as, the forward belt. There is a gap of from 8 to 10 miles between the two belts, with isolated fortified works located at critical points.

c. Typical section of fortified belt.—A section of one of the fortified belts of the West Wall involves the following series of fortifications:

(1) A continuous band of antitank obstacles.
(2) One or more continuous bands of wire entanglements.

(3) A deep zone of fortified works, the fire from which covers the obstacles and all the terrain.

(4) Fortified shelters, without armament, for quartering troops. (See fig. 186.)

(5) Artillery emplacements.

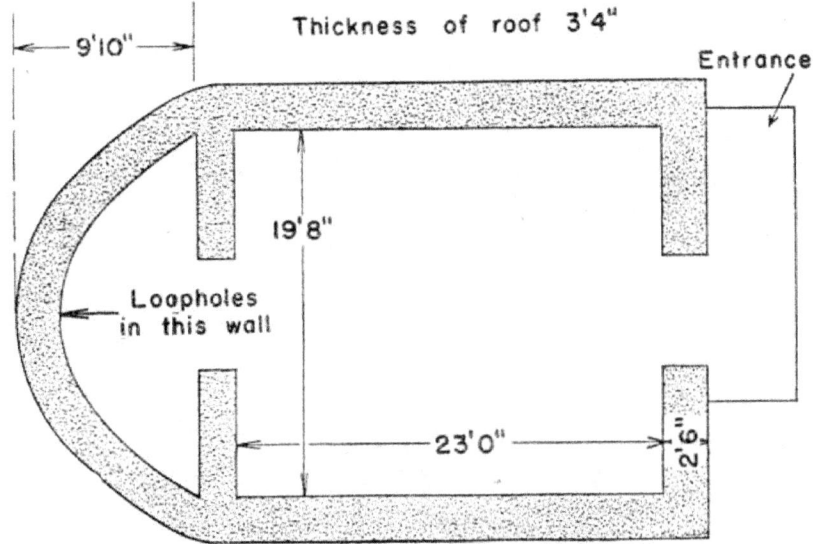

Figure 184.—Underground emplacement.

d. Individual defenses.—(1) *Antitank obstacles.*—The most commonly used antitank obstacle of the West Wall is the so-called "dragon's teeth" (fig. 187). This consists of four to eight rows of truncated pyramids made of reinforced concrete, cast in a single-block base. The truncated pyramids increase in height from front to rear, and an additional "tooth" is placed in each interval of the rear row. On occasion, the obstacle is reinforced by an antitank ditch dug immediately in front of it. The dragon's teeth obstacle has been developed as the result of experience. Originally it consisted only of four rows of "teeth"; additional

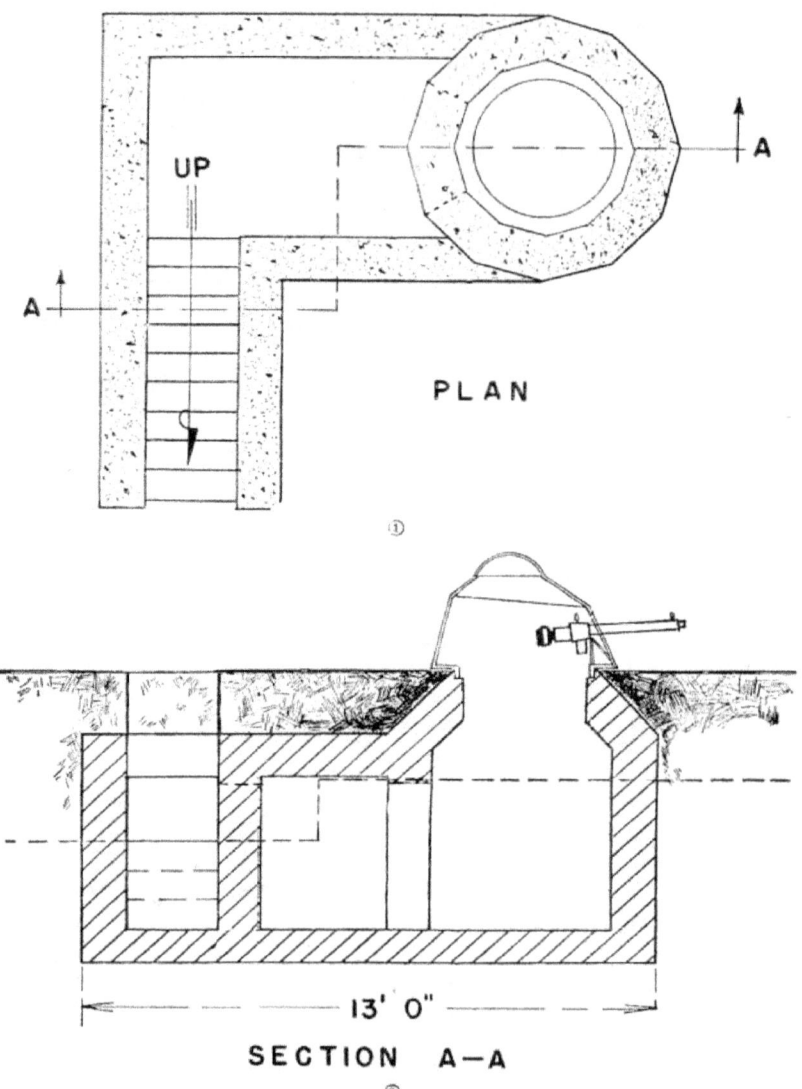

Figure 185.—Emplacement with a tank turret.

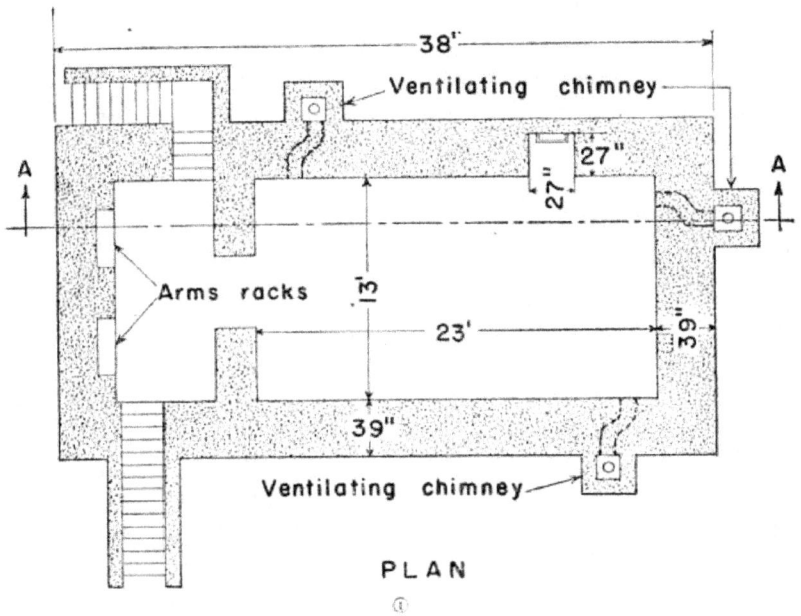

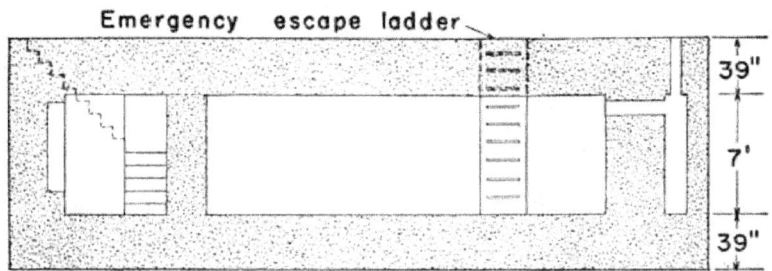

Figure 186.—Rectangular shelter.

rows, the antitank ditch, and the "tooth" between each of the rear intervals were added in order to withstand improved models of tanks. The obstacle may be overcome by bridging, by demolitions, or by gunfire. The gunfire method may be applied by tank units themselves. About 5 to 10 rounds per tooth from a 75-mm gun would be required in order to effect a passage for tanks. The other type of antitank obstacle used extensively in the West Wall is the so-called "angle-iron grill" consisting of a continuous row of frames made up of steel sections. The forward face of the obstacle presents a concave wall which cannot be climbed by a tank. The curved-frame obstacle may be destroyed by engineer demolition or by gunfire.

(2) *Wire entanglements.*—The standard German wire entanglement is similar to, but lower and wider than, the U. S. double-apron fence. The wire entanglements of the West Wall are placed immediately in the rear of the antitank obstacles.

(3) *Fortified works.*—The fortified works in the West Wall are of several types with many variations in detail. In general, the works are designed to deliver fire both to the front and to the flanks. In this respect they differ from French works in that the latter were often designed for fire to the flank only. The German works are rarely provided with turrets, and such turrets as they have, unlike those of the Maginot Line, are of the fixed (nonrevolving, nondisappearing) type. The German works are located so as to be mutually supporting. They are usually entered by tunnels leading from defiladed points in the rear. The same system of tunnels may serve many individual works.

(4) *Artillery emplacements.*—The bulk of the artillery used to defend the West Wall would be held mobile so as to be employed for mass effect at decisive points. Artillery positions are prepared throughout the defended zones. These positions are constructed in order to afford some protection for personnel and ammunition, and are provided with an underground communication system. Observation posts are located in permanent works, usually turreted bunkers.

Figure 187.—Dragon's teeth antitank obstacles.

(5) *Intermediate works.*—The individual fortifications located in the area between fortified belts are similar to the works described above. They are also protected by obstacles on all sides.

(6) *Antiaircraft defense.*—The antiaircraft defenses of the West Wall include the following:

(*a*) Antiaircraft listening devices.

(*b*) Antiaircraft searchlight batteries.

(*c*) Aircraft warning service.

(*d*) Balloon barrage system.

(*e*) Air-raid alarm service.

(*f*) Smoke screen facilities.

(*g*) Antiaircraft guns of all calibers.

(*h*) Pursuit aircraft.

(7) *Camouflage.*—All fortifications, emplacements, and other parts of the West Wall system are carefully camouflaged according to the most modern methods.

125. Beach defenses.—*a. General.*—The Germans have built or are building fortifications and defensive works all the way along the Atlantic coast line from North Cape to the Bay of Biscay. These works vary greatly, depending on local topography and the relative importance of the areas in which they are located. In addition to the defense works in the west, the Germans are strengthening the coastal defenses of southern France and the Balkans, as well as those of the island of Crete. For many months, tens of thousands of men have been employed on the coastal defenses of Europe in an effort to place insuperable difficulties in the way of Allied landings. In general, beach defenses are characterized by the use of obstacles, road blocks, pillboxes, and gun emplacements, ranging from small defense works containing only a machine gun and its crew to vast concrete structures equipped with heavy, long-range artillery and protected by a series of outer works and antiaircraft batteries, some of which are mounted on concrete antiaircraft towers. Plans and pictures of various types of coastal defenses are shown in figures 188 to 191.

PERMANENT FORTIFICATIONS 125

b. *Underwater and beach obstacles.*—(1) *Steel stakes.*—At beaches where the Germans feel that landing attempts may be made, they have driven rows of steel stakes off the shore line with the tops of the stakes pointing out to sea. Additional stakes are set in concrete emplacements on the beaches themselves to prevent tanks from landing.

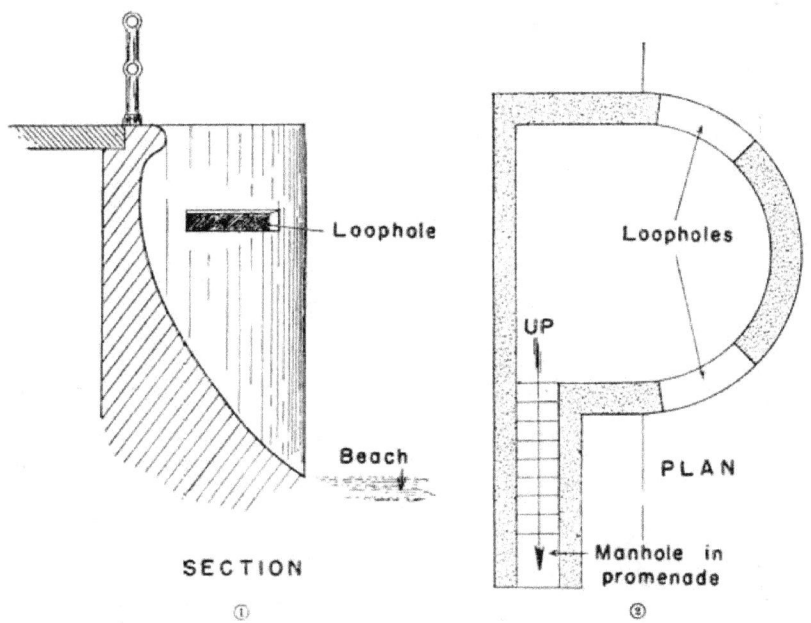

Figure 138.—Promenade emplacement designed for enfilading fire.

(2) *Beach wire.*—In shallow water at threatened beaches the Germans have placed thick belts of wire, trip wire, and wire fences to impede troops disembarking from landing craft. On the beaches themselves they have used wire entanglements consisting of extra heavy wire strung in aprons, with concertina-type coils and trip wires placed in front of it. Additional wire fences and coils of

341

125 HANDBOOK ON GERMAN MILITARY FORCES

wire are used to block ravines and gulleys leading from beaches to higher land to prevent their use by advancing troops (fig. 192).

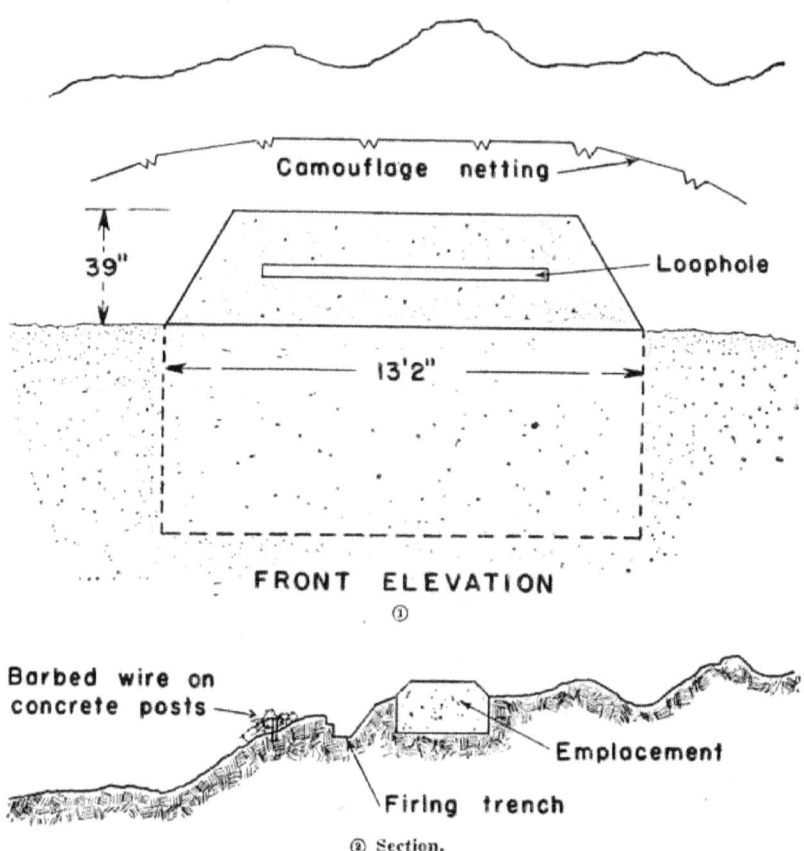

Figure 189.—Emplacement in the sand dunes in the Wassenaar district of the Netherlands.

(3) *Mines.*—The Germans have planted mine fields on beaches which might be used by landing troops. These are believed to consist mostly of mines of the 19-pound *Teller* type. In addition,

342

PERMANENT FORTIFICATIONS   125

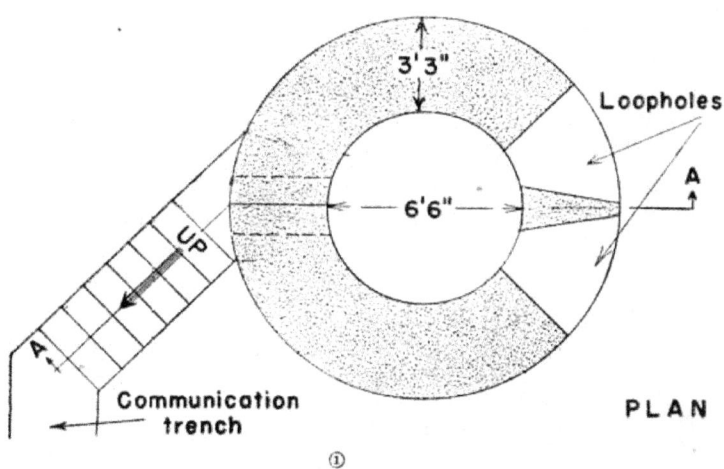

①

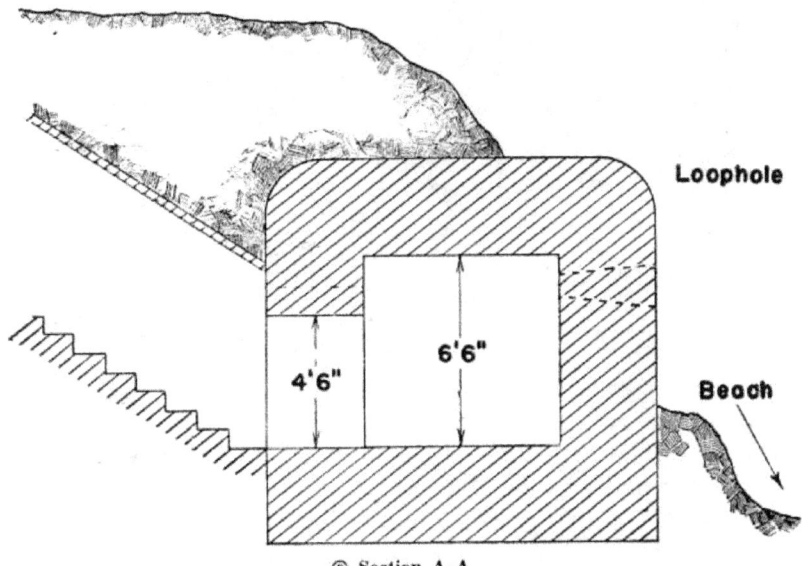

② Section A-A.
Figure 190.—Cliff pillbox.

antipersonnel mines and booby traps are used to hinder the work of removing the larger type of mines. The mine fields may also be covered by fire from artillery and machine guns.

(4) *Other obstacles.*—Near threatened beaches the Germans have constructed concrete antitank obstacles, such as "dragon's teeth," which would prevent tanks from maneuvering, while additional antitank obstacles block roads leading from landing beaches.

Figure 191.—Gun emplacement on a beach protected by barbed wire.

Such blocks are guarded by antitank guns as well as by machine-gun nests to prevent their removal by personnel. Reinforced concrete walls have been built on the shore side of beaches to make doubly certain that no attacking tanks reach open country.

(5) *Fortification of coastal towns.*—The Germans have turned many of the little towns along the French coast into semifortresses. They have walled up the windows and doorways of houses that

looked out over the sea, placed reinforced concrete machine-gun and antitank-gun emplacements along the quays, and constructed concrete walls between houses across most streets leading from the waterfront section to other areas in the town. Streets which are not blocked by walls are provided with "chevaux-de-frise," which can be moved into place at a moment's notice.

(6) *Heavier defenses.*—Further inland or on cliffs overlooking the sea and possible landing beaches the Germans have built tre-

Figure 192.—Antitank obstacles of the chevaux-de-frise trestle type.

mendous reinforced-concrete gun emplacements holding long-range artillery of the heaviest calibers. Some of these emplacements have thick reinforced concrete roofs and are protected by elaborate outworks, including concrete antiaircraft towers, four-barreled 20-mm antiaircraft guns (*Vierlingsflak*) mounted on elevators, open concrete emplacements for Army artillery, and, near the beaches, concrete emplacements for antitank guns as well as light field artillery.

345

Section XVIII
COINAGE, WEIGHTS, AND MEASURES

	Paragraph
Currency	126
Weights	127
Measures	128

126. Currency.—*a. General.*—There have been changes in the composition of German currency during the war. These changes have been caused by the scarcity of certain metals; by the demand for certain denominations owing to the increased number of small income earners; by the changes in trading practices; and by the rationing system, which tends to increase the frequency of purchases and to reduce the amount of each individual purchase. The net effect of these changes is the complete disappearance of the 2 *Pfennig* coin and the 500 *Reichsmark* note, and the replacement of 1 *RM* coins by notes. It is interesting to note that, contrary to the policy pursued under German pressure in many satellite countries, the circulation of silver coins has, as yet, not been interfered with.

b. Table of equivalents.—The *Reichsmark*, which is equivalent to 40 cents in U. S. currency, is the standard unit of money in Germany.

German	U. S. equivalent
Copper and zinc coins:	
1 Pfennig	0.4 cent.
2 Pfennige	0.8 cent.
5 Pfennige	2 cents.
10 Pfennige	4 cents.
50 Pfennige	20 cents.
Nickel and silver coins:	
1 Reichsmark	40 cents.
2 Reichsmark	80 cents.
5 Reichsmark	$2.00.
Paper currency:	
10 Reichsmark	$4.00.

127. Weights.—*a. Solids.*

German	U. S. equivalent
Gramm	15.43 grains troy.
Milligramm	0.01543 grain.
Zentigramm	0.15432 grain.
Dezigramm	1.543 grains.
Dekagramm	6.43 pennyweight.
Hektogramm	3.527 ounces avoirdupois.
Kilogramm	2.204 pounds avoirdupois.
Zentner	110.2 pounds avoirdupois.
Doppelzentner	220.4 pounds avoirdupois.
Tonne	0.9842 ton (2,000 pounds).

b. Liquids.

Liter	1.759 pints.
Zentiliter	0.017 pint.
Deziliter	0.17 pint.
Dekaliter	2.200 gallons.
Hektoliter	22.00 gallons.

128. Measures.—*a. Linear.*

Kilometer	3,280.8 feet.
Meter	3.2808 feet.
Millimeter	0.039370 inch.
Zentimeter	0.393701 inch.
Dezimeter	3.9370 inches.

b. Square.

Quadratmeter	1.1960 square yards.
Quadratzentimeter	0.15500 square inch.
Ar	119.60 square yards.
Hektar	2.4711 acres.

c. Cubic.

Kubikmeter	1.3079 cubic yards.
Kubikzentimeter	0.06100 cubic inch.

d. *Calibers of guns.*[1]

German	U. S. equivalent
1 mm	.0393 inch.
7.92 mm	.311 inch.
10 mm	.393 inch.
13.2 mm	.518 inch.
2 cm	.79 inch.
3.7 cm	1.45 inches.
4.7 cm	1.85 inches.
7.5 cm	2.95 inches.
7.7 cm	3.03 inches.
8.1 cm	3.16 inches.
8.8 cm	3.46 inches.
10.5 cm	4.14 inches.
15 cm	5.91 inches.
17 cm	6.69 inches.
21 cm	8.26 inches.
28 cm	11.02 inches.
35 cm	13.78 inches.
38 cm	14.96 inches.
42 cm	16.53 inches.

[1] See p. 73, note 1, and par. 55.

INDEX

	Paragraph	Page
Active service	21	27
Adjutant's Office	14	19
Administration, command, and staff:		
Organization of High Command in War	14	16
Organization of subordinate commands	15	21
Regional organization	16	24
Administration Office	14	21
Administration Service	94	217
Aerial bombs	92	190
Aerial defense system	107	244
Aerial spray	92	190
Agents, chemical	92	188
Airborne forces	107	253
Airborne troops	111	317
Aircraft:		
Arado 196, standard catapult plane	109	294
Blohm-Voss 138, flying boat	109	294
D.F.S. 230, glider	109	294
Dornier 217, long-range bomber	109	284
Fieseler Storch 156, short-range reconnaissance plane	109	290
Focke-Wulf 189, short-range reconnaissance plane	109	290
Focke-Wulf 190, single-engine fighter	109	271
Focke-Wulf 200 Kurier, long-range bomber	109	286
Gotha 242, glider	109	296
Gotha 244, glider	109	296
Heinkel 111, twin-engine medium bomber	109	282
Heinkel 177, long-range bomber	109	286
Henschel 126, Army cooperation plane	109	290
Henschel 129, ground-attack plane	109	280
Junkers 52, transport plane	109	276
Junkers 87 (*Stuka*), dive bomber	109	276
Junkers 88, long-range bomber	109	284
Junkers 88C, twin-engine fighter	109	276

INDEX

	Paragraph	Page
Aircraft—Continued.		
Messerschmitt 109, single-engine fighter	109	270
Messerschmitt 110, twin-engine fighter	109	273
Messerschmitt 210, twin-engine fighter	109	273
Messerschmitt 323, glider-transport	109	296
Aircraft armament:		
M.G. 15, standard rifle-caliber free gun	109	301
M.G. 17, standard rifle-caliber fixed gun	109	301
M.G. 81, newest rifle-caliber free gun	109	301
M.G. 131, standard defense weapon	109	302
M.G. 151, Mauser cannon	109	302
M.K. 101, 30-mm gun	109	302
Oerlikon FF, standard fixed gun	109	302
Air defense	107	244
Air Force:		
Aircraft	109	269
Arms and services	107	243
Army and Navy cooperation	108	264
Chain of command	106	232
Equipment	109	269
Fighting units	107	257
General Staff	105	228
High Command	105	228
Organization	104	227
Parachute and airborne troops	107	253
Rear echelon	105	229
Reconnaissance units	113	322
Supply	105	229
Tactics	111	310
Training	110	304
Uniforms and insignia	32	43
Air gunner training	110	308
Air Ministry	105	228
Air raid precautions	107	247
Air Signal Service	107	249
Air transport	107	257
Ammunition supply	55, 62, 68, 92	82, 102, 128, 200
Antiaircraft defenses	107, 124	243, 340
Antigas equipment	91	186
Antipersonnel traps and mines	78	154

INDEX

	Paragraph	Page
Antitank:		
Battalions	64	104
Mines	78, 79	153, 155
Obstacles	79, 124	155, 335
Units	64	104
Weapons	53, 68	75, 120
Arado 196, standard catapult plane	109	294
Argus 410, 12-cylinder airplane engine	109	299
Armament:		
Artillery regiments (divisional)	57	86
Bicycle battalions	48	63
Engineer battalions	70	129
Infantry battalion	38	55
Infantry division	9	11
Infantry regiment	37	53
Light division	13	13
Motorcycle battalion	42	59
Motorized antiaircraft machine-gun battalion	44	60
Motorized infantry division	10	11
Motorized infantry regiment (*Mot.*)	39	57
Motorized infantry regiment (*Panzer-Grenadier*)	40	58
Mountain division	12	13
Mountain infantry regiment	41	58
Panzer division	11	13
Reconnaissance battalions	47	62
Signal battalions	84	163
Tank units	64	104
Armament of signal personnel	86	167
Armed Forces	14	16
Armed Forces GHQ signal regiment	83	162
Armed Forces High Command	14	16
Armed Forces Operations Staff	14	17
Armies	7	7
Armored cars	67	118
Armored combat vehicles	67	111
Armored division. (*See* Panzer troops.)		
Arms and services (Air Force)	107	243
Arms and services (Army)	6	6
Army:		
Attached officers	15	23
GHQ allotment	8	7

INDEX

	Paragraph	Page
Army—Continued.		
Insignia	31	41
Pay and allowances	27	35
Recruitment and mobilization	20, 29	27, 37
Types of armies	7	7
Uniforms	30	38
Army and Navy cooperation (Air Force)	108	264
Army antiaircraft battalion (GHQ)	59	100
Army auxiliaries	103	225
Army corps and *Wehrkreise*	7, 16	6, 24
Army General Staff	14	19
Army GHQ signal regiment	83	162
Army group (*Heeresgruppe*)	7	7
Army High Command	14	18
Artillery. (*See* Field Artillery.)		
Artillery commanders	58	96
Artillery emplacements	124	338
Artillery regiments	57	86
Artillery gas shells	92	191
Artillery staff	58	96
Assault Badge	35	49
Assault boats	75	144
Assault detachments	71	135
Attached officers	15	23
Attacks, kinds of	117	325
Automatic small arms	52	69
Auxiliary organizations	33, 103	44, 225
Bangalore torpedoes	80	157
Battalions:		
Antitank	64	107
Bicycle	48	63
Chemical warfare	90	184
Engineer	70	129
GHQ	59, 65, 71	97, 108, 135
Infantry	38	55
Motorcycle	42	59
Motorized antiaircraft machine-gun	44	60
Motorized machine-gun	43	60
Reconnaissance	47	62
Signal	84	163
Tank	64	104

INDEX

	Paragraph	Page
Bayonets	51	68
Beach defenses	125	340
Bicycle battalions	48	63
Blister gases	92	189
Blohm-Voss 138, flying boat	109	294
B.M.W. 801, 14-cylinder airplane engine	109	300
Boats	75	144
Bomber crew training	110	305
Bombing	111	311
Bombs, aerial	92	190
Bombs, incendiary	92	200
Breaking off combat (tactics)	121	332
Bridge-building battalions	71	135
Bridge column trailers	81	158
Bridges	75, 76, 77	144, 151, 153
Bridging columns	70, 71	131, 135
B ponton and trestle equipment	75	144
Calibers of guns	128	348
Camouflage	124	340
Campaign decorations	35	49
Cantonments	26	34
Carbine	51	67
Cartographic battalions	59	100
Cavalry and reconnaissance units:		
Bicycle battalions	48	63
Mounted cavalry units	49	64
Reconnaissance battalion	47	62
Chain of command	106	232
Chemical aerial bombs	92	190
Chemical (smoke) regiments	90	184
Chemical warfare troops:		
Battalions	90	185
Defense	91	185
Equipment	91, 92	186, 190
Offensive warfare	92	188
Organization and administration	90	183
Regiments	90	184
Uniform	30	40
Weapons	92	190
Chief of Signal Communications	83	161

INDEX

	Paragraph	Page
Chief of the Mobile Troops	14	21
Choking gases	92	189
Cipher equipment	87	179
Classification (active and reserve)	21	27
Coast defense	109, 125	294, 340
Coinage, weights, and measures:		
Currency	126	346
Measures	128	347
Weights	127	347
Colors	31, 32	41, 43
Combat engineers (GHQ)	71	135
Combat reconnaissance	113	321
Combat vehicles	67	111
Commander-in-Chief of the Air Force	105	228
Communications. (See Signal troops.)		
Composition and Strength. (See Armament, Personnel, Transport.)		
Compressors	74	142
Construction troops	72	139
Corps	7, 8, 15, 84	6, 8, 23, 165
Counterattack	120	332
C ponton and trestle equipment	75	148
Crew training (Air Force)	110	309
Crimea Shield	35	50
Criminal Investigation Police	101	225
Currency	126	346
C. V. P. 1 antitank mine (Hungarian)	78	154
Czech *CZDV8H* tank	67	118
D.B. *605*, 12-cylinder airplane engine	109	300
D.B. *606*, 24-cylinder airplane engine	109	300
Decontaminating material	91	187
Decontamination battalion	90	185
Decontamination vehicles	91	187
Decorations and awards	35	47
Defensive belts (fortifications)	124	334
Delaying actions (tactics)	120	331
Demolition equipment	73	140
Deployment of troops	116	325
Detectors, gas	91	188
D.F.S. *230*, glider	109	294

INDEX

	Paragraph	Page
Direction finders	87	172
Distinguishing colors	31, 32	41, 43
Dive bombers	109	276
Dive bombing	111	313
Divisional artillery	57	86
Divisions:		
Cavalry	7, 49	6, 64
Frontier guard	7	6
Infantry	7, 9	6, 11
Light	7, 13	6, 13
Mobilization	7	6
Motorized	7, 10	6, 11
Mountain	7, 12	6, 13
Panzer	7, 11	6, 13
Reserve	7	6
Security	7	6
Special duty	7	6
Do-Gerät	92	191
Dogs	85	166
Dönitz, Karl	14	17
Dornier 217, long-range bomber	109	284
D ponton and trestle equipment	75	148
Draft procedure	22	28
Dragon's teeth	79	156
Dual-purpose machine gun	52	72
East Medal	35	50
80-mm mortar	52	74
Einheit principle	5	3
Electrical and mechanical equipment	74	142
Elementary booby traps	78	154
Elite Guard	100	222
Engineers:		
Antitank obstacles	79	155
Battalions	70	129
Construction troops	72	139
Demolition equipment	73	140
Electrical and mechanical equipment	74	142
Fixed bridges	76	151
Floating equipment	75	144
GHQ units	71	135
Mines	78	153

INDEX

	Paragraph	Page
Engineers—Continued.		
Organization	69	128
Portable tank bridges	77	153
Special equipment for use in assault	80	156
Vehicles	81	158
Engineer landing companies	71	136
Engineer parks	71	137
Engineer specialist companies	71	138
Engines	109	296
Enveloping attack (tactics)	117	329
Equipment:		
Air Force	109	269
Chemical warfare	91, 92	186, 190
Demolition	73	140
Electrical and mechanical	74	142
Engineer	73, 74, 75	140, 142, 144
Floating	75	144
Personal	30	39
Signal troops	87	167
Exploders	73	142
Explosives	73	140
Felled trees	79	156
Female signal operations battalion	83	163
Ferry construction battalions	71	136
Field artillery:		
Ammunition	62	102
Commanders and staffs	58	96
Divisional	57	86
GHQ units	59	97
Methods of fire	61	102
Nomenclature	60	101
Organization	56	83
Field blouse	30	39
Field cap	30	39
Field generating sets	74	142
Field Postal Service	97	220
Field searchlight projectors	74	142
Field uniform	30	38
Fieseler Storch 156, short-range reconnaissance plane	109	290

INDEX

	Paragraph	Page
50-mm antitank gun, *Pak 38*	53	78
50-mm mortar	52	73
Fighter tactics	111	315
Fighting units (Air Force)	107	257
Firepower. (*See* Armament.)		
Flame-throwers	80, 92	156, 194
Flame-thrower GHQ tank battalion	65	108
Flanking attack	117	329
Fliegerdivision (Air Force)	106	234
Fliegerführer	106	238
Fliegerkorps	106	233
Flight engineer training	110	308
Floating equipment	75	144
F.M.W. 132, 9-cylinder airplane engine	109	299
Focke-Wulf 189, short-range reconnaissance plane	109	290
Focke-Wulf 190, single-engine fighter	109	271
Focke-Wulf 200 Kurier, long-range bomber	109	286
Food rations	93	215
Foreign tanks	67	118
Formation of staffs	15	22
Fortified works	124	338
Fortress engineers (GHQ)	71	139
Frontages	117, 119	325, 330
Frontal attack	117	329
Fuel supply	93	216
Fuzes	73	141
Gas	92	188
Gas defense training	91	185
Gas detectors	91	188
Gas grenades	92	192
Gas masks	91	186
Gas mines	92	194
Gas protective ointment	91	188
Gastilt	91	187
Gendarmerie	101	225
General Army Office	14	20
General principles of organization	5	3
General *SS*	100	222
General Staff	14, 105	19, 228
German Cross	35	48

INDEX

	Paragraph	Page
German time-delay railway mine	78	154
Gewehr 41, 7.92-mm rifle 41	51	68
GHQ troops:		
Army allotment	8	8
Artillery units	59	97
Bicycle battalion	48	63
Chemical warfare units	90	184
Corps allotment	8	8
Engineer units	71	135
Organization	8	7
Panzer units	63	103
Signal units	83	161
Tank units	65	108
Gliders	109	294
Göring, Hermann	14	17
Gotha 242, glider	109	296
Gotha 244, glider	109	296
Grenade charge	80	157
Grenades	51, 92	68, 192
Grenadier, motorized infantry (Panzer)	40	58
Grof, medium-weight flame-thrower	80	157
Ground-attack planes	109	280
Ground listening sets	87	172
Gruppe	106	236
Guns, artillery	57	91
Half-track tractor (engineer)	81	158
Hand grenades	51	68
Heavy antitank battalion (GHQ)	65	108
Heavy artillery	60	101
Heavy chemical (smoke) regiment	90	184
Heavy machine gun	52	71
Heavy tank battalion (GHQ)	65	108
Heavy tanks	67	118
Heinkel 111, twin-engine medium bomber	109	282
Heinkel 177, long-range bomber	109	286
Helmet	30	39
Henschel 126, Army cooperation plane	109	290
Henschel 129, ground-attack plane	109	280
Herbert bridge	75	149
High Command	14, 105	16, 228
Higher units, organization of	7	6

INDEX

	Paragraph	Page
Himmler, Heinrich	99	222
Hitler, Adolf	14	17
Hitler Youth	103	227
Hollow demolition charges	80	157
Hollow ring charges	80	158
Horse protection	91	188
Housing	26	34
Howitzers	54	80
Identification, means of	34	45
Identification tag	34	45
Igniters	73	141
Improvised bridges	76	153
Incendiaries	92	200
Independent chemical warfare battalions	90	184
Independent signal companies	83	162
Infantry:		
Ammunition	55	82
Infantry battalion	38	55
Infantry division	9	11
Infantry regiment	37	53
Motorcycle battalion	42	59
Motorized antiaircraft machine-gun battalion	44	60
Motorized infantry regiment (*Mot.*)	39	57
Motorized infantry regiment (*Panzer-Grenadier*)	40	58
Motorized machine-gun battalion	43	60
Mountain infantry regiment	41	58
Organization	36	52
Security regiment	45	61
Weapons	50	65
Infantry ammunition	55	82
Infantry Assault Badge	35	48
Infantry battalions	38	55
Infantry division:		
Antitank battalion	64	107
Armament	9	11
Artillery regiment	57	87
Engineer battalion	70	129
Infantry regiment	37	53
Organization	9	11
Personnel	9	11
Reconnaissance battalion	47	62

INDEX

	Paragraph	Page
Infantry division—Continued.		
Signal battalion	84	163
Transport	9	11
Infantry divisional reconnaissance	47	62
Infantry regiment	37	53
Infantry support artillery	54	80
Infantry weapons:		
Ammunition	55	82
Antitank weapons	53	75
Automatic small arms and mortars	52	69
Infantry support artillery	54	80
Small arms and hand grenades	51	65
Insignia:		
Air Force	32	43
Army	31	41
Militarized and auxiliary organizations	33	44
National Socialist Aviation Corps	33	45
National Socialist Motor Corps	33	44
Rank	31, 32	42, 43
Reich Labor Service	33	45
Storm Troopers	33	44
Technical Emergency Corps	33	45
Unit	31	41
Waffen-SS	33	44
Inspectorate of Cadet Schools	14	21
Inspector of Signal Troops	83	161
Interception receivers	87	172
Iron Cross	35	47
Jumo 207, airplane engine	109	300
Jumo 211, airplane engine	109	300
Junkers 52, transport plane	109	276
Junkers 87 ("Stuka"), dive bomber	109	276
Junkers 88, long-range bomber	109	284
Junkers 88C, twin-engine fighter	109	276
Keitel, Wilhelm	14	17
Kholm Shield	35	50
Kleif, light-weight flame-thrower	80	156
Korten, Günther	14	17
K ponton and trestle equipment	75	148
Labor service	33, 103	45, 226
Landwehr units	21, 28	27, 37

INDEX

	Paragraph	Page
Level bombing	114	311
Light division	13	13
Light machine gun	52	71
Light signals	87	180
Light support weapons	52	69
Light tanks	67	111
Light-weight *Kleif*, flame-thrower	80, 92	156, 194
Line construction	87	180
Long-range air reconnaissance	108	267
Long-range bombers	109	280
L.P.Z. antitank mine	78	153
Luftflotte	106	233
Luftgau	106	239
Luger pistol	51	65
L.Z. bridge	76	151
Machine guns:		
M.G. *34*, 7.92-mm	52	71
M.G. *42*, 7.92-mm dual-purpose	52	72
Maintenance of tanks	66	108
Maneuvers	25	33
March-combat groups	5	5
Marches (tactics)	114	322
Mauser carbine, model 98 K	51	67
Means of identification	34	45
Measures	128	347
Mechanical equipment	74	142
Medals	35	47
Medical Service	95	218
Medium artillery	60	101
Medium tanks	67	113
Medium-weight *Grof*, flame-thrower	80	157
Meeting engagement (tactics)	115	324
Meisel, Wilhelm	14	17
Memel Medal	35	51
Memorial Medal	35	51
Message throwers and projectors	87	180
Messengers	85	166
Messerschmitt 109, single-engine fighter	109	270
Messerschmitt 110, twin-engine fighter	109	273
Messerschmitt 210, twin-engine fighter	109	273

INDEX

	Paragraph	Page
Messerschmitt 323, glider-transport	109	296
Meteorological services	107	262
Methods of fire	61	102
M.G. 15, standard Air Force rifle-caliber free gun	109	301
M.G. 17, standard Air Force rifle-caliber fixed gun	109	301
M.G. 34, 7.92-mm machine gun	52	71
M.G. 42, 7.92-mm dual-purpose machine gun	52	72
M.G. 81, newest Air Force rifle-caliber free gun	109	301
M.G. 131, standard Air Force defense weapon	109	302
M.G. 151, 15-mm aircraft cannon	109	302
Militarized and auxiliary organizations	33, 103	44, 225
Militarized police	102	225
Military districts	16	24
Military Police	98	221
Military service law	18	26
Mine detectors	74	142
Mine exploding nets	80	158
Mines	78, 79, 125	153, 155, 342
Minister of Aviation	105	228
M.K. 101, 30-mm aircraft gun	109	302
Mobile laundries	91	187
Mobilization	28, 29	37
Model 98K, Mauser carbine	51	67
Mortars	52	73
Motorboats	81	158
Motorcycle battalion	42	59
Motorized antiaircraft machine-gun battalion	44	60
Motorized antitank battalion	64	107
Motorized artillery regiment	57	93
Motorized decontamination companies	90	185
Motorized engineer battalion	70	131
Motorized infantry division:		
Antitank battalion	64	107
Armament strength	10	11
Artillery regiment	57	93
Engineer battalion	70	131
Infantry regiment	39	57
Motorcycle battalion	10	11
Organization	10	11

INDEX

	Paragraph	Page
Motorized infantry division—Continued.		
Panzer battalion	64	106
Panzer reconnaissance battalion	47	63
Personnel strength	10	11
Signal battalion	84	164
Transport strength	10	11
Motorized infantry regiment (*Mot.*)	39	57
Motorized infantry regiment (*Panzer-Grenadier*)	40	58
Motorized machine-gun battalion	43	60
Motorized reconnaissance battalion	47	62
Motor transport. (See Transport.)		
Mountain antitank battalion	64	107
Mountain artillery regiment	57	94
Mountain bicycle battalion	48	64
Mountain division:		
Antitank battalion	64	107
Armament strength	12	13
Artillery regiment	57	94
Bicycle battalion	48	64
Engineer battalion	70	133
Infantry regiment	41	58
Organization	12	13
Personnel strength	12	13
Signal battalion	84	165
Transport strength	12	13
Uniform	30	40
Mountain engineer battalion	70	133
Mountain infantry regiment	41	58
Mountain signal battalion	84	165
Mounted cavalry units	49	64
Narvik Shield	35	49
National colors	31	41
National devices	31	41
National rosette	31	41
National Socialist Aviation Corps	33, 103	45, 227
National Socialist Motor Corps	33, 103	44, 226
Navy High Command	14	16
Nebelwerfer (smoke weapon)	92	191
Neutralization of enemy artillery	116	325
9-mm submachine gun, *Schmeisser M.P. 38*	52	69
9-mm submachine gun, *Schmeisser M.P. 40*	52	69

INDEX

	Paragraph	Page
Nitrogen mustards	92	189
Nomenclature of German artillery	60	101
Noncommissioned Officer Corps	24	31
Normal military training	25	32
Normal type GHQ tank battalion	65	108
Nose gases	92	189
Observer Corps	107	246
Observer training	110	307
Obstacles, antitank	79, 124	155, 335
Officer Corps	24	30
105-mm gun	57	93
105-mm gun-howitzer	57	87
150-mm gun	57	92
150-mm gun-howitzer	57	89
150-mm infantry howitzer	54	80
Operational reconnaisance	113	320
Operational training school	110	309
Order for attack	116	324
Ordnance	14	20
Organic tank units	64	104
Organization:		
Air Force	104	227
Cavalry and reconnaissance units	46, 47	61, 62
Chemical warfare troops	90	183
Engineer troops	69	128
Field artillery	56	86
GHQ troops	8	7
High Command	14	16
Higher units	7	6
Infantry division	9, 36	11, 52
Light division	13	13
Motorized infantry division	10	11
Mountain division	12	13
Panzer division	11	13
Principles	5	3
Signal troops	83	161
Subordinate commands	15	21
Tank units	64	104
Pack flame-thrower	80	156
Pak 37, 37-mm antitank gun	53	77
Pak 38, 50-mm antitank gun	53	78

INDEX

	Paragraph	Page
Panzer division:		
Antitank battalion	64	107
Armament strength	11	13
Artillery regiment	57	93
Engineer battalion	70	132
Motorcycle battalion	42	59
Motorized infantry brigade	40	58
Organization	11	13
Personnel strength	11	13
Reconnaissance battalion	47	62
Signal battalion	84	163
Tank battalion	64	106
Tank regiment	64	104
Transport strength	11	13
Panzer-Grenadier regiment. (*See* Motorized infantry regiment (*Panzer-Grenadier*).)		
Panzer troops:		
Antitank weapons	68	120
Armored combat vehicles	67	111
GHQ tank units	65	108
Organic tank units	64	104
Tank maintenance	66	108
Uniform	30	40
Parachute troops	30, 32, 107	40, 44, 253
Pay	27	35
Paybook	34	46
Permanent fortifications:		
Basic principles	123	333
Beach defenses	125	340
West Wall	124	334
Personnel strength:		
Artillery regiments	57	86
Bicycle battalions	48	63
Engineer battalions	70	129
Infantry battalion	38	55
Infantry division	9	11
Infantry regiment	37	55
Light division	13	13
Motorcycle battalion	42	60
Motorized antiaircraft machine gun battalion	44	60
Motorized infantry division	10	11
Motorized infantry regiment (*Mot.*)	39	57

INDEX

	Paragraph	Page
Personnel strength—Continued.		
Motorized infantry regiment (*Panzer-Grenadier*)	40	58
Mountain division	12	13
Mountain infantry regiment	41	58
Panzer division	11	13
Reconnaissance battalions	47	62
Signal battalions	84	168
Tank units	64	104
Pilot training	110	305
Pistole 08 (Luger)	51	65
Pistole 38 (Walther)	51	65
Pistols	51	65
Pneumatic boats	75	144
Pole charge	80	157
Police. (*See SS*, police, and other militarized organizations.)		
Pontons	75	144
Portable tank bridges	77	153
Power tools	74	142
Premilitary training	25	32
Preparation for attack	116	324
Principles of organization	5	3
Professional cadre	24	30
Projectors	92	191
Protection of horses	91	188
Protective clothing	91	188
Pursuit (tactics)	118	330
Pz.B. 38, 7.92-mm antitank rifle	53	75
Pz.B. 39, 7.92-mm antitank rifle	53	75
Pz.Kw. I (*Sd. Kfz. 101*), light tank	67	111
Pz.Kw. II (*Sd. Kfz. 121*), light tank	67	111
Pz.Kw. III (*Sd. Kfz. 141*), medium tank	67	113
Pz.Kw. IV (*Sd. Kfz. 161*), medium tank	67	114
Pz.Kw. V, heavy tank	67	111
Pz.Kw. VI, heavy tank	67	118
Radio	82, 87	161, 167
Railway bridges	76	153
Railway engineer parks	71	139
Railway engineer units	71	138
Railway mines	78	154
Ranks	14, 24, 31	16, 30, 42

INDEX

	Paragraph	Page
Ration supply system	93	214
Rear echelon	105	229
Reconnaissance	108, 113	266, 320
Reconnaissance battalions	47	62
Reconnaissance units	113	322
Recruitment and mobilization:		
Active and reserve categories	21	27
Housing, cantonments, and training areas	26	34
Military service law	18	26
Mobilization in the past	28	37
Pay and allowances	27	35
Period of service	19	26
Present principles of mobilization	29	37
Professional cadre	24	30
Recruitment procedure	20	27
Replacement training system	23	28
Training	25	32
Wartime modifications of draft procedure	22	28
Regiments:		
Artillery	57	86
Chemical warfare	90	183
Infantry	37	53
Motorized infantry (*Mot.*)	39	57
Motorized infantry (*Panzer-Grenadier*)	40	58
Mountain infantry	41	58
Security	45	61
Signal	83	161
Tank	64	104
Regional organization	16	24
Regular police	101	225
Reich Labor Service	33, 103	45, 226
Replacement training system	23	28
Reserve Training Unit	110	309
Reserve units, mobilization	21	27
Ricochet fire	61	102
Rifles	51	67
Road decontamination battalion	90	185
Rural Police	101	225
Schmeisser M.P. 38, 9-mm submachine gun	52	69
Schmeisser M.P. 40, 9-mm submachine gun	52	69
Sea Rescue Service	107	261

INDEX

	Paragraph	Page
Security Police	101	225
Security regiment	45	61
Self-propelled guns	59, 67	100, 111
S ponton and trestle equipment	75	149
Services. (*See* Supply and administrative services.)		
7.92-mm antitank rifle, *Pz.B. 38*	53	75
7.92-mm antitank rifle, *Pz.B. 39*	53	75
7.92-mm dual-purpose machine gun, *M.G. 42*	52	72
7.92-mm machine gun, *M.G. 34*	52	71
7.92-mm Mauser carbine	51	67
7.92-mm rifle 41 (*Gewehr 41*)	51	68
75-mm infantry howitzer	54	80
75-mm mountain howitzer	57	94
75-mm self-propelled gun	59	100
Short-range air reconnaissance	108	266
Shrapnel mines	78	154
Signal battalions	84	163
Signal troops:		
Additional communication methods	85	166
Armament of signal personnel	86	167
Composition and allotment of units	84	163
Equipment	87	167
Organization	83	161
Transportation	88	182
Weapons	86	167
Single-engine fighters	109	270
Sleeve Band for Crete	35	50
Small arms	51	65
Smoke mortars	92	192
Smoke screens	92	200
Smoke units	92	198
Somua tank (French)	67	118
Special duty uniforms	30	40
Special equipment for use in assault	80	156
SS, police, and other militarized organizations:		
Elite Guard	100	222
Militarized police	102	225
Organizations used as Army auxiliaries	103	225
Police	101	225
SS Security Service	100	225
Staff control of supply	93	201

INDEX

	Paragraph	Page
Staffel (Air Force unit)	106	237
Staff organization	15	22
State Police	101	225
Steel helmet	30	39
Storm troopers	33, 103	44, 227
Strength. (*See* Armament, Personnel, Transport.)		
Submachine guns:		
Schmeisser M.P. 38, 9-mm	52	69
Schmeisser M.P. 40, 9-mm	52	69
Subordinate commands	15	21
Sudeten Medal	35	51
Supply and administrative services:		
Administrative Service	94	217
Field Postal Service	97	220
Medical Service	95	218
Military Police	98	221
Supply	93	201
Veterinary Service	96	219
Supply columns	93	205
Supply of ammunition	93	209
Supply of fuel and tires	93	215
Supply of rations	93	214
Supply labor units	93	207
Supply repair units	93	208
Supply services	93	204
Supply service units	93	204
Supply staff control	93	201
Supply storage units	93	207
Supply transportation officers	93	204
Supply transport units	93	206
Supply troop commander	93	203
Survey and cartographic battalions	59	101
Switchboards	87	175
Tactical reconnaissance	113	320
Tactics:		
Air Force	111	310
Attack	117	325
Breaking off combat	121	332
Defense	119	330
Delaying actions	120	331
Doctrine	112	319

INDEX

	Paragraph	Page
Tactics—Continued.		
Marches	114	322
Meeting engagement	115	324
Preparation for attack	116	324
Pursuit	118	330
Reconnaissance	113	320
Withdrawal	122	332
Tank Badge	35	48
Tank battalions	64, 65	106, 108
Tank maintenance	66	108
Tank regiment	64	104
Tanks:		
Foreign	67	118
Heavy	67	118
Light	67	111
Medium	67	113
Tank units	64	104
Task force	14	17
Technical battalions	71	136
Technical Emergency Corps	103	226
Telegraph	87	175
Telephone	87	177
Tellermine	78	153
37-mm antitank gun, *Pak 37*	53	77
Time-delay railway mine	78	154
Tires	93	215
Todt Organization	103	225
Torpedo bombing	111	314
Tractors	81	158
Trailers	81	158
Training	25, 90, 110	32, 183, 304
Training areas	26	34
Training recruits	25	32
Transportation officers	93, 14	204, 19
Transportation, signal	88	182
Transport planes	109	276
Transport:		
Artillery regiments	57	86
Bicycle battalions	48	63
Engineer battalions	70	129
Infantry battalion	38	55

INDEX

	Paragraph	Page
Transport—Continued.		
Infantry division	9	11
Infantry regiment	37	53
Light division	13	13
Motorcycle battalion	42	59
Motorized antiaircraft machine-gun battalion	44	60
Motorized infantry division	10	11
Motorized infantry regiment (*Mot.*)	39	57
Motorized infantry regiment (*Panzer-Grenadier*)	40	58
Mountain division	12	13
Panzer division	11	13
Reconnaissance battalions	47	62
Signal battalions	84	168
Tank units	64	104
Traps and mines (antipersonnel)	78	154
Trestle equipment	75	144
Tross (train)	5	3
Trucks	81	158
Twin-engine fighters	109	272
Unger bridge	77	153
Uniforms, insignia, and identifications:		
Army uniforms	30	38
Army insignia	31	41
Air Force uniforms and insignia	32	43
Decorations and awards	35	47
Means of identification	34	45
Uniforms and insignia of militarized and auxiliary organizations	33	44
Vehicles:		
Armored combat vehicles	67	111
Decontaminating vehicles	91	187
Gas detection car	91	188
Light telephone limbered wagon	88	182
Signal limber (horse transport)	88	182
Tanks	67	118
Tractors	81	158
Trailers	81	158
Trucks	81	158
Veterinary Service	96	219
Visual equipment	87	179
Waffen-SS	100	223

INDEX

	Paragraph	Page
Walther pistol	51	65
War Merit Cross	35	47
War-time training of recruits	25	33
Weapons: (*See also* Armament.)		
Air Force	109	269
Antitank	53, 68	75, 120
Artillery	57, 60	86, 101
Automatic small arms	52	69
Bayonet	51	68
Chemical warfare	92	190
Engineer	80	156
Hand grenades	51	68
Infantry support artillery	54	80
Machine guns	52	71
Mortars	52	73
Pistols	51	65
Projectors	92	191
Rifles	51	67
Signal troops	86	167
Small arms	51	65
Submachine guns	52	69
Werfer, 15-cm, 41 (smoke weapon)	92	191
Wehrkreise	16	24
Weights	127	347
West Wall	112, 124	319, 334
Wire entanglements	124	338
Wireless operation training	110	308
Withdrawal (tactics)	122	332
Wound Badge	35	49
Zeitzler, Kurt	14	17

German Army rank	Literal translation	Corresponding U. S. Army rank (according to function)	German Navy rank
Generalfeldmarschall	General Field Marshal	(None)	*Grossadmiral*
Generaloberst	Colonel General	General	*Generaladmiral*
General der Infanterie	General of Infantry	Lieutenant General	*Admiral*
Artillerie.	Artillery.		
Kavallerie.	Cavalry.		
Pioniere.	Engineers.		
Panzertruppe, etc.	Armored Troops, etc.		
Generalleutnant	Lieutenant General	Major General	*Vizeadmiral*
Generalmajor	Major General	Brigadier General	*Konteradmiral*
Oberst	Colonel	Colonel	*Kapitän zur See*
Oberstleutnant	Lieutenant Colonel	Lieutenant Colonel	*Fregattenkapitän*
Major	Major	Major	*Korvettenkapitän*
Hauptmann,	Captain,	Captain	*Kapitänleutnant*
Rittmeister.	Captain of Cavalry.		
Oberleutnant	First Lieutenant	First Lieutenant	*Oberleutnant zur See.*
Leutnant	Lieutenant	Second Lieutenant	*Leutnant zur See.*
Stabsfeldwebel	Staff Sergeant	Master Sergeant	*Stabsoberfeldwebel*
Stabswachtmeister.	Staff Cavalry Sergeant.	Regimental Sergeant Major.	
Stabsfeuerwerker.	Staff Ordnance Sergeant.		
Wallstabsfeldwebel	Staff Fort Sergeant.		
Festungspionierstabsfeldwebel	Staff Fortification Engineer Sergeant.		
Stabsfunkmeister.	Staff Radio Sergeant.		
Stabsbrieftaubenmeister.	Staff Carrier Pigeon Sergeant		
Stabsschirrmeister.	Staff Maintenance Sergeant.		
Hauptfeldwebel, Hauptwachtmeister.	Chief Sergeant. Chief Cavalry Sergeant.	First Sergeant	*Oberfeldwebel*
Oberfeldwebel	First Sergeant	Master Sergeant	*Stabsfeldwebel*
Oberwachtmeister.	First Cavalry Sergeant.		
Oberfähnrich.	Ensign (officer candidate).		
Oberfeuerwerker.	First Ordnance Sergeant.		
Walloberfeldwebel.	First Fort Sergeant.		
Festungspionieroberfeldwebel.	First Fortification: Engineer Sergeant.		
Oberfunkmeister.	First Radio Sergeant.		
Oberbrieftaubenmeister.	First Carrier Pigeon: Sergeant.		
Oberschirrmeister.	First Maintenance: Sergeant.		
Feldwebel	Sergeant	Technical Sergeant	*Feldwebel*
Wachtmeister.	Cavalry Sergeant.		
Feuerwerker.	Ordnance Sergeant.		
Wallfeldwebel.	Fort Sergeant.		
Festungspionierfeldwebel.	Fortification Engineer: Sergeant.		
Funkmeister.	Radio Sergeant.		
Brieftaubenmeister.	Carrier Pigeon Sergeant.		
Schirrmeister.	Maintenance Sergeant.		
Fähnrich.	(Officer candidate)	(None)	*Fähnrich zur See.*
Unterfeldwebel, Unterwachtmeister.	Junior Sergeant, Junior Cavalry Sergeant.	Staff Sergeant	*Obermaat*
Unteroffizier, Fahnenjunker-Unteroffizier.	Noncommissioned Officer Cadet	Sergeant	*Maat*
Stabsgefreiter	Staff Lance Corporal	(None)	*Hauptgefreiter*
Obergefreiter	Chief Lance Corporal	Corporal	*Obergefreiter*
Gefreiter, Fahnenjunker-Gefreiter	Lance Corporal. Junior Cadet.	Acting Corporal	*Gefreiter*
Obergrenadier	Chief Infantryman	Private, First Class	
Oberjäger.	Chief Chasseur.		
Oberreiter.	Chief Cavalryman.		
Oberkanonier.	Chief Gunner.		
Oberpionier.	Chief Engineer.		
Oberfunker.	Chief Radioman.		
Oberfahrer.	Chief Driver.		
Oberkraftfahrer.	Chief Motor Driver.		
Grenadier	Infantryman	Private	*Matrose*
Jäger.	Chasseur.		
Reiter.	Cavalryman.		
Kanonier.	Gunner.		
Funker.	Radioman.		
Fahrer.	Driver.		
Kraftfahrer.	Motor Driver.		
Pionier.	Engineer.		
Schütze.	Rifleman.		

Figure 13.—Ranks in the Ger

German Air Force rank	Medical Corps	Veterinary Corps	Bandmasters
Reichsmarschall			
Generalfeldmarschall			
Generaloberst			
General der Flieger Flakartillerie. Luftwaffe. Luftnachrichten- truppen, etc.	*Generaloberstabsarzt*	*Generaloberstabsveterinär*	
Generalleutnant	*Generalstabsarzt*	*Generalstabsveterinär*	
Generalmajor	*Generalarzt*	*Generalveterinär*	
Oberst	*Oberstarzt*	*Oberstveterinär*	
Oberstleutnant	*Oberfeldarzt*	*Oberfeldveterinär*	*Obermusikinspizient*
Major	*Oberstabsarzt*	*Oberstabsveterinär*	*Musikinspizient*
Hauptmann	*Stabsarzt*	*Stabsveterinär*	*Stabsmusikmeister*
Oberleutnant	*Oberarzt*	*Oberveterinär*	*Obermusikmeister*
Leutnant	*Assistenzarzt*	*Veterinär*	*Musikmeister*
Stabsfeldwebel Stabswachtmeister. Stabsfeuerwerker.	*Sanitätstabsfeldwebel*	*Oberhufbeschaglehrmeister*. Hufbeschaglehrmeister. Stabsbeschlagmeister.	
Hauptfeldwebel, Hauptwacht- meister. *Oberfeldwebel* Oberwachtmeister. Oberfeuerwerker. Oberfähnrich.	*Sanitätsoberfeldwebel* Unterarzt.	*Oberbeschlagmeister* Unterveterinär.	
Feldwebel Wachtmeister. Feuerwerker.	*Sanitätsfeldwebel*	*Beschlagmeister*	
Fähnrich	*Fähnrich im Sanitäts-Korps*	*Fähnrich im Veterinär-Korps*	
Unterfeldwebel Unterwachtmeister.	*Sanitätsunterfeldwebel*	*Beschlagschmiedunterwachtmeister*	
Unteroffizier Fahnenjunker-Unteroffizier.	*Sanitätsunteroffizier*	*Beschlagschmiedunteroffizier*	
Hauptgefreiter			
Obergefreiter	*Sanitätsobergefreiter*	*Beschlagschmiedobergefreiter*	
Gefreiter Fahnenjunker-Gefreiter.	*Sanitätsgefreiter*	*Beschlagschmiedgefreiter*	
		Oberbeschlagschmiedschütze Oberbeschlagschmiedreiter.	
Flieger Kanonier. Funker.	*Sanitätssoldat*	*Beschlagschmiedschütze* Beschlagschmiedreiter.	

Name	Type	Weight	Country of origin	Crew	Armor (maximum)	Armament	Ammunition	Engine
Pz.Kw. I (Sd. Kfz. 101).	Obsolete, but may still be used as reconnaissance, liaison, and command vehicle.							
Pz.Kw. II (Sd.Kfz. 121).	Light	9 tons	Germany	3	40-mm	One 20-mm Hv MG, one LMG.		6-cyl Maybach air-cooled.
Pz.Kw. IIF (Sd. Kfz. 121) aus A.	Light	12 tons	Germany	3	30-mm	One LMG, two flame-throwers mounted on each track guard.	1,800 rds. of SAA, 35 gals of oil.	
CZDV8H Pz.Kw. 38 (t)	Light medium.	16.5 tons	Czechoslovakia.	4	38-mm	One 47-mm gun, one Hv MG coaxially mounted, one Hv MG to left of driver.	90 rounds for 47-mm gun, 3,000 for Hv MG's.	245 hp V8
Pz.Kw.III(Sd. Kfz. 141).	Light medium.	18-20 tons	Germany	5	50-mm	One 50-mm gun, one LMG coaxially mounted, one LMG in hull.		320 hp V121 water-cooled
Pz.Kw.IV(Sd.Kfz. 161).	Medium	22 tons	Germany	5	60-mm	One 75-mm gun, one LMG coaxially mounted, one LMG on ball mount to right of driver.		320 hp V121 water-cooled
Somua (S. 40)	Medium	18 tons	France	3	40-mm	One 47-mm, one MG.		190 hp water-cooled.
Pz.Kw.VI ("Tiger").	Heavy	56-62 tons	Germany	5	102-mm	One 88-mm, two MG's, one MG to right of driver, others mounted coaxially, three smoke grenade dischargers.		680 hp

Figure 87.—Charac

Road speed	Radius	Spanning ability	Vertical obstacle	Fording ability	Climbing ability	Suspension system
25 mph	125 miles	4 ft 11 in	1 ft 11 in	2 ft 6 in	45°	5 wheels; older type has 4 small bogies, 3 connected by girder.
34 mph	155 miles	4 ft 11 in	1 ft 11 in	2 ft 6 in	45°	large bogies, 4 return rollers.
27 mph	77 miles	7 ft 6 in	3 ft 3 in	3 ft 3 in	41°	9 bogie wheels, 1 independent; 4 pairs of bogies each with semi-elliptic leaf springing connected by outside bearer girder.
28 mph	100 miles	5 ft 7 in	2 ft	2 ft 11 in (approximately).		(a) Latest type with 6 small rubber bogies, independently sprung. (b) 5 small bogie wheels. (c) 8 small bogies in 4 pairs with leaf springing, but all have 3 return rollers.
25 mph		9 ft	2 ft 3 in	3 ft 6 in		8 small bogie wheels, 4 pairs with leaf springing.
29 mph	140 miles	7 ft 10 in	2 ft 11 in	3 ft 3 in	40°	9 small bogies protected by armor plating with 2 return rollers.
22 mph	75 to 85 miles	Unknown	Unknown	Unknown	Unknown	8 axles, 24 Christie-type wheels on each side.

GERMAN RADIO TRANSM[ITTERS]

Translation of apparatus nomenclature	Transmitters and tubes	Power in antenna (watts)	Wave band		Antenna	Working methods
			Meters	Kc		
Heavy radio set a.	1–5 kw transmitter. Two RE .084K. Seven RS .282. Two RS .329. Three RGN .2004.	1,500	500–3,000	100–600	80-foot mast with 6- or 12-spoke umbrella.	Local or remote keying, hand-speed or high-speed CW or ICW teleprinter picture transmission.
Heavy radio set b.	1 kw transmitter. Two RF .084K. Seven RS .282. Two RS .329. Three RGN .2004.	1,000	45–275	1,090–6,700	80-foot masts with single-wire antenna, 83 feet long for medium waves or 33 feet long for short waves.	As for Serial No. 1.
Medium radio set a.		80	100–268	1,120–3,000		CW local keying and voice; picture transmission.
Medium b. Medium armored b. Fu. II SE 100. 100 WS.*	100-watt transmitter. Two RS .237. One RS .241.	100-watt can be switched to provide ⅒ output.	250–1,500	200–1,200	33-foot mast with 4-spoke umbrella, 20-foot sectional mast with 3-spoke umbrella; roof masts according to type of truck in which carried.	CW local and remote keying; local voice. picture transmission (television).
Medium c. Fu. 12 SE 120 U.	120-watt transmitter.	120	5.5–7.1	42,100–54,000	70-foot mast with vertical stub aerial on top.	CW and ICW local and remote keying and voice; hand-speed and high-speed keying; teleprinter; picture telegraphy.
Light a. Light b. Light mountain b. Fu. 9 SE 5. 5 WS/24b–104.*	5-watt transmitter with two RS .241.	5	96–316	950–3,150	21-foot sectional mast with high antenna 1/1 or 2/2; 5-foot mast antenna with low antenna 1/1, two 7-foot ground antennas; roof antenna (Kfz. 17).	CW local keying and speech.
Light c. Light armored c. Light mountain c. Fu. 7 SE 20 U. 20 WSd.*	20-watt transmitter with five RL 12 T 15.	20	6.3–7.1	42,100–47,800	16-foot mast with 5-foot stub aerial on top and four counterpoises.	ICW local keying and voice.
Light d. Light armored d. Fu. 8 SE 30. Fu. 10 SE 30 (TE) 30 W/246–120.*	30-watt transmitter with five RS .241 or 30-watt transmitter a.	30 30	180–316 100–268	950–1,670 1,120–3,000	21-foot sectional mast with high aerial 3/3. 5-foot mast with low aerial 3/3; roof antennas on trucks.	ICW local keying and voice.
Pack a. SE a 2/24b–202.*	Pack transmitter a. with— Three RE .084 K. Two RE .134. One H 406D or One RES .094.	2	45–100	3,000–6,670	Low dipole antenna; ground antenna.	ICW local keying. Local or remote voice.
Pack a. 2	Pack transmitter a. 2 with— Two RE .084K. Two RES .164. One H 406D or One RES .094.	1	45–100	3,000–6,670	Single-wire antenna with 8 rods; single-wire antenna with 3 rods.	ICW local keying. Local or remote voice.
Pack b. 1. Torn Fu. b. 1.*	Pack transmitter b. 1 with— Seven RV 2 P 800. One RL 2 P3.	0.65	60–100	3,000–5,000	7½-foot mast single-wire antenna with 8 rods; single-wire antenna with 3 rods; vehicle aerial, Kfz. 2 or 15.	ICW local keying. Local or remote voice.
Pack d. 1.	Pack transmitter d. 1 with— Eight RV 2 P 800. One RL 2 T 2.	1	7.9–8.8	33,800–38,000	7-foot mast, 6-foot roof antenna on trucks, Kfz. 2 or 15.	ICW local keying. Local or remote voice.
Pack d. 2.	As for d. 1.	1	7.9–8.8	33,800–38,000	7-foot mast, 6-foot roof antenna on trucks, Kfz. 2 or 15.	ICW local keying. Local or remote voice.
Pack f. Fu. 13 TF. Torn Fux.*	Pack transmitter f. with— Seven RV 2 P 800. One RL 2 P 3.	0.65	45–67	4,500–6,670	As for Serial No. 11.	ICW local keying. Local or remote voice.
Fu. 5 SE 10 U. 10 W Sc.* 10 W Sh.*	10-watt transmitter a., b., or c. with— One RV 12 P 4,000. Two RL 12 P 35.	10	a. 10–11 b. 9–10 c. 9–11	27,200–30,400 30,200–33,400 27,200–33,400	7-foot mast antenna on armored Kfz 121, Kfz 141, or Kfz 622.	CW local keying and voice.
Fu. 6 SE 20 U.	20-watt transmitter c. with five RL 12 T 15.	20	9–11	27,200–33,400	7-foot mast antenna on armored trucks Kfz 265, 266, 267.	CW local keying and voice.

Figure 134.—Principal German radios with compa[rison]

ITTERS

Range (miles)			Source of energy	Remarks	Similar to Signal Corps radio
CW	ICW	Voice			
725	725	180-370	Type A machine connected to convertor type U 1,500.	*Circuit.* (a) R. F. master oscillator (RS .282) amplifier (two RS .282 in parallel), output (two RS .329 in parallel). (b) Audio frequency amplifier (two RS .282, two RE .084 K). (c) Keying, two RG .282, three rectifiers RGN .2004. *Use.*—AHQ.	
725	725	300	As above		
125 100 25-50		45 30 6-12½	Type C machine connected to convertor type U. 100a or U. 100 with 12-volt storage battery.	*Circuit.*—Master oscillator, power amplifier, modulation in the grid circuit of the power amplifier by means of vacuum tube control; arrangements for "break-in" operation; motorized. *Weight.*—75 pounds. *Use.*—Army, corps, and divisional signaling battalions. For use at AHQ corps headquarters.	177 B
45 30 10 15		12½ 10 1 5	Convertors U. 5a. or U. 5a. 1, connected to a 12-volt storage battery.	Used with pack receiver a. (See (2), below for types of receivers.) Both transmitter and receiver in three boxes, each 24 by 18 by 15 inches; total weight, 200 pounds; can be operated on the move when carried in a vehicle. *Use.*—Division headquarters.	284A
	30	30	As for Serial No. 6	For use at AHQ	583 ( )
	75 55 25-35	25 16 6-12	As for Serial No. 6	*Use.*—Division headquarters	284A
	15 5	5 1½	Two 90-volt plate batteries, one storage battery type NC10.	Used with pack receiver b. (See (2), below for types of receivers.) Both together form two loads: transmitter, receiver, aerial in one; batteries, accessories, spares, in other; total weight of each load, about 22 pounds.	609 ( )
	18	4-7	Same as Serial No. 9	See Serial No. 9	
	13	4			
	15	7½	Two 90-volt plate batteries, one storage battery type 2 B .38.	Used with pack receiver b. (See (2) below for types of radio receivers.) Transmitter and receiver housed in one box, batteries and accessories in second box; total weight, 120 pounds; automatic switching to send/receive carried out by key or push button. *Use.*—In forward areas.	511 ( ) Alternative 194 195 300
	15 10 10	7½ 4 4			
	10 7½	4 2	Same as Serial No. 11	Can be carried together with its receiver by one man; consists of two half knapsacks which can be clamped together to form one load; crystal control on two fixed frequencies. *Weight.*—40 pounds.	
	10 7½	4 2	As for Serial No. 11	As for Serial No. 12	
	15 15 10	7½ 7½ 4	As for Serial No. 11	*Use.*—Batteries of field artillery.	511 ( )
4		2½	Convertor U 10 with 12-volt storage battery.	*Use.*—Armored fighting vehicles.	508
6		5	Convertor U 20 a. 2 with 12-volt storage battery.	Is believed to have been replaced by Serial No. 20 below.	508

Aircraft manufacturer and model	Engines, model and hp rating	Weight (gross lbs)	Speed (maximum mph)	Service ceiling (ft)	Cruising range (miles)	Armament (caliber in mm)	Bomb load (lbs)
Focke-Wulf, F.W. 190A, Fighter or Fighter-Bomber.	BMW 801D 1 x 1,695 hp at S. L. (fully rated).	8,580 to 10,803 maximum.	392 at 17,250 ft.	36,500	Normal 380. Maximum 960.	2 x MG 151/20+2 x MG 17/7.9+2 x FF/20 MG 17 and FF Oerlikon may be omitted on fighter-bombers.	Normal 1 x 550 or 1 x 1,100. Maximum 1 x 2,200 (overload).
Messerschmitt, Me. 109 G, Fighter or Fighter-Bomber.	DB 605 1 x 1,425 hp at 21,300 ft.	8,000 to 8,500. (estimated)	385 at 25,000 ft.	40,000+ (estimated)	Normal 400. Maximum 1,020 (fighter with external tanks).	3 x MG 151/20+2 x MG 131/13.	550.
Messerschmitt, Me. 110 TE, Fighter-Bomber.	DB 601A 2 x 1,150 hp at 2,400 rpm.	15,300	365 at 19,000 ft.	33,300	Normal 920. Maximum, 1230.	Normal 4 x MG 17/7.9 +2 x FF/20+1 x MG 15/7.9.	Normal, none. Occasionally 615.
Messerschmitt, Me. 210 TE, Fighter-Bomber.	DB 601F 2 x 1,400 hp at 14,500 ft.	20,250 (estimated)	365 at 20,000. (estimated)	33,000 (estimated)	1,300 with 1,100 lb bombs at 323 mph.	2 x MG 151/20+2 x MG 17/7.9 at 2 x MG 131/13 in Barbattes.	Normal 1,100. Maximum 3,300.
Henschel, Hs. 129, Ground-Attack Dive Bomber.	Gnome-Rhone, 14M 2 x 820 at 10,500 ft.	12,000	275 at 11,000 ft.	25,300	Normal 460. Maximum 520.	2 x MG 151/15+2 x MG 17/7.9 and 1 x MK 101/30.	Maximum 770. When MK 101/30 is carried load is 2x 110 or 45 x 4.4.
Junkers, Ju. 88 C 6 TE, Fighter-Bomber Night Fighter.	BMW 801 Dz 2 x 1,650 at 15,000 ft.	24,000	345	32,500	Normal 820. maximum 1,660 with fuel overload.	3 x FF/20+3 x MG 17/7.9. (May vary.)	Normal, none. Maximum 1,100.
Junkers, Ju. 89 A-4, Bomber and Dive Bomber.	Jumo 211J 2 x 1260 at 12,500 feet.	29,300	300	19,500 to 30,000.	Normal 1,130; maximum Bombers 680. Maximum fuel 2280.	4 to 5 MG 81/7.9	Normal 4,400. Maximum 6,600.
Junkers, Ju. 87D, "Stuka" Dive Bomber.	Jumo 211J 1 x 1260 at 12,500.	9,400 to 10,500.	245 at 15,000 feet.	24,500	425 to 950	2 x MG 17/7.9+2 x MG 81/7.9.	Normal 1,100. Maximum 3,100 or 1 x 2,200 rocket bomb or 1 x 3,000+4 x 100.
Heinkel, He. 111 H6, Bomber and Dive Bomber.	Jumo 211F 2 x 1,200 at 13,300 feet.	25,300 to 31,000.	255 at 16,000 feet.	26,500	840/900 to 1,760/1,900 maximum.	1 x FF/20+2 x MG 15/7.9+2 x MG 81/7.9+1 x MG 17/7.9.	Normal 4,400. Maximum 6,200 bombs or torpedoes.
Focke-Wulf, FW. 200K, Bomber and L. R. Recn.	Bramo-Fafnir 323R 4 x 940 at 12,000 feet.	50,500	250 at 13,000 feet.	21,500	1,250 to 2,430.	2 x MG 131/13+2 x MG 151/20+1 x MG 15/7.9. (May vary.)	Normal 3,300. Maximum 11,000. May carry mines or torpedoes.
Dornier, Do. 217E2, Bomber and Dive Bomber.	BMW 801A 2 x 1,650 at 15,300 ft.	32,000 to 34,000.	325 at 17,000 ft.	22,500	1,090 to 2,150 maximum.	3 x MG 131/13 + 2 x MG 81/7.9. (May vary.)	Normal 4,400. Maximum 6,600. May carry torpedoes.
Heinkel, He. 177, Heavy Bomber.	DB 606 2 x 2,300 mounted in pairs =4 x 1,150.	6,700 (estimated)	270/300 at 18,000 ft. (estimated)	21,000 ft (estimated)	3,400 maximum. (estimated)	3/6 MG 131/13 + 1 x MG 151/15 or 20.	Normal 13,200. Maximum 16,000 or 8 torpedoes.
Junkers, Ju. 52, Transport.	BMW 132A or T 3 x 660 hp. at S L.	23,100 maximum	165 mph	16,000	Maximum load 530. Maximum fuel 4,000 lb. load 790.	2 to 4/7.9 MG	22 fully equipped troops or 5,000 lb. freight.
Messerschmitt, Me. 323, Transport.	Gnome-Rhone 14 M 6 x 820 hp at 10,000 ft.	65/70,000 lbs. (estimated)	140 at S L. (estimated)	? Low flying.	?	6 MG	(Estimated). 120 fully equipped troops, motorcars or small tanks 20/25,000 lb. freight.

Figure 161.—Characteristics of German airplanes.

GERMAN RADIO TRANSMITTE[RS]

Translation of apparatus nomenclature	Transmitters and tubes	Power in antenna (watts)	Wave band		Antenna	Working methods
			Meters	Kc		
Fu. 15 SE dm			0.53-57	526,310–566,000		
Radio telephone "Fildfunk Fu. Sprechera."	Pack transmitter—6 RV 12 P 2000. 1 RL 12 P 10.	6	10.1-11	27.5-29.8	Short wave or rod; 1,000 ohms best.	Local voice for transmitting survey results.
Radio set for sound-ranging position.	20-watt transmitter with five RL 12 T 15.	20	11-12	25,000–27,200		
Transmitter for use in tanks.	20-watt transmitter	20	9.6-11	27,200–31,200	7-foot rod with counterpoise.	Local keying and voice.
AKS 25	25-watt transmitter	25	25-100	3,000–12,000	33-foot antenna on one 33-foot mast; counterpoise four 33-foot wires.	Local keying and voice.
	8-watt transmitter	8 switch provided to reduce power by ¼.	100-300	1,000–3,000		Local keying and voice; send/receive operates by push button in radiotelephone.
	Ultra high frequency transmitter with two Acorn D. S. 202/2. Two R. L.	40-60 m. w	.59-.66	454,000–508,000	Saw-tooth antenna (double diamond with reflector); highly directional.	Local or remote keying and voice ICW.
Not sender (Floatable Rescue set).	Crystal controlled 2 R. L. (Osc. & Mod.).		600	500	260 feet stainless steel wire on balloon, or kite.	Auto. keyman and manual CW.

GERMAN RADIO RECEIVERS

Type	Wave range		Tubes	Source of energy	Working time (hours)
	Meters	Kc			
Pack receiver a (445 Bs)*	45-3,000	100-6,670	Four RE 074 N	One storage battery, type 4.8 NC 10.	
Pack receiver b	43-3,000	100-6,670	Four RV 2 P 800	One 90-volt plate battery. One storage battery, type 2 B 38. One 90-volt plate battery or 1 converter.	
Long wave receiver a	197-4,000	75-1,525	Eight RV 2 P 800	One storage battery, type 2 B 38. One 90-volt plate battery.	
Fa H Eu* Intercept and monitoring.		.5-25 mc			
Medium wave receiver b.	150-517	580-2,000	Six RV 12 P 4,000	One converter, type EU a.	
Medium wave receiver c.	100-360	835-3,000		One convertor, type EU a.	
Short wave receiver a	30-3,000	1,000-10,000	Eleven RV 2 P 800	One storage battery, type 2 B 38. One 90-volt plate battery.	
Ultra short wave receiver b.1	11-12	25,000-27,200	Nine RV 12 P 4,000	One convertor, type EU a 8.	
Ultra short wave receiver c.1	9-11	27,200-33,300	Eight RV 12 P 4,000	One convertor, type EU a.	
Ultra short wave receiver d. UKWEh* (b.1). UKWEc* (c.1).	6.3-7.1	42,100-47,800	Eight RV 12 P 4,000	Two 90-volt plate batteries or 1 converter, type EU a.	

Figure 134.—Principal German radios with comparable U. S. Army

8—Continued

Range (miles)			Source of energy	Remarks	Similar to Signal Corps radio
CW	ICW	Voice			
--------	--------	--------	--------------------	No details are available.	
--------	--------	5	Convertor U 20 a. S with 12-volt storage battery.	Used as U H F telephone for RCN in forward echelon.	{509} {609}
(?)	(?)	(?)	12-volt storage battery and motor generator.	*Circuit.*—Crystal oscillator, heterodyne oscillator, mixer, power stage; aerial is semiflexible, with "Set" at any random angle, if hit; can be straightened by hand. *Weight.*—18 pounds.	
(?)	(?)	(?)	--------------------	*Circuit.*—Three radio frequency stages— (a) Master oscillator. (b) Neutralized buffer amplifier. (c) Neutralized push-pull amplifier. Modulation in grid of power amplifier tube; keying in grid circuit of all stages. *Uses.*—Divisions, infantry and artillery regiments.	
--------	(?)	(?)	90-volt battery and 2.4-volt Edison cell.	*Circuit.*—Two stages, master oscillator and power amplifier; grid modulation in latter; used with receiver Serial No. 14, (2) below; to be standard portable set for forward and mobile troops. *Transmitter.*—Weight, about 25 pounds; size 24 by 18 by 15 inches. *Receiver.*—Weight, about 28 pounds; size as for transmitter.	
Quasi-optical path.	Quasi-optical path. 125(?)	Quasi-optical path. 125(?)	2-volt lead storage battery. Two 90-volt plate batteries.	Used with receiver serial No. 15, (2) below, in five boxes. (a) Transmitter and receiver. (b) Accessories. (c) Stand, etc. *Circuit.*—Series tuned Hartley; plate modulation through 1:1 transformer; MCW by keying modulator tube, which acts as A. F. oscillator.	
250	--------	--------	Hand driven generator.	6.2W into antenna	SCR 578

8

Working time (hours)	Allocation to transmitters	Remarks	Similar to Signal Corps Radio
50 40 42 40	Serial Nos. 1 and 2 can be used with any of the following transmitters: Heavy a and b. Medium b. Medium armored b. Light and pack a, b, and d. Light armored d. Light mountain d. Fu. 1 TE. Fu. 9 SE 5. Fu. 10 SE 30 (TE). Fu. 11 SE 100. Intercept a and b.		{BC 312} {BC 342}
20 8	Heavy a and b Fu. 8 SE 30 Fu. 8 SE 30 Fu. 4 E.	5 Bands—all wave	BC 123
--------	Fu. 4 E.		
13 10	Heavy a and b. Serial 19 of transmitters. For sound-ranging position. Fu. 2 EU. Fu. 6 SE 20. Light c. Light armored c. Light mountain c. Fu. 3 EU. Fu. 7 SE 20 U.		538 ( ) 538 ( )

Army sets.—Continued.

www.ingramcontent.com/pod-product-compliance
Lightning Source LLC
Chambersburg PA
CBHW082104230426
43671CB00015B/2607